PT BOATS AT WAR
World War II to Vietnam

Norman Polmar and Samuel Loring Morison

MBI Publishing Company

First published in 1999 by MBI Publishing Company, 729 Prospect Avenue, PO Box 1, Osceola, WI 54020-0001 USA

MBI Publishing Company books are also available at discounts in bulk quantity for industrial or sales-promotional use. For details write to Special Sales Manager at Motorbooks International Wholesalers & Distributors, 729 Prospect Avenue, Osceola, WI 54020-0001 USA.

Library of Congress Cataloging-in-Publication Data
Polmar, Norman.
   PT boats at war: World War II to Vietnam/Norman Polmar & Samuel Loring Morison.
      p. cm.
   Includes index.

ISBN 0-7603-0499-8 (alk. paper)
   1. Torpedo–boats––United States––History––20th century. 2. United States––History, Naval––20th century. I. Morison, Samuel L.
V833.P65   1999
359.3'258––dc21   99-13550

All photos are from the private collections of Samuel Loring Morison, Norman Polmar, Al Ross, and A. D. Baker III, except as noted. The authors are indebted to the National Air and Space Museum (NASM) and to the U.S. Naval Institute (USNI) for the use of photos from their special collections. Many of the U.S. Navy photos were provided by the Naval Historical Center and the Office of Information, Department of the Navy

On the front cover: The 80-foot Elco PT 141 at high speed. She was also assigned to MTB Squadron 4, the PT boat training unit and saw no combat during the war. *U.S. Navy*

On the back cover, top: MTB Squadron 2 departs the Washington Navy Yard in January 1941. There are several 70-foot Elco PT boats and the PT 9 (center left). Beyond the PT boats are the presidential yacht *Potomac* and her tender *Cuyahoga*, both ex-Coast Guard cutters; the later was returned to the Coast Guard in 1941. *U.S. Navy*

On the back cover, bottom: An Elco-type PT boat fires two Mark VIII torpedoes. This scene, repeated hundred of times in combat, struck fear in the hearts of the captains of enemy warships. This was a test firing off the Naval Torpedo Station at Newport, Rhode Island. *U.S. Navy*

Edited by Michael Haenggi
Designed by Rebecca Allen

Printed in the United States of America

Contents

Preface

I wish to have no Connection with any Ship that does not sail fast, for I intend to go in harm's way.

—John Paul Jones

These oft-quoted words of America's first naval hero personified the PT boat of World War II. The PT boat was fast, heavily armed, manned by men of indomitable courage, and it sought out the enemy.

PT boats saw extensive action in the Philippines during America's dark days of 1941–1942 as Japanese air, ground, and naval forces assaulted Allied possessions in the Far East. PTs subsequently saw almost continuous combat in the fighting in the South Pacific, Mediterranean, and English Channel. In addition, American-built motor torpedo boats saw combat in the British and Soviet navies.

In particular, the bleak days of December 1941 to the spring of 1942 gave birth to the image of the PT boat as the "David" taking on the enemy "Goliath." The PTs attacked enemy cruisers, destroyers, and even submarines, all larger and more heavily armed. This audacity, lionized in the well-crafted book *They Were Expendable*, by E. L. White, published in 1942, further contributed to the image of the PT boat. The 1945 movie *They Were Expendable*, starring Robert Montgomery and John Wayne, added still more to that reputation. Books, articles, and movies all publicized the dash and adventure of PT boats, calling them "mosquito boats" and "Peter Tares," the latter term based on the phonetic military alphabet for the letters PT.

The crowning publicity for the PT boat occurred when John F. Kennedy, a young Boston politician, campaigned in 1960 for the presidency of the United States. In World War II Kennedy had been in PT boats and was the commanding officer of the *PT 109* in the Solomon Islands when the craft was rammed and sunk by a Japanese destroyer. The *PT 109* event was controversial—reportedly Kennedy's father, former U.S. ambassador to Britain, wanted the Medal of Honor for his son while General Douglas MacArthur, the theater commander, wanted to court-martial the young officer.

But nothing could tarnish the image of the PT boat, not even its limited accomplishments. PT boat sailors claimed the sinking of enemy cruisers, destroyers, submarines, and lesser vessels in far greater numbers than actually occurred. This was due partly to PT boats making most of their attacks at night, not being able to remain on the scene to rescue enemy survivors or otherwise access their effectiveness, and a lack of knowledge about how poorly U.S. torpedoes were performing.

PT boats did sink scores of Japanese and German troop and supply barges as well as several enemy warships. Equally important was the impact of the PT boat on enemy planning, forcing the enemy to employ less effective and more costly means of moving troops and supplies because of the fear of PT boat attacks.

The PT boat—in the guise of the fast patrol boat (PTF)—also served in the Vietnam War. These activities contributed significantly to the escalation of American participation in that conflict.

As described in the following pages, even though the craft were small, the size of the PT program was awesome. During the late 1930s and World War II, American shipyards produced 757 PT boats for the U.S. Navy, Royal Navy, and Soviet Navy; the yards also produced 42 similar PTC submarine chasers plus

58 so-called BPT torpedo boats under British contract. During this period the U.S. Navy also acquired seven foreign-built torpedo boats, one built in Britain and six in Canada. After the war scores of U.S. PT boats were transferred to other countries.

In the postwar era American shipyards produced four prototype PT boats and ten PTFs; another 14 PTFs were acquired from Norway. Although the PTFs did not carry torpedoes—they could be so equipped if needed—they continued the tradition of being fast ships that went in "harm's way."

PT Boats at War seeks to describe the development, construction, and employment of PT boats, from the U.S. Navy's entry into this field in the late 1930s through the Vietnam War. The authors have made an effort to place the PT boat into the proper perspective with regard to U.S. naval strategy and operations. In addition, we have provided—for the first time in a single volume—detailed data on the construction and fate of every PT boat built for the U.S. Navy, including prototypes, those intended specifically for foreign transfer, and the several constructed outside of the United States. The PT boat has contributed an important chapter to the history of the U.S. Navy. We hope that this book adequately reflects that history.

The PT boat has long been gone from the U.S. Navy. However, five PT/PTFs are retained for exhibition as memorials, plus one hulk:

Number	Owner	Location
PT 309	Admiral Nimitz Museum of the Pacific War	LaPorte, Tex.
PT 617	USS Massachusetts memorial	Fall River, Maine
PT 658	Save the PT Boats, Inc.	Portland, Ore.
PT 659	American Patrol Boat Association	Portland, Ore.
PT 796	USS Massachusetts memorial	Fall River, Mass.
PTF 17	Buffalo & Erie County Naval & Serviceman's Park	Buffalo, N.Y.

The *PT 309* is the only surviving World War II-era PT boat that served in combat. The *PT 659* is a hulk, having been stripped to restore the *PT 658*.

Several individuals have been most helpful in producing this book. In particular we would like to acknowledge the help of Bernard F. Cavalcante and Cathy Lloyd of the operational archives, Naval Historical Center; Alyce Gutherie of PT Boats, Inc.; Charles Haberlein and Jack A. Green of the photographic section, Naval Historical Center; Glenn Helms, Navy Department Library; Dawn Stitzel of the photo archives of the U.S. Naval Institute; and Tom Wildenberg, author and Ramsey Fellow, National Air and Space Museum.

PT Boats Inc., Post Office Box 38070, Germantown, TN, 38183-0070, provided considerable assistance for this project.

Norman Polmar
Samuel Loring Morison

Chapter 1

The Torpedo and the Torpedo Boat

The invention of the self-propelled or "automobile" torpedo in the late 1800s led to new types of naval warfare as the torpedo became a potent weapon for use by submarines, small surface craft, and, eventually, aircraft. The torpedo is a particularly potent weapon because, unlike cannon fire and bombs, it always strikes below the ship's water line. Like the effects from the detonation of a naval mine, a torpedo's blast admits water into the ship, causing major damage if not sinking the ship. Indeed, many ships, including battleships and at least one aircraft carrier, have been sunk by a single torpedo.

Credit for the first practical self-propelled torpedo must go to the team of *Fregattenkapitan* Giovanni de Luppis, a retired Austrian naval officer, and Robert Whitehead, the English manager of a marine engine factory at Fiume, Hungary. Their collaboration resulted in the development of the first practical self-propelled torpedo in 1866. The initial weapon was propelled by a compressed-air engine, carrying a charge of 18 pounds of dynamite, with speed of six knots and a range of a few score yards. When first demonstrated to the Austrian government, its depth keeping proved to be erratic; the problem was quickly solved by Whitehead with a control device that he called "The Secret." In fact it was a simple pendulum-type mechanism.

In 1868, Whitehead offered to sell exclusive rights for the torpedo to the Austrian government. When the Austrians refused to finance the project, in 1869 Whitehead offered the torpedo to other European nations. Subsequently, Austria, Great Britain, France, Germany, Italy, Sweden, and Russia acquired production rights for what came to be called the Whitehead torpedo.

Britain was first to use the torpedo in combat, when the cruiser *Shah* launched a torpedo against the Peruvian monitor *Huascar* in 1877. That attack failed, as did the Russian use of Whitehead torpedoes later in the same year against the Turks. Finally, in January 1878, the Russian steamer *Constantine* sank a Turkish steamer in the Black Sea—the first success for a Whitehead torpedo.

The first specialized torpedo boat was built in England by Thornycroft, the 27-ton *Lightning*, launched in 1876. The craft had a single torpedo tube in her bow and could reach a speed of 18 knots. Her success led the British Admiralty to order 12 such craft with one, produced by Yarrow, reaching the record speed of 21.9 knots. The French purchased some of these torpedo boats and then initiated construction in their own yards. (Far less successful was the first French torpedo boat, a 101-ton warship built in 1877; the craft, later named *Isand*, carried two torpedo tubes—one forward and one aft—but could make only 14 knots.)

Several European nations produced more-capable torpedo boats. And, larger warships, including battleships, also were fitted with torpedo tubes. The potential destructive power of the torpedo and the ability to carry torpedoes in small surface craft and even submarines (while large naval guns required massive battleships and cruisers) led to the proposal that such torpedo craft could be produced in large numbers at far less cost than a conventional battle fleet. It was estimated that as many as 60 torpedo boats could be procured for the cost of one battleship. (As early submarines developed, they were generally grouped with surface torpedo craft under the collective term "torpedo boats.")

The idea that the torpedo boat was truly the warship of the future found particularly strong advocates in France, chiefly among a group of younger officers who, under the leadership of Admiral Theophile Aube, became known as *la jeune école* (the young school). The brilliant writer Gabriel Charmes formulated and expounded the new torpedo boat theories in his book *La Reforme de la Marine*, published in 1886. Charmes argued that in a modern navy small torpedo boats could defend the coasts and larger ones could drive enemy battleships and cruisers from the oceans. Large numbers of small, high-speed torpedo craft would be practically invulnerable to any defensive weapons as they raced to attack large, outdated battleships.

When Admiral Aube became France's Minister of Marine in 1886 he immediately ordered the suspension of battleship construction, laying down instead 14 cruisers and ordering 34 torpedo boats, as well as supporting the development of submarine torpedo boats. More torpedo boat orders would follow. And, to encourage and train officers, he established the Torpedo School.

But these torpedo boats, which were given extensive sea trials and exercises, were not successful. They proved too slow (making only 19 knots at sea), and they were too small for long-range operations or heavy seas. Two capsized. Others were rebuilt to improve seakeeping (which further reduced their speed) while France's overseas interests and the subsequent building of the High Seas Fleet by Germany led France to continue the construction of major, oceangoing warships.

The U.S. Navy had considerable interest in torpedoes, and American engineers greatly improved upon and supplemented the Whitehead weapons. In August 1886, Congress voted $100,000, for which "The President is hereby authorized to have constructed, one first class torpedo boat. . . . That the vessels herein authorized shall be built of steel of domestic manufacture. . . ."

But before that craft could be constructed, the Navy purchased the first U.S. torpedo boat,

The privately built *Stiletto*, although not considered a successful torpedo boat, was the first U.S. Navy ship to launch a self-propelled torpedo. The craft's single torpedo tube, mounted in the stem, is shown launching a torpedo. *U.S. Navy*

the *Stiletto*. This was a wood-hulled, steam-powered boat built as a private venture by the Herreshoff Manufacturing Company in Bristol, Rhode Island. It was a 94-foot, 31-ton craft fitted with a single torpedo tube fitted in the boat's stem. The *Stiletto* was launched in 1885 and purchased for naval use under an Act of Congress dated March 3, 1887.

The *Stiletto* entered service in July 1887, the U.S. Navy's first craft capable of launching self-propelled torpedoes. The Navy used her for experimental work at the Torpedo Station in Newport, Rhode Island, until discarding her in 1911.

The first Navy-built torpedo boat, the *USS Cushing*, was laid down in April 1888 and placed in commission on April 22, 1890, as Torpedo Boat No. 1. The craft was named for Commander William Cushing, a hero of the American Civil War unsurpassed for his daring and courage. He was commended four times by the Navy Department and received the formal thanks of Congress for his destruction of the Confederate ironclad *Albemarle* in Plymouth, North Carolina, in 1864, using a 30-foot, steam-driven boat with a "spar torpedo"—an explosive charge affixed to the end of a spar projecting from the bow of the craft.

The 140-foot torpedo boat *Cushing* displaced 116 tons and her coal-burning steam-propulsion plant could drive her at 23 knots, the fastest of any ship in the fleet at the time. The *Cushing* was fitted with two small deck guns and three torpedo tubes.

The *Cushing*—named for a Civil War "torpedo boat" hero—was the first torpedo boat built by the U.S. Navy. She was the progenitor of 35 such U.S. craft. This type of torpedo boat was succeeded by the larger and more versatile torpedo boat destroyer. *U.S. Navy*

Beginning in 1890, Congress authorized a series of torpedo boats, and 34 were constructed through 1902. Each series or class of torpedo boats was larger, providing better sea-keeping qualities. Speed usually increased with each successive class, with some boats designed for 30 knots. Most carried three tubes (a few had two) for launching 18-inch-diameter torpedoes.

Although suitable for coastal defense, these ships had limited range and sea-keeping qualities. But by the turn of the century the United States was acquiring an overseas empire, with political-economic interests far from American shores. The country needed larger and longer-range warships. At the same time, the development of torpedo boats had caused some navies to develop ships to protect their battleships and cruisers from torpedo boats—torpedo boat destroyers. The first of these ships in the U.S. Navy was the *USS Bainbridge*, completed in 1902. The *Bainbridge* was more than twice as large as the later torpedo boats, displacing 420 tons, and had a primary armament of guns. And like virtually all battleships and cruisers being built, the destroyers would also have torpedo tubes.

The appearance of the destroyer, which would evolve into a multipurpose warship, would end the further development of specialized torpedo boats in the U.S. Navy for almost three decades. In Europe several navies did develop small, fast, hit-and-run motor torpedo boats, with Italian craft having particular success against Austro-Hungarian warships in World War I.

During the war the Electric Boat Company of Groton, Connecticut, built several motor torpedo boats for Italy and hundreds of fast patrol launches for Britain. Electric Boat and several other U.S. firms did produce small, high-speed craft as patrol and anti-submarine craft for the Navy, but none is known to have been fitted with torpedo tubes. A variety of torpedo-armed craft were proposed to the Navy, and the Navy's General Board, the senior advisory body to the Secretary of the Navy, considered building a flotilla of torpedo boats to attack German naval bases. But the Navy rejected the proposal, primarily because it believed the labor and material could be better used to produce destroyers, submarine chasers, aircraft, and other proven naval weapons.

Commercial firms continued to propose torpedo craft to the Navy after the war. Some proposals called for highly innovative craft, including one that could be flooded down during an attack, reducing the craft's freeboard and hence vulnerability to detection. In the early 1920s the U.S. Navy acquired two British motor torpedo boats, a 45-foot and a 55-foot torpedo boat built by Thornycroft. Trials were conducted for several years, with the larger craft being used sporadically until 1930. No procurement followed.

By the late 1930s, however, with war raging in the Far East and threatening in Europe, the U.S. Navy developed renewed interest in motor torpedo boats.

The *Morris* at high speed, launching a torpedo from her triple bank of 18-inch torpedo tubes, which rotated outboard for firing. The ship—designated TB No. 14—had a top speed of 23 knots. The *Morris* and other U.S. torpedo boats saw no action in World War I. *U.S. Navy*

Chapter 2

The American
Torpedo Boat

The U.S. Navy had little interest in Motor Torpedo Boats (MTBs) until the 1930s. Because of the isolated position of the United States, which would place its enemies on the other side of the Atlantic or Pacific Oceans, there was little need for small combat craft. And many observers looked at MTBs as defensive weapons, and defense was certainly not the forte of the U.S. Navy.

America's renewed interest in MTBs came about in the mid-1930s, in part because the U.S.-controlled Philippine Islands came under threat

from Japanese expansion in the Far East. On December 5, 1936, Rear Admiral Emery S. Land, chief of the Navy's Bureau of Construction and Repair, wrote to the Chief of Naval Operations that "Developments since the war of the motor torpedo boat type, then known as Coastal Motor Boats, have been continuous and marked in most European Navies. . . . The results being obtained in foreign services are such to indicate that vessels of considerable military effectiveness for the defense of local areas are being built, the possibilities

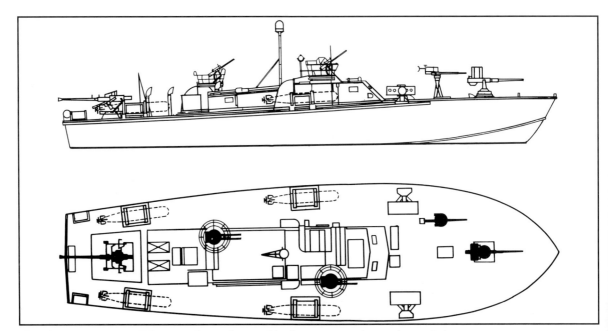

The "ultimate" American PT boat: an Elco 80-footer with a heavy gun, rocket, and torpedo battery.

Few photos exist of the *PT 1*, shown here on the seaplane tender *Pocomoke*. The belated U.S. entry into MTB development would be assisted by British experience and the innovation of American boat builders. *U.S. Navy*

The *PT 3* churns the Potomac River during a 1940 demonstration for members of Congress and senior naval officers. Although impressive, mosquito boats did not fit into the U.S. naval strategy of the period, which stressed open-ocean warfare. Note the two aft-firing torpedo "chutes." *U.S. Navy*

The *PT 4* without torpedo-launching apparatus. Several foreign MTBs featured rear-firing torpedoes, but the scheme was not adopted by the U.S. Navy. There are two "gun tubs" abaft the bridge for twin .50-caliber machine gun mounts. *James C. Fahey collection (USNI)*

of which should not be allowed to go unexplored in our service. It is, of course, recognized that the general strategic situation in this country is entirely different from that in Europe, so that motor torpedo boats could not in all probability be used offensively by us. It appears very probable, however, that the type might very well be used to release for offensive service ships otherwise unavoidably assigned to guard geographic points such as an advance base itself."

Indeed, since 1900 U.S. war planning called for the rapid transfer of U.S. warships in the Atlantic to the Pacific (around South America until the Panama Canal was completed in 1914). The fleet would then embark Army troops and Marines at San Francisco and steam westward. Stops for coal for the warships and transports would be made at Hawaii (where there was not yet a naval base), Midway, Guam, and finally the Philippines. Thus, torpedo boats could be useful for defending advance bases and fleet anchorages against Japanese raids.

The Navy's leadership reviewed Rear Admiral Land's proposals. The General Board agreed that "it is clearly evident that because of our strategic situation the [MTB] type is of much less initial value to our Navy . . . future situations can occur under which it would be possible for such small craft to be used on directly offensive missions—as is no doubt contemplated in certain foreign navies." The board recommended that the Navy initiate an experimental torpedo boat program.

The Secretary of the Navy, Claude A. Swanson, approved the board's recommendation on

May 7, 1937. President Franklin D. Roosevelt, who as Assistant Secretary of the Navy during World War I had become convinced of the value of small craft, personally supported the proposal. A year later, in a supplementary budget appropriation, Congress voted "the sum of $15,000,000 to be expended at the discretion of the President of the United States for the construction of experimental vessels none of which shall exceed three thousand tons displacement." The Navy rapidly announced a competition for American shipyards to submit designs for advanced anti-submarine craft and motor torpedo boats.

American boat builders had gained considerable experience in small, high-speed boats from the late 1920s, as they had produced "rum runners" to carry illegal liquor during the Prohibition era. In addition, American design firms had kept track of the proliferation of small craft designs in Europe between the wars.

U.S. boat-building yards and designers thus were ready to respond to the Navy Department's invitation on July 11, 1938, to submit plans for a 165-foot submarine chaser, a torpedo boat 70 to 80 feet long, and a torpedo boat 54 to 60 feet long. Each torpedo boat type was to carry two torpedoes plus depth charges and .50-caliber machine guns. The winner in each category would receive a prize of $15,000, a significant sum for the day.

When the competition closed on September 30 the Navy had received 24 designs for the smaller torpedo boat and 13 designs for the larger. The Navy selected three and five of the designs, respectively, and requested more-detailed

The sister boats *PT 3* and *PT 4* at high speed. These craft were too small for U.S. Navy requirements. They had Packard diesel engines providing a speed of 32 knots; the tubes on the after decks are diesel exhausts. *James C. Fahey collection (USNI)*

The Higgins *PT 5* (foreground) and *PT 6* were the first PT boats with the basic MTB configuration adopted by the U.S. Navy. The *PT 5*, however, had unreliable supercharged Vilmart gasoline engines and was unsuccessful; the *PT 6*, powered by three Packard diesel engines, was sold to Finland. *Fred Freeman collection (USNI)*

This is the second *PT 6*, on high-speed trials in the spring of 1941. Canvas covers the two stern-firing 18-inch torpedo tubes and the two depth charge racks fitted between them.

A broadside view of the *PT 9* shows the design's relationship to the Elco MTBs. The "shadow" numbers were used for early U.S. PT boats. They were impressive on light hulls. The *PT 9* lacks a mast and the cannon and open machine gun mounts found in later PT boats.

The *PT 7* and *PT 8* had sleek lines, resembling several European MTB designs. Their design severely limited the weapons that they could carry. *James C. Fahey collection (USNI)*

The *PT 7* and *PT 8* were U.S. Navy designs that displayed numerous shortcomings. The *PT 7* was built of wood, the *PT 8* of aluminum. Their two 21-inch torpedo tubes were forward-firing. *U.S. Navy*

The Scott-Paine *PT 9*, brought to the United States by the Electric Boat firm, became the prototype for the highly successful Elco series of MTBs. The *PT 9* was photographed departing from New York on January 14, 1941, en route to Florida with other PT boats. *Rudy Arnold collection (NASM)*

data. On March 21, 1939—with war already raging in Asia and little more than five months away in Europe—the Navy announced the design winners: Sparkman and Stephens, noted sailboat designers, had won the competition for the 70-foot torpedo boat, and Professor George Crouch, working for the firm of Henry B. Nevins, was selected for the 54-foot boat.

Next, the Navy selected shipyards to construct these designs, now designated as PT for motor torpedo boat. PT was derived from the Navy classification scheme, with *P* indicating the category of patrol craft and the *T* for torpedo.

The *PT 1* and *PT 2* would be built by the Fogal Boat Yard (later known as the Miami Shipbuilding Co. in Florida), and the *PT 3* and *PT 4* by the Fisher Boat Works in Detroit, Michigan, all four to a modified Crouch design. The *PT 5* and *PT 6* would be built by Higgins Industries in New Orleans, founded by innovative small-craft designer Andrew J. Higgins, to the Sparkman and Stephens design as an 81-foot torpedo boat. And the *PT 7* and *PT 8* would be 81-foot torpedo boats built at the Philadelphia Navy Yard to a design produced by the Bureau of Ships (successor to the Bureau of Construction and Repair).

But "as it turned out, the winning designs already were obsolete," wrote PT-boat historian Robert J. Bulkley, Jr., in his history *At Close Quarters*. The British had an intensive motor torpedo boat program and the Electric Boat Company (Elco) had good relations with the Royal Navy. In Britain, Hubert Scott-Paine had designed a 70-foot

MTB that could carry two 21-inch-diameter or four 18-inch-diameter torpedoes plus machine guns. Powered by Rolls-Royce gasoline engines, the Scott-Paine boat was fast, maneuverable, and sturdily constructed. The Royal Navy and other navies soon ordered large numbers of these craft.

Elco executives looked at the Scott-Paine boat as well as MTBs produced by Thornycroft and Vosper. The Scott-Paine craft was judged to be superior to the other designs and with the personal approval of President Roosevelt, a 70-foot MTB and manufacturing rights were purchased by Elco for the U.S. government on June 1, 1939. This would be the direct progenitor of the several hundred PT boats and PTC and BPT derivatives that U.S. shipyards would construct during the next six years.

The Scott-Paine boat—now designated *PT 9*—arrived at the port of New York on September 5, 1939, as deck cargo on the *SS President Roosevelt* (named for Theodore Roosevelt). The *PT 9* was then carried by barge to the Elco yard at Groton, Connecticut, where Scott-Paine himself sailed the craft for Navy trials. Commander Robert B. Carney, one of the inspecting officers and a future Chief of Naval Operations, would report, "I started out on the trials frankly skeptical about the claims I have heard for this boat during the past year, and I asked for every condition which I thought might bring out weaknesses in the boat's performance; Mr. Scott-Paine was more than glad to go anywhere at any speed or on any course that I requested, and on the run

The Elco-built *PT 10* through *PT 19* were the U.S. Navy's first series built MTBs. Here the *PT 10* at high speed shows her torpedo tubes and aircraft-type Dewandre gun turrets, each with twin .50-caliber Browning machine guns. *James C. Fahey collection (USNI)*

Torpedoes were the principal weapon of MTBs. Here, a 21-inch-diameter tube for Mark VIII torpedoes is installed on a PT boat. The device at left—at the rear of the tube—contains the high-pressure firing charge.

The 70-foot Elco PT boats and some other early MTBs carried twin-mount .303-caliber Lewis machine guns forward of the bridge. These World War I-era machine guns had rotating drum magazines fitted atop the twin barrels. *Electric Boat Co.*

The chief engineer's position atop one of the three Packard gasoline engines of a 70-foot Elco PT boat. The triple-engine propulsion plants had potential dangers because of their high-octane gasoline, but they proved reliable. *Electric Boat Co.*

from Watch Hill to Race Light he handled the boat much more roughly than was necessary to demonstrate the qualities of the boat."

With Britain and France at war against Germany since September 3, there was now an urgency to begin producing torpedo boats. The Navy took the $5 million remaining from the original funds voted for competitive MTB prototypes and, with President Roosevelt's permission, contracted with Electric Boat to mass produce the Scott-Paine design. The President's interest was important to the procurement of MTBs because of the massive U.S. naval building program of aircraft carriers, battleships, cruisers, destroyers, auxiliaries, and other small ships and craft. The allocation of resources—labor, shipyard space, and materials—was becoming critical.

Elco offered to produce 23 near-duplicates of the *PT 9* which, with the British-built prototype, would provide two 12-boat MTB squadrons. On December 7, 1939—an ominous date—the Navy Department awarded Elco a contract to construct 11 MTBs *(PT 10–20)* and 12 MTB "chasers" *(PTC 1–12)*, the latter to carry additional depth charges for "chasing submarines" in place of torpedoes. The American boats would be near duplicates of the Scott-Paine design, but with three

1,200-horsepower Packard engines in place of the Rolls-Royce engines.

Slowly the American-built prototypes were delivered. None of them could be considered successful. The Miami-built *PT 1* and *PT 2* were delayed because of their engines, which were being delivered in December 1941; they were quickly reclassified as small boats.

The Fisher Boat Works' *PT 3* and *PT 4* were unsuccessful mainly because they were too small, being 58-foot craft like the Miami boats. The Higgins-built *PT 5* suffered from poor performance, while the similar *PT 6* was never placed in U.S. service, but sold to Finland. Significantly, Andrew Higgins then—at his own expense—built a boat to his own design that, when delivered in February 1941, proved an outstanding performer. This boat was also given the designation *PT 6*.

The two Navy-designed boats, the *PT 7* and *PT 8*, were also unsuccessful. The *PT 8* was unique in having an aluminum hull; all the other PT prototypes had been constructed of wood. Both boats were overweight, in part because the

Philadelphia yard used destroyer parts in their construction.

Instead, it would be the Elco design—derived from the Scott-Paine boat—that would provide the U.S. Navy's first operational MTBs. The *PT 10* was delivered to the Navy on November 4, 1940, and four days later MTB Squadron 2 was commissioned with Lieutenant Earl S. Caldwell as squadron commander. MTB Squadron 1 had been commissioned earlier on July 24, 1940 (also under Caldwell) for *PT 1* through *PT 8*. The failure of those prototypes meant that MTB Squadron 2 was the first truly operational PT-boat unit.

The first ten Elco boats, *PT 10* through *PT 19,* were 70-foot boats delivered through December 1940. MTB Squadron 2's boats were put through their paces on a cruise to Cienfuegos, Cuba. They proved to be good sea boats. By the time the last of them was delivered it was obvious that the design was already outdated, as Elco and Higgins had already developed superior MTB designs. Accordingly, beginning in April 1941, the ten boats were transferred to Britain under the Lend-Lease program. All saw combat in the Mediterranean and several were lost.

The three 4M-2500 Packard engines of a 70-foot Elco PT boat. The American-built Packards had many features adopted from British engines; in turn, many American-built Packards went to Britain under Lend-Lease arrangements. *Electric Boat Co.*

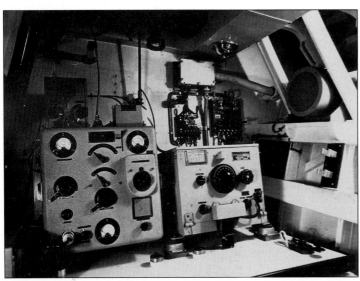

The radio room of a 70-foot Elco PT boat. The lone radio operator on an MTB was generally kept busy during combat operations listening for friendly and as well as enemy radio transmissions. *Electric Boat Co.*

A 21-inch torpedo tube on a 77-foot Elco boat. The muzzle cover on the tube was removed before entering combat. The ventilators carried air into the engineering spaces for the gasoline engines and the below-decks crew. *U.S. Navy*

Also transferred to Britain were the *PT 3*, *PT 4*, *PT 5*, *PT 6*, and *PT 7*, while the British-built *PT 9* was also returned to her homeland in 1941. The unsuccessful *PT 6* and *PT 8* were sent to Newport, Rhode Island, to train MTB sailors, while the *PT 16* through the *PT 19* served there briefly before going to Britain. Thus, 16 of the Navy's first 19 MTBs were sent to sea under the White Ensign in 1941.

Elco offered an improved 77-foot MTB to the Navy, which quickly awarded it a contract for 49 boats covering hull numbers *PT 20* through *PT 68*. These craft, with a standard displacement of 33 tons, would carry four 21-inch torpedo tubes (or two tubes plus eight depth charges, the latter not normally carried). All four tubes fired forward; just prior to firing the tubes were trained outboard along a short track

Close-up of the aircraft-type Dewandre gun turret fitted on the *PT 9*. These turrets, designed by a Dutch firm, were electrically powered. They proved too complex, too restrictive, and easily fogged over. Subsequently, all machine gun mounts were open.

Fixed 21-inch torpedo tube on a 70-foot Elco boat built for the Royal Navy. There are twin .303-caliber Lewis guns forward; the .50-caliber machine gun mounts amidships have had the turret domes removed. These guns have ammunition boxes fitted. *U.S. Navy*

The *PT 11* after running aground on the Isle of Pines, off Cuba. The boat was stripped of guns, engines, and other gear to permit her to be floated off. The craft was then rehabilitated and returned to service. *Al Ross collection*

The *PT 14* after transfer to the Royal Navy and reconfiguration as the *MTB 263*. Twin Lewis guns are fitted forward, the twin machine gun mounts are open, the after tubes are removed (with two depth charges fitted), and a 20-mm gun with shield is fitted aft. *Elco*

The *PT 11* and *PT 18* show the standard plan view of MTBs. Two or four torpedo tubes were mounted outboard of the small bridge superstructure of U.S. torpedo boats.

The January 1941 transit of these seven PT boats from New York to Florida demonstrated the open-sea cruising capability of these diminutive craft. The Elco *PT 12* is in the lead as the MTBs leave New York harbor. *Rudy Arnold collection (NASM)*

mounted under the front of each tube. No torpedo reloads were carried.

Each MTB had two aircraft-type turrets for twin .50-caliber Browning machine guns. These were hydraulically powered mountings with a high rate of fire to provide defense against air attack. Forward of the bridge were two mountings for .30-caliber twin Lewis machine guns.

The boats were constructed of wood—the hull was double-planked mahogany with canvas stretched between the planking, laid with marine glue. The deck was made of double planking with canvas in between, the inner layer of mahogany, and the outer deck of teak. Inside the hull and small deck house, designers used wood (including balsa) and aluminum to save weight. There was, of course, no armor on the boats.

The three Packard engines could produce 3,600 hp to drive the boat at a maximum speed of 41 knots. Popular press reports generally accorded the boats "super speeds" of 50 and even 60 knots! Manned by two officers and ten enlisted

PT boat accommodations were tight. Here, officers and enlisted men share the invariably simple meal in the combination crew's quarters and mess space. MTBs required support from bases ashore and tenders. *Rudy Arnold collection (NASM)*.

MTB Squadron 2 departs the Washington Navy Yard in January 1941. There are several 70-foot Elco PT boats and the *PT 9* (center left). Beyond the PT boats are the presidential yacht *Potomac* and her tender *Cuyahoga*, both ex-Coast Guard cutters; the latter was returned to the Coast Guard in 1941. *U.S. Navy*

Three Elco 70-foot PT boats race in formation a few days after the Japanese attack on Pearl Harbor. They were powered by three Packard gasoline engines, each rated at 1,200 horsepower, providing a speed of 45 knots when the boats were in good condition. Those engines would be standard for war-built MTBs. *Rudy Arnold collection (NASM)*

men, these craft would prove to be reliable, maneuverable, and rugged.

Meanwhile, Higgins Industries had designed a so-called "Dream Boat," 76 feet long, also with three 1,200-hp Packard engines. Since other builders wished to compete in future MTB contracts, the Chief of Naval Operations, Admiral Harold R. Stark, ordered competitive trials held on July 21–24, 1941. At this so-called "Plywood Derby" ten MTBs raced over a 190-mile course from New London around Block Island, New York; these were:

Higgins	PT 6	81-foot
Navy	PT 8	81-foot (aluminum)
Elco	PT 20	77-foot
Elco	PT 26	77-foot
Elco	PT 30	77-foot
Elco	PT 31	77-foot
Elco	PT 33	77-foot
Huckins	PT 69	72-foot
Higgins	PT 70	78-foot

Also participating was a Higgins 70-foot boat built for the British.

The Elco *PT 20* won the first race in smooth water by turning up an average of 38 knots, and *PT 31* of the same series won the second, in rough water, with an average speed of 25 knots. With Elco's demonstrated superiority the firm was given a contract for the mass production of the 77-footers.

The later Higgins design placed so well in the derby that the 78-foot craft was also ordered into production. The Huckins Yacht firm of Jacksonville, Florida, having entered its single prototype, was given a smaller production contract, bringing to three the number of U.S. yards engaged in producing MTBs.

Meanwhile, the Elco 77-footers were coming off the production line at Bayonne, New Jersey, at a prodigious rate. MTB Squadron 3 was placed in commission on August 12, 1941, under Lieutenant John D. Bulkeley. The squadron was specifically intended for operations in the Philippines, where U.S. leaders expected the Japanese to strike first when they went on the offensive against the United States.

Both MTB Squadrons 1 and 3 were to be shipped to the Pacific. Under Lieutenant Commander William C. Specht, all 12 Elco boats of Squadron 1 were dispatched to Pearl Harbor in late 1941—the *PT 20* through *PT 30* and the *PT 42*. The first six boats of Squadron 3—*PT 31* through *PT 35* and *PT 41*—with Bulkeley in charge, departed the New York Navy Yard on August 19 aboard the fleet oiler *Guadalupe*. The oiler passed through the Panama Canal and, after stopovers at Long Beach, California, and Pearl Harbor, arrived at Manila on October 5.

Because of the impending hostilities, it was decided that six MTBs of Squadron 1 would be shipped from Pearl Harbor to the Philippines as deck cargo aboard the Navy oiler *Ramapo* to complete Squadron 3. On Sunday morning, December 7, 1941, the *Ramapo* was moored with other auxiliary ships and warships at the Pearl Harbor Navy Yard. The *PTs 27, 29, 30,* and *42* were resting in cradles on the oiler's deck; on the adjacent pier were the *PT 26* and *PT 28,* in their cradles, about to be lifted by the yard's huge hammerhead crane onto the *Ramapo.*

As the first Japanese planes screamed over Pearl Harbor the six MTBs of Squadron 1 were in the water, moored in a nest at the submarine base, adjacent to the repair barge *YR 20,* which served as a floating base for the boats. Most of their crews were aboard the barge finishing breakfast.

PT-boat crewmen raced to their boats' guns. In a few seconds the .50-caliber Brownings on all six boats were firing skyward. Credit was claimed for shooting down two Japanese torpedo planes that streaked over the PT boats. But with so many ships firing at the attackers it was impossible to make definitive claims.

A few hundred yards south of the submarine base, PT boat crews similarly raced for the guns aboard the four boats already loaded on the oiler *Ramapo.* For their shipment the boats' empty fuel tanks had been filled with carbon dioxide to prevent fires from gasoline fumes. Thus the crews could not start the gasoline engines to compress

Looking aft from the midships bridge structure of the oiler *Guadalupe* are four PT boats, the *PT 34* and *PT 35* farther aft; two additional boats forward. The six other Squadron 3 boats were being loaded aboard an oiler at Pearl Harbor when the Japanese attacked. *U.S. Navy*

The Navy oiler *Guadalupe* was employed to carry six PT boats of MTB Squadron 3 to the Philippines in the fall of 1941. She was one of 12 tankers built just before the war under a joint Navy-Maritime Commission project; all wore Navy gray during the war, with four being converted to escort aircraft carriers. *U.S. Navy*

A close-up of the *PT 34* aboard the *Guadalupe*. The .50-caliber Dewandre turrets are covered with canvas for the transit. Note the MTB Squadron 3 pennant flying from boat's stub mast. A U.S. heavy cruiser passes in the background. *U.S. Navy*

air, which was needed to force hydraulic oil into the turret training mechanisms.

The sailors quickly cut the hydraulic lines, permitting several men to slew each turret manually, while a gunner fired at the Japanese planes. The .50-caliber guns on the PT boats fired more than 4,000 rounds of ammunition. Claims were made that these gunners hit at least one attacking plane.

Neither the *Ramapo*, whose guns also blazed away during the attack, nor any of the PT boats suffered any damage. U.S. PT boats had fought their first action, four while high and dry on the deck of a fleet oiler, and two on a pier. With the attack over, the Navy decided that it would be too dangerous for the *Ramapo* to proceed to the Philippines. She would instead sail for the West Coast. Her six PT boats would be kept at Pearl Harbor to help with the base defenses. The dozen MTBs of Squadron 1 would be especially useful in the face of rumors that the Japanese would be making amphibious (and possibly airborne) landings on Oahu.

Meanwhile, the six PT boats in the Philippines were also coming under Japanese fire.

Chapter 3

"They Were Expendable"

War came to the United States at 7:55 A.M. (local time) on Sunday, December 7, 1941, when the Japanese struck Pearl Harbor. More than 4,000 miles to the west, in Manila, the capital of the Philippines, it was 2:25 A.M. on Monday morning, December 8.

Moments after the attack on Pearl Harbor began, the Navy headquarters there sent the momentous radio message, AIR RAID PEARL HARBOR. THIS IS NO DRILL. Admiral Thomas Hart, commander of the U.S. Asiatic Fleet, with headquarters in Manila, received the message, but inter-service relations were such that he did not pass the message to his Army counterpart, Lieutenant General Douglas MacArthur.

MacArthur had been the U.S. Army's Chief of Staff from 1930 to 1934; upon retiring from the Army he had gone to the Philippines as head of military forces of the Philippine Commonwealth with the rank of field marshal. There he tried to build up the military strength of the islands to resist the expected Japanese assault. By July 1941, when MacArthur was recalled to active U.S. service and named commanding general of U.S. Army Forces in the Far East, he had 130,000 troops under his command, but of those 100,000 were Filipino troops who were poorly trained and armed. MacArthur had 277 Army aircraft, but the only modern planes were 35 early B-17 Flying Fortress bombers and 72 P-40 fighters, the latter greatly inferior to the contemporary Japanese A6M Zero fighter.

The Asiatic Fleet had three cruisers, 13 destroyers, and 29 submarines; most of these were outdated. And there were the six PT boats and 83 officers and enlisted men of MTB Squadron 3 under Lieutenant John D. Bulkeley, which had arrived in Manila two months before. The boats were the *PT 31* through *PT 35* and *PT 41*. In 1937—before the first U.S. funding of MTB development—MacArthur, in planning for the defense of the Philippines, had expressed the belief that 100 torpedo boats could fend off a Japanese invasion.

On December 8, several hours after the attack on Pearl Harbor, Japanese bombers and fighters struck U.S. airfields on Luzon, destroying half the B-17 force (the other half had earlier flown to the southern island of Mindanao) and most of the P-40s. The Asiatic Fleet had been partially scattered for several days in anticipation of the outbreak of war. This initial Japanese air attack concentrated on U.S. air bases. Those ships remaining in the Manila area mostly escaped damage, as did the six PT boats.

At dawn on December 9, Japanese forces had made an unopposed amphibious landing on tiny Batan Island off Luzon and seized its air strip. At dawn on the following day more Japanese troops went ashore at two points on northern Luzon, Aparri and Vigan, again with no opposition during the landing and easily captured nearby airfields.

And on December 10 Japanese bombers struck the Cavite Navy Yard at the eastern end of

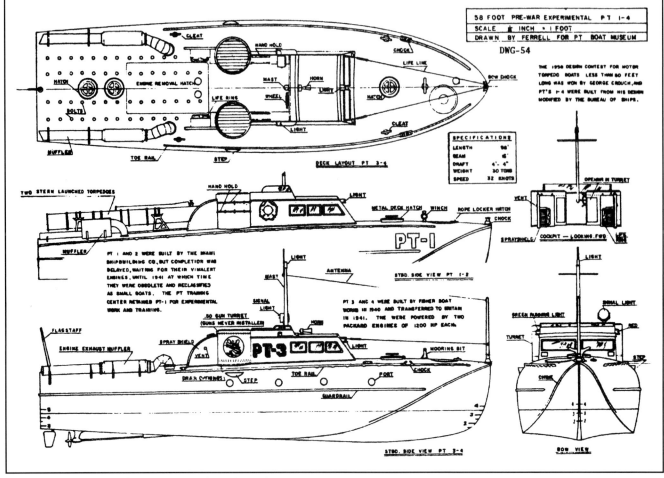

A line drawing of the 58-foot experimental PT1 through PT4. *Courtesy PT Boat Museum*

Manila Bay. This was a high-level bombing raid, the planes flying at some 20,000 feet, high above the range of the machine guns fitted in the PT boats as well as the Army's 3-inch anti-aircraft guns. The MTBs, based at Cavite, maneuvered in the bay. Several Japanese bombers dived on the torpedo boats. The small craft easily avoided their bombs, while the PT-boat gunners claimed to have shot down three of their antagonists.

Meanwhile, waves of twin-engine Japanese bombs struck the Navy Yard. Virtually every building within the facility was destroyed or heavily damaged. A submarine undergoing repairs was heavily damaged (and later scuttled by U.S. forces). The PT boats' spare parts and equipment, and thousands of drums of 100-octane gasoline were destroyed. Nine replacement Packard engines that were stored in private Manila garages were saved for the moment, but they would never be installed in the boats.

As the bombers departed, the MTBs transported wounded from the burning Navy Yard to the hospital at Cañacao. They then took aboard their support personnel and such equipment as could be salvaged from the wreckage and proceeded to a nearby fishing village to set up base. Immediately the boats began local patrols around Manila Bay and along the Bataan Peninsula.

There were increasing reports of Japanese landing craft and even submarines in the area. The PT boats were dispatched to check out these reports, initially working with some of the small patrol craft still in the area. Although Japanese naval ships and small craft were operating along the northern coasts of Luzon, the PT boats were kept on a tight rein. A few of the surviving B-17s did carry out bombing attacks on Japanese ships, but with little result. Their bases untenable, they soon fled to Australia.

The PT boats required continued maintenance. With the Cavite Navy Yard devastated, repairs to the MTBs were undertaken by the submarine tender *Canopus*, anchored at Mariveles, and the *Dewey* floating dry dock. While each boat, in turn, underwent maintenance, the *PT 32* suffered an engine room explosion and spent several weeks undergoing repairs.

The PT boats took time out from their almost routine patrols on the night of December 17 when the passenger ship *Corregidor* struck a mine. She had been loaded with hundreds of passengers attempting to escape the Philippines. The *PT 32*, *PT 34*, and *PT 35* joined other small craft in pulling survivors from the oil-covered waters. The three diminutive boats took aboard 296 passengers; the *PT 32*—manned by a crew of about 12—took on 196 survivors.

The Japanese, with control of the air, were able to carry out their invasion plan with little interference from U.S. forces. The main Japanese landing force, embarked in 76 transports and landing ships, reached Lingayen Gulf, on Luzon's west coast, on December 22. The closest landing was about 100 miles from Manila Bay. The Japanese troops raced for the capital.

General MacArthur—without consulting with the senior U.S. Navy commander—declared the capital an open city on December 26 and withdrew his remaining ground troops to the Bataan Peninsula; the day before MacArthur had moved his headquarters to the tunnels cut into the island of Corregidor in Manila Bay. Lieutenant General Masaharu Homma, the overall Japanese commander, chose to take Manila—with his troops entering the city on January 2—rather than immediately pursue MacArthur's troops to Bataan. This gave the U.S.-Filipino troops time to set up a defense line on the peninsula.

The Bataan Peninsula is about 25 miles long and 20 miles across at its widest point. Earlier Army plans had called for the peninsula to have defenses and provisions to hold out against attacks for six months, until a relief force could reach the Philippines. But MacArthur felt such plans were defeatist. Now tens of thousands of U.S. and Filipino troops as well as civilian refugees streamed to the peninsula. These gallant defenders were only delaying the inevitable.

The PT boats could give them little support. On the night of December 24 the *PT 33*, while patrolling south of Manila Bay, ran aground. On Christmas Day other MTBs attempted to pull her off the reef, but without success. The craft was stripped of useful parts, equipment, and weapons, and set afire to prevent her being captured by the Japanese. The remaining food was also taken from the *PT 33*, as shortages had caused naval personnel in the area to be limited to two meals a day. There were more serious

problems: Little high-octane gasoline for the PT boats was available and much of what was had been "sabotaged," with wax deposits in the gasoline that clogged gas strainers and carburetors. Army forces also found the lubricating oil to be contaminated with sand. Consequently, careful straining was added to the task of refueling the boats by hand.

The PT boats continued their generally uneventful patrols of Manila Bay, and on January 9 a PT boat carried General MacArthur from Corregidor to Bataan. On Bataan he assured everyone he spoke with that he could hold the peninsula for "several months." He then returned to Corregidor after this, his only visit to the Bataan battlefield.

The PT boats were belatedly ordered into action against major Japanese ships on the night of January 18–19 in response to reports of Japanese ships off the western coast of Bataan, at the northern end of Subic Bay. Lieutenant Bulkeley led the *PT 31* and *PT 34* to investigate.

The boats were fired on by Japanese shore batteries. Bulkeley, in the *PT 34*, sighted a Japanese freighter and fired two torpedoes. One launched properly and moments later there was an explosion. The second torpedo stuck partially out of the tube. Every time the speeding craft hit a wave the water turned the small impeller in the nose of the torpedo. With sufficient turns the torpedo would be armed, and vulnerable to detonation by a hard wave slap. A sailor straddled the torpedo tube and stuffed toilet paper into the impeller blades to stop them from turning (the torpedo was later jettisoned).

U.S. troops ashore reported that the *PT 34* had sunk a Japanese merchant ship, estimated at 5,000 tons. Japanese records examined after the war, however, showed no sinking.

The night action cost the *PT 31*. Early in the boat's patrol on the night of January 18, two of its engines stopped from wax in the fuel. Then the third engine suffered a breakdown of its water-cooling system. The boat drifted aground. Under fire from Japanese shore guns, the crew tried to get the boat off the reef. Finally, the crew abandoned the craft, setting it on fire and blowing holes in the hull with hand grenades. Ten crewmen survived; three were lost.

The four surviving PT boats continued to search for reported Japanese activity in Manila Bay, patrolled the waters off Bataan, and on occasion provided gunfire support for troops ashore. Japanese forces hit the boats with small-caliber bullets, wounding one officer. U.S. troops shot up one Japanese barge, and Bulkeley boarded the craft to retrieve documents. Two wounded Japanese were taken as prisoners.

The PT boats made periodic attempts to attack a freighter sighted offshore. On the night of February 1–2 the *PT 32*, patrolling in Subic Bay, sighted what appeared to be a Japanese cruiser. The MTB closed on the ship. At a distance of 5,000 yards she was sighted by the cruiser, which illuminated her with a searchlight and began firing. The *PT 32* fired two torpedoes at the warship and withdrew under heavy fire. Two torpedo hits were reported. But Japanese records show only that the small, 1,135-ton minelayer *Yaeyama* suffered minor damage at the time, and even that was attributed to shore fire.

The most daring and, in some respects, important accomplishment of Bulkeley's PT boats was to remove General MacArthur, his family, and several staff officers from Luzon. Several thousand U.S. soldiers, sailors, airmen, and Marines had taken refuge on the fortified island of Corregidor in Manila Bay. MacArthur, his family, and staff lived with them in the massive underground tunnels of Corregidor as Japanese aircraft and bombarded the island.

On February 20, Manuel L. Quezon, president of the commonwealth, his family, and staff were evacuated from Corregidor by a U.S. submarine and taken to the island of Panay, between Manila and the southernmost island of Mindanao. Three days later the U.S. high command in Washington ordered MacArthur to immediately go to the central Philippines to ascertain the feasibility of a prolonged defense, and to then proceed to Australia to take command of the U.S. forces that would be built up there. General MacArthur, however, delayed leaving Corregidor.

There were several thousand American and Filipino troops on Corregidor, already living on half-rations, and under constant Japanese attack. In response to several additional directives from Washington, MacArthur finally decided to follow orders. He planned to leave Corregidor in the submarine *Permit*, but she could not reach the island until March 13 at the earliest. Further, there was a sudden increase in Japanese naval activity in the area and hence concern that the Japanese would intercept the submarine in the restricted waters of Manila Bay.

Accordingly, on March 1, while four of the few surviving P-40 fighters operated over Manila Bay, General MacArthur and his wife, Jean, embarked in the *PT 41* for a brief excursion in the bay to determine the feasibility of escape by PT boat. While the brief cruise demonstrated nothing

practical to MacArthur, the decision was made to escape in the MTBs.

Lieutenant Bulkeley had four of his original six boats remaining. All were kept running by using equipment from the discarded boats and improvised parts. Their engines were long overdue for overhaul and as a result none of the boats could reach maximum speed. The plan was for them to carry MacArthur to Mindanao in the central Philippines, from where an aircraft would fly him to Australia.

On the evening of March 11 the *PT 41* came alongside Corregidor's north dock. Passengers for the other MTBs were ferried by small boat from Corregidor to the boats in nearby coves to avoid the Japanese observing a concentration of the four boats at the island. There were 18 passengers: MacArthur boarded Bulkeley's *PT 41*, accompanied by his wife, Jean, their young son, his Chinese nurse, and his chief of staff. The other passengers—ten Army officers, two naval officers, and an Army sergeant—were embarked in the three other boats. (Among the thousands of Americans left behind on Corregidor were one hundred Army nurses.)

General MacArthur was the last to board the *PT 41*. In his book *Reminiscences*, MacArthur wrote,

"Darkness had now fallen, and the waters were beginning to ripple from the faint night breeze. The enemy firing had ceased and a muttering silence had fallen. It was as though the dead were passing by the stench of destruction. The smell of filth thickened the night air. I raised my cap in farewell salute, and I could feel my face go white, feel a sudden convulsive twitch in the muscles of my face. I heard someone ask, 'What's his chance, Sarge, of getting through?' and the gruff reply, 'Dunno. He's lucky. Maybe one in five.'

"I stepped aboard *PT 41*. 'You may cast off, Buck,' I said, 'when you are ready.' "

MacArthur had told the general he left in command, Jonathan M. Wainwright, that he hoped that Corregidor and the troops still fighting on the Bataan Peninsula could survive until July 1. By that time he intended to return at the head of a massive U.S. military force to lift the siege of the island from its attackers. He would return—in two and a half years. (The surviving U.S. and Filipino troops on the Bataan Peninsula would surrender to the Japanese on April 9; Corregidor would hold out until May 6.)

The four boats were to rendezvous at the entrance to Manila Bay at 8 P.M. and then proceed

PT boats in action: Artist James Session's rendering of Lieutenant John D. Bulkeley in the *PT 34* attacking a Japanese freighter on the night of January 18–19, 1942, off the coast of Bataan. MTBs operated against enemy ships mainly at night, when few photographers were present. *U.S. Navy*

south. Should any boat break down, her passengers would be transferred to another and she would try to proceed independently; if unable to continue, she would be scuttled. If Japanese ships were sighted, the MTBs would try to evade them; if forced to fight, the *PT 41* would attempt to escape while the others would attack.

The four boats rendezvoused and, led by the *PT 41*, slipped out of Manila Bay in column. There was an easterly wind and the seas were rough. The boats had planned to travel in a diamond formation, the *PT 41* in the lead. The *PT 34* had trouble keeping up; the *PT 32* had only two working engines. All boats had to stop periodically to work on their engines. With the engines stopped, the boats rolled violently, making passengers ill (MacArthur's young son was already running a fever). Unavoidably, the PT boats became separated during the night.

The next morning the *PT 32* saw what the crew believed to be a Japanese destroyer closing from astern. In the early light the MTB tried to escape, throwing over the drums of gasoline lashed to the deck. As the sun came up it became obvious that the overtaking "ship" was the *PT 41*.

At a small island the *PT 32*'s passengers were transferred to other boats. The MTB was to then try to reach another island where it was hoped

gasoline would be available. The *PT 35* had not yet arrived at the island, and that evening Bulkeley with MacArthur in the *PT 41* and the *PT 34* got under way for another night run to the south.

On the morning of March 13 the two boats arrived at Cagayan on the island of Mindanao, the southernmost of the major Philippine islands, having sailed 560 miles from Manila Bay through Japanese-controlled waters. The *PT 35* arrived later that day. As he went ashore, General MacArthur declared, "Bulkeley: I'm giving every officer and man here the Silver Star for gallantry. You've taken me out of the jaws of death, and I won't forget it."

But the three B-17 Flying Fortresses that were to have flown up from Australia had not arrived. Two B-17s did arrive on the 17th. All 17 passengers were crammed into the two bombers, and MacArthur's party was flown to Australia. There, at Adelaide railroad station, MacArthur gave a brief speech, telling how President Roosevelt had ordered him to "break through the Japanese lines" to organize the American offensive against Japan and the relief of the Philippines. "I came through and I shall return," he concluded.

While awaiting the B-17s to carry MacArthur's party to safety, Bulkeley had his three boats repaired as best they could be at Cagayan. He also

Lieutenant John D. Bulkeley of MTB Squadron 3 on the bridge of a PT boat. His squadron's exploits in the Philippines in the early days of World War II would capture the nation's imagination and would be immortalized in print and film. *U.S. Navy*

secured the use of a small aircraft to search the area for the *PT 32*. However, the *PT 32* had remained at Tagauayan. On the morning of March 13 the submarine *Permit* arrived at the island. The *PT 32* was no longer considered seaworthy. Her captain took the 15 crewmen of the PT boat aboard the submarine, and the MTB was destroyed by gunfire from the *Permit*.

The *Permit* continued on to Corregidor. There, eight of the PT-boat sailors were put ashore (along with most of the 3-inch rounds and small arms on the submarine). The submarine then took on 40 personnel from Corregidor, most of them code-breaking specialists whom the United States desperately wanted kept out of Japanese hands. Counting these men, the seven PT-boat personnel, and 64 submariners, the *Permit* set out from Corregidor with 111 men on board. (Despite her human "cargo," the *Permit* was ordered to make an attack on Japanese warships. She was unable to score against them, and Japanese destroyer attacks forced the submarine to remain submerged for 22 hours. On April 7 the submarine reached Australia.)

President Quezon, who had been taken to Panay by submarine, had moved to the nearby island of Negros to establish a new government. The Japanese advance made that impossible. The U.S. Army high command asked Bulkeley to bring Quezon to Mindanao so that he, too, could be flown to Australia.

On the evening of March 18, Bulkeley led the *PT 35* and *PT 41*—the only two MTBs still operational—to Negros. When they reached the island, a run of 100 miles, the *PT 41* entered a small port while the *PT 35* remained offshore, watching for reported Japanese destroyers.

President Quezon was reported to be farther up the coast, and the *PT 41* went back to sea. The *PT 35* had struck a submerged object, which had opened a large hole in her bow. Bulkeley took aboard the *PT 35*'s crew and the damaged boat was beached.

Quezon was finally located. He came aboard the *PT 41* with his wife, two daughters, vice president, and an entourage. With his group, the boat's crew and that of the *PT 35*, plus a mass of Quezon luggage, the small MTB was badly overcrowded. Rough seas made the trip hazardous as well as uncomfortable. Quezon and his party were safely delivered to Mindanao on the morning of March 19. He was then flown to Australia, and went on to Washington where he established a government-in-exile.

With his VIP-carrying duties completed, Bulkeley returned to Negros to recover the *PT 35*, which he towed to Cebu City, where there was a marine railway. After undergoing preliminary repairs, the craft was able to travel—at 12 knots—to Cebu, where more substantial repairs could be undertaken. Meanwhile, on April 8, Bulkeley led the *PT 41* and *PT 34* to sea to attack two Japanese destroyers reported to be in the area.

Late that night these MTBs sighted a Japanese ship. At a range of 5,000 yards the enemy was identified not as a destroyer, but as the light cruiser *Kuma*. The PT boats attacked. They each fired two torpedoes. Then, caught in the cruiser's searchlights and with shells flying overhead, they made a second torpedo attack. At times, the PT boats closed to within 300 yards of the cruiser.

As the MTBs attempted to escape, a second Japanese ship, a destroyer, appeared on the scene, joining the cruiser in blasting away at the torpedo boats. The *PT 34* had her stub mast shot away and took many small-caliber shell hits.

The crews of the two PT boats believed that they had sunk the cruiser. In fact, of the eight torpedoes fired, only one 21-inch torpedo struck the cruiser, and that one failed to explode. The Japanese ships escaped undamaged. Historian Robert Bulkley wrote in *At Close Quarters*, ". . . the magnitude of the damage, or lack of it, neither increases nor diminishes the courage of the officers and men who pressed home a close-range attack on a dangerous enemy 100 times their size."

The next morning the damaged *PT 34*, with one sailor wounded in attacking the cruiser, was attacked by four Japanese floatplanes. During the 15-minute aerial attack the Japanese planes dropped eight small bombs and strafed the boat. All of her guns were knocked out, and two crewmen were killed and others wounded. She was beached. One Japanese plane may have been shot down.

Efforts were begun to salvage the *PT 34*, but several hours later three of the planes returned. Bombing and strafing, they set the boat afire and she exploded.

Next the *PT 35* was destroyed. She was still at Cebu when Japanese troops entered the city on April 12. She was burned. Lieutenant Bulkeley now had only the *PT 41*. He had not been able to replace his torpedoes after attacking the Japanese cruiser. On April 13, on direct orders from General MacArthur, he was flown to Australia. (In early April two U.S. submarines had unloaded 14 torpedoes at Cebu to make space for food to be carried to Corregidor through the Japanese blockade. Thus, torpedoes were available for the PT boats.)

The Army planned to disassemble the *PT 41* and transport her 15 miles inland to Lake Lanao on Mindanao. It was intended to use her as a gunboat to prevent Japanese floatplanes from using the lake. She was stripped and partially disassembled. Before she could be moved to the lake, however, she was destroyed to prevent her capture by the Japanese. (Her three Packard engines, taken separately by truck, did reach the lake.)

Officers and sailors of MTB Squadron 3 continued fighting the Japanese ashore. Eighteen others died aboard PT boats or ashore fighting the Japanese. The Japanese took 38 prisoners; nine died in prison camps. Including those who reached Australia, 56 men from the squadron survived the war. Bulkeley, after reaching Australia, was ordered to Washington. There, he was personally awarded the Medal of Honor by President Roosevelt.

The six MTBs of Bulkeley's squadron had fought a heroic delaying action in the Philippines against Japanese aircraft, warships, and artillery. Although their score against Japanese ships was virtually nil, they were still heroes, just like the defenders of Wake Island and the soldiers, sailors, and Marines on Corregidor and Bataan.

A 1942 book based on the squadron's adventures, *They Were Expendable*, by W. L. White, became one of America's great war stories. The book was made into a movie of the same name, in which Robert Montgomery, who was a U.S. Navy captain in the war, and John Wayne (who saw no military service) played PT-boat officers. The book and film title came from a remark by Bulkeley about the expendability of PT men and boats: "In a war, anything can be expendable—money or gasoline or equipment or most usually men. They are expending you and that machine gun to get time. They don't expect to see either one again. They expect you to stay there and spray that road with steel until you're killed or captured, holding up the enemy for a few minutes or even a precious quarter of an hour."

Chapter 4

Building and Manning PT Boats

The first series production of MTBs for the U.S. Navy were the 49 boats by the Electric Boat Company (Elco), the 77-foot *PT 20* through *68*. These were also the first U.S. torpedo boats to see combat at Pearl Harbor, in the Philippines, and at the Battle of Midway.

With Europe and Asia at war, by early 1941 the U.S. Navy had undertaken a massive warship building program—battleships, carriers, cruisers, destroyers, submarines, and auxiliaries were being constructed in prodigious numbers. While many of the previous objections to building PT boats remained valid, such as the U.S. Navy planning to fight enemy fleets at long distances, it also became evident that German U-boats could bring the war to American shores. Also, the defense of the Philippines could require large numbers of MTBs while the Lend-Lease program, which went into effect on March 11, 1941, meant that Britain and possibly other nations would want U.S. torpedo boats, as their shipyards were already overloaded with war program construction.

Although the Navy attempted to standardize on single designs for most types of large warships, throughout the war it sought to produce several classes of PT boats as well as prototypes. Further, numerous small shipyards were capable of producing wood-hull PT boats but not larger or more complicated steel ships. Thus, efforts were made to employ all aspects of the massive American shipbuilding industry.

Three classes dominated PT boat construction in the United States:

80-foot Elco
78-foot Higgins
70-foot Vosper

The 358 "standard" 80-foot Elco boats were built by Electric Boat at Bayonne, New Jersey (see Appendix A). Joining the fleet from June 1942 onward, these craft were considerably larger than the previous 77-foot Elco boats because of their higher freeboard. Further, these boats were more rugged than their predecessors. Accommodations were well arranged, providing bunks and mess spaces for the crew of two officers and nine enlisted men.

The boats mostly were built with four 21-inch torpedo tubes and four M2 .50-caliber machine guns in twin open mounts. Boats could be fitted with only the forward two tubes, providing space aft for 12 300-pound depth charges or (rarely carried) mines.

A 20-mm Oerlikon cannon was soon fitted aft in these boats, after which the armament was increased based on local conditions and availability. Various boats were fitted with combinations of a second 20-mm cannon, or 37-mm, 40-mm Bofors, and even 75-mm cannon, mortars, and rocket launchers. Some boats were also fitted with "Mousetraps" to launch ahead-firing anti-submarine projectiles. (With additional weapons, more crewmen were added, requiring some sharing of bunks—"hot bunking.")

A final "weapon" was stern-mounted smoke generators. These were valuable for daylight operations, to cover withdrawal, or hide a damaged boat.

Radars were provided to PT boats at an early stage. Early small craft radars that proved very unreliable were installed in Elco boats, the first in November 1942. Improved sets were soon being produced. These were microwave (3 and 10 centimeters) surface search sets in the SO-series produced by Raytheon. The original SO radar set weighed 420 pounds; it had a 24-inch-diameter antenna rotating within a radome, with the total weight of the radome being 65 pounds. Typical detection ranges for the early SO-series were 15 miles for a low-flying aircraft, 20 miles for a battleship, 10 miles for a destroyer, and 5 miles for a surfaced submarine. More reliable versions of the radar were provided through the end of the war.

A few PT boats had a second search radar installed. Also fitted in the later stages of the war were Radio Direction Finders and Identification Friend or Foe systems to help detect enemy ships. U.S. motor torpedo boats were thus

An Elco-type PT boat fires two Mark VIII torpedoes. This scene, repeated hundreds of times in combat, struck fear in the hearts of the captains of enemy warships. This was a test firing off the Naval Torpedo Station at Newport, Rhode Island. *U.S. Navy*

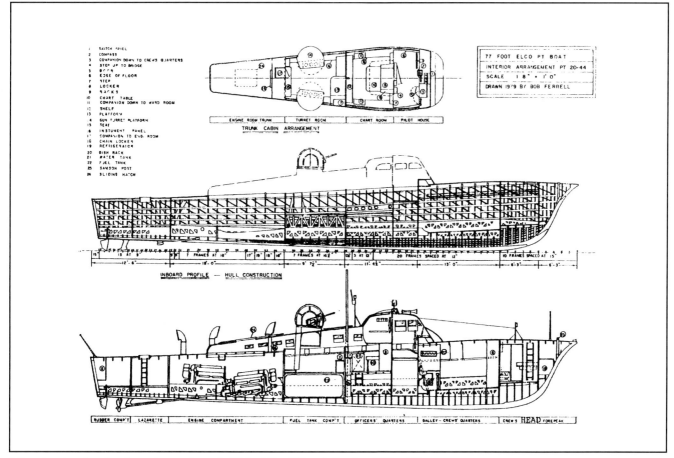

A line drawing showing the cutaway view of a 77-foot Elco PT boat. *Courtesy PT Boat Museum*

The 80-foot Elco MTB was produced in larger numbers than any other U.S. PT boat design. The *PT 105* was an early boat of this design; later boats were provided additional guns, usually four torpedo tubes or launchers, and—highly significant—search radar. *U.S. Navy*

provided with better electronics than the small craft of any other nation.

Throughout the war the Elco design was improved and modified, especially with regard to armament. The Elco production boats (beginning with *PT 103*) had a full load displacement of 51 tons while the latter boats were 60 tons, 15 of which were weapons and ammunition.

The Elco yard at Bayonne also produced 59 smaller PT boats and a dozen PTC "chasers."

The second PT class, in terms of numbers produced, was the 78-foot Higgins boat. These 221 boats were produced at New Orleans, where Higgins Industries also turned out swarms of landing craft. Higgins completed the first of these torpedo boats in July 1942.

Pilot houses situated relatively far forward with a V-face distinguished these craft. Like the Elcos, these Higginses originally had four torpedo tubes. Gun armament originally consisted of two

The *PT 140* shows off the basic Elco 80-foot design. This photo, taken during a training run, shows the boat with torpedo tubes and .50-caliber machine guns, prior to the installation of a battery of cannon. A balsa life raft stowed forward. A censor has painted out the radar mast. *James C. Fahey collection (USNI)*

.50-caliber twin mounts and two single 20-mm guns (both aft). Crews numbered 12 to 14.

The Vosper design, at 70 feet, was the smallest mass-produced PT boat. The U.S. Navy ordered 136 boats from U.S. yards, most of which went to Britain and the Soviet Union under Lend-Lease; in addition, other Vospers built under British contracts in U.S. yards did not have hull numbers. These PT boats were built at several small yards: Annapolis Yacht in Maryland; Herreshoff of Bristol, Rhode Island; and Robert Jacob of City Island, New York.

Finally, in a form of "reverse Lend-Lease," in 1942, the Navy procured four Vosper MTBs built by Canadian Power Boat in Montreal (*PT 368* through *PT 371*). These boats were originally ordered by the Netherlands Navy, but the Germans had occupied Holland before they could be delivered.

The Vosper MTBs had only two 21-inch torpedo tubes with two .50-caliber twin machine gun mounts and a single 20-mm cannon. Their crews numbered 12 men.

Beyond the nine early prototypes *PT 1* through *PT 9* and the four Canadian-built *PT 368*

Radar had a profound impact on all aspects of Allied naval operations, including the nocturnal operations of PT boats. This is a PT boat's SO-series radar set.

The highly successful 80-foot Elco design, showing, from bow, a 37-mm cannon and a 20-mm cannon forward of the bridge; 5-inch rocket launchers, twin .50-caliber machine gun mounts, and, aft, a single 40-mm gun. A pair of Mark XIII torpedo-launching racks are on each side of the *PT 588*. *U.S. Navy*

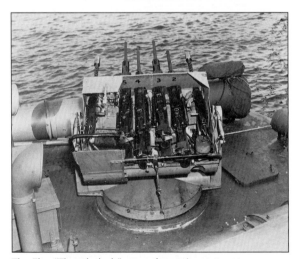

The Elco "Thunderbolt" was a dramatic attempt to increase the close-in firepower of MTBs. At top is the "business end" of the mount, which consisted of four drum-fed 20-mm cannon and two belt-fed .50-caliber machine guns, all aimed and fired by a single gunner who sat in the mount. The *PT 138* was the first boat to have the mount, fitted aft; production versions dispensed with the machine guns. *Electric Boat Co.*

through *PT 371*, U.S. shipyards produced 758 wartime PT boats. Another 58 BPTs were built in a separate series specifically for transfer to Britain in addition to the scores of "straight" PTs going to Britain, the Soviet Union, and Yugoslavia.

The PTC motor torpedo boat chaser was a standard PT boat with depth charges in place of torpedo tubes. Their ASW capability was limited because of their size and hence their range. Attempts to provide them with underwater listening gear failed. Their crews were to locate submarines by sighting them on the surface or spotting their periscopes.

The PTCs had two .50-caliber twin machine-gun mounts and carried eight depth charges. Like their PT cousins, they had wood hulls, but instead of the three Packard engines fitted in all PT boats, the PTCs had two Hall-Scott Defender gasoline engines that provided 30 knots of speed.

Elco and the John Trumpy yacht yard in Camden, New Jersey, constructed only 42 of these craft for the U.S. Navy. (Elco built *PTC 1* through *PTC 12* and Trumpy, *PTC 37* through *PTC 66*). Most of these craft went to Britain or

Another effort to increase PT boat firepower consisted of mounting two pairs of .50-caliber machine guns on the bow, fired remotely from the bridge. This installation on the *PT 564* shows the control cables running across the forecastle. The craft's radar mast is lowered.

the Soviet Union, with only the *PTCs 50, 51, 52,* and *53* remaining under U.S. colors. The planned *PTC 13* through *24* were completed as the *PT 33* through *PT 44*, and the *PTC 25* through *PTC 36* were completed as *PT 59* through *68*.

The principal weapon of the MTB was the torpedo, although its guns often inflicted considerably more damage on their targets. American-built MTBs initially had two or four 21-inch-diameter torpedo tubes. In Elco boats the tubes were fitted on the fore-and-aft axis; the forward tubes could be trained outboard 8 degrees, while the after tubes were trained out 12 degrees. The training gear was hand operated. On the Higgins boats the tubes were fixed, angled out 12 degrees from the centerline.

Torpedoes could be fired electrically from a cockpit position, or manually by a crewman striking the firing mechanism with a mallet!

U.S. PT boats initially carried the Mark VIII torpedo. This "fish" was 21 inches in diameter, 256 inches long, and weighed 2,600 pounds with a warhead of 466 pounds of TNT. The Mark VIII became operational in 1911(!) and most of the torpedoes in the fleet when the war began had been produced in the 1920s.

The torpedo required constant maintenance and adjustments. The PT boat had to be on a near even keel when launching the torpedoes because of their gyroscope guidance system. The steam turbine could propel the Mark VIII at a maximum speed of 36 knots and a range of 16,000 yards.

Subsequently, PT boats were armed with the smaller Mark XIII torpedo, designed initially for use by aircraft. While the newer torpedo's speed

Sailors man the 20-mm Oerlikon cannon on the stern of a torpedo boat (possibly the *PT 62*) during a training evolution at Melville, Rhode Island. Up to three men manned this highly effective gun. *U.S. Navy*

(33.5 knots) and range (6,300 yards) were less than those of the Mark VIII, this weapon was lighter, more reliable, and could be launched from a moving PT boat by being released over the side from a lightweight, side-launching rack. The release was accomplished electrically from the cockpit. Dispensing with the bulky torpedo tubes saved weight aboard the boats and, after the torpedoes were launched, more deck space was available.

The Mark XIII, introduced into the fleet in 1938, was 22.5 inches in diameter and 161 inches long. It weighed 2,216 pounds and had a potent

The *PT 564's* bow-mounted 50-caliber machine guns. Ammunition feeds came from boxes welded to the deck. The guns were difficult to aim, as the craft's bow would rise out of the water at higher speeds.

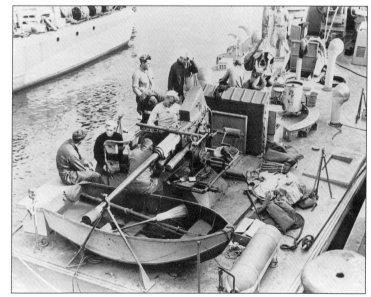

A 40-mm Bofors cannon fitted on a PT boat. These were the largest guns normally mounted on U.S. MTBs, making them effective in the motor gunboat role. U.S. warships from battleships and aircraft carriers down to PT boats and landing craft gunboats carried the weapon.

The bridge of the Elco *PT 552*. One man could control both the helm and the throttles. The location of the forward .50-caliber gun mount restricted visibility from the bridge, but gave the guns better firing arcs. *U.S. Navy*

The basic gun armament on all U.S. PT boats were twin .50- caliber Browning M2 machine guns. One sailor could train, elevate, and fire the guns, which could issue 750 to 850 rounds per minute per barrel. Note the jam-free belt loading arrangement on the *PT 107*. *Fred Freeman collection (USNI*

warhead of 600 pounds of the improved explosive Torpex (TPX). A replacement for the Mark XIII, the Mark 25, with an alcohol turbine to provide a speed of 40 knots, was not put into service due to the large inventory of Mark XIIIs available.

U.S. PT boats experienced very poor performance with their torpedoes. Many failed to function properly, especially at the very shallow settings required for attacking small ships and craft. Equally significant, PT crews received relatively little realistic training in torpedo attacks, and once deployed, there was little opportunity and too few torpedoes for them to continue their training. Fortunately, their guns proved to be highly effective against a variety of targets.

The principal gun armament of early PTs was paired .50-caliber Browning machine guns in power-driven, aircraft-type turrets. These gun mounts had plexiglass domes. In early combat the plexiglass was found impractical, restricting visibility and fogging over from the heat of the gun barrels; the hydraulic system would work only when the ship was powered.

Accordingly, the .50-caliber guns were mounted on open scarf rings so that they could be manually trained. These guns, which could fire 600 rounds per minute per barrel, were found to be effective against aircraft, small craft, and even personnel ashore. Ammunition was belted and automatically fed into the guns; a curved feed system helped to alleviate jamming. One man could easily operate the twin .50-caliber gun mount.

The Swiss-design 20-mm Oerlikon cannon was installed in U.S. warships from late 1941. (It was earlier adopted by the Japanese and British navies.) The Oerlikon operated on the blow-back principle, with the explosive force of the propellant

The *PT 200* was a standard Higgins 78-foot MTB. Radar was not available when this boat was photographed on trials in January 1942. The paired .50-caliber guns fitted outboard of the bridge give the illusion of a four-barrel mount. There is a 20-mm gun fitted aft, forward of a smoke generator. *James C. Fahey collection (USNI)*

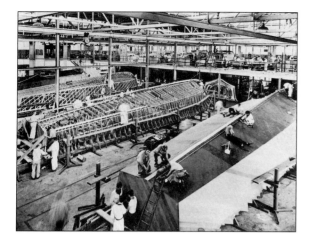

The Electric Boat Company's Elco plant at Bayonne, New Jersey, produced more PT boats than any other American yard. At upper left, 80-foot MTB hulls are assembled; above, workmen assemble the deck house for the *PT 108*; and at left, the *PT 624* is being completed. *Electric Boat Co.*

The 78-foot Higgins *PT 70* was an experimental design with an unusual torpedo configuration. The boat is flying the Higgins banner and manned by company personnel as she goes through speed trials. There are three gun "tubs"; depth-charge rails are fitted at the stern.

moving the breach to accept the next round. The gun's high rate of fire (450 to 480 rounds per minute), its light weight, and its ability to be bolted to the deck without electrical connections made it highly suitable for MTBs. It was produced in single, twin, triple, and even quad mounts. The 20-mm gun was fired by a gunner and ammunition loaders, and either a radio talker or pointer pointed out approaching aircraft to the gunner. The 20-mm guns had either a simple open sight or a gyroscopic sight that took into account the ship's pitch, roll, yaw, and speed changes. Ammunition was normally provided in 60-round drums.

The Oerlikon had a relatively short range, about 4,000 yards, which gave it a limited effec-

tiveness against aircraft. Still, it provided more hitting power than machine guns.

The other standard PT-boat gun was the Swedish-design 40-mm Bofors. This was the most widely used anti-aircraft gun of the war; both the Allied and Axis armed forces used it. The Bofors—which came in single, twin, and quad mountings—was reliable and efficient. It was installed in U.S. Navy ships from mid-1942 and was first fitted to PT boats in mid-1943.

The 40-mm Bofors had a cyclic rate of fire of 160 rounds per minute per barrel; however, because it was manually loaded in four-round clips, a 60 to 90 rounds-per-minute rate was realistic. The single-barrel Bofors fitted in PT boats was fired by two gunners and several loaders, plus either a radio talker or pointer. The guns had an open sight (with radar directors provided for 40-mm guns in larger ships).

The Bofors could reach a maximum altitude of 7,600 yards at 90 degrees elevation, while maximum range was 11,000 yards at 42 degrees elevation. The range and hitting power of the four-pound 40-mm rounds made this a most effective weapon for close-in fighting.

A variety of other guns were fitted on PT boats, some for combat and some for experiments. A popular weapon was the 37-mm cannon, removed from the less-popular P-39 Airacobra fighter. This was subsequently produced specifically for use aboard PT boats. Mounted forward on the boats, the 37-mm cannon could fire 120 rounds per minute with a maximum range of 8,875 yards and could reach an altitude of 6,200 yards against aerial targets. It was fed by a circular magazine.

Another popular weapon, developed late in the war by Elco, was the "Thunderbolt," a power-driven turret mounting four 20-mm cannon. The gunner sat within the mounting. This weapon, although used in only a few actions, delivered an impressive amount of firepower. But for the weight, the PT-boat crews preferred the heavier rounds fired by the 40-mm Bofors.

The first Thunderbolt installation was on the *PT 138* late in 1942. This first mount was not satisfactory in tests, and was washed off the craft in heavy seas. Improved mounts were subsequently provided to MTB Squadron 29 in July 1944 in the Mediterranean. The squadron deployed teams of one Thunderbolt-armed PT boat accompanied by two armed with 40-mm Bofors in the Mediterranean. "The combination of the Thunderbolt's withering volume of 20-mm fire and the slower but more potent 40-mm fire from the other boats proved particularly effective," wrote historian Robert J. Bulkley in *At Close Quarters*. The squadron commander, Lieutenant Commander S. Stephen Daunis, called the Elco Thunderbolt, "an exceptional weapon."

A late model Higgins boat, the *PT 631* seen with a heavy armament. Note the SO3 radar antenna atop her lattice mast. Guns, rockets, and even mortars in reality made U.S. PT boats combination MTBs and motor gunboats. *U.S. Navy*

The Higgins Industries' production line at City Park, in New Orleans, Louisiana. In addition to PT boats, American shipyards produced several hundred wooden minesweepers and SC-series submarine chasers during World War II. *Higgins Industries*

Stern aspect of the *PT 462* on trials. She has two 20-mm cannon amidships in addition to twin .50-caliber machine gun mounts. More weapons would be fitted before she went into combat in the Pacific. *U.S. Navy*

The 78-foot Higgins *PT 462* on Navy trials. She has four lightweight launchers for Mark XIII torpedoes in place of the heavy tubes found in early PT boats. The Higgins-designed PT boats had a short forecastle. *U.S. Navy*

Larger guns, up to 75 mm, were tried on PT boats, the model being experimentally fitted to New Guinea boats that were actually lighter than the 40-mm mount. However, the higher rate of fire of the 40-mm cannon was more valuable in PT operations. A heavier gun battery could be provided from 1942 onward when the Mark XIII torpedo was introduced with side-launching racks in place of the heavier Mark VIII torpedoes and launch tubes.

Since PT boats operated in inshore waters to provide fire support ashore, 60-mm mortars were mounted to provide additional firepower. The 60-mm weapon fired a 31-pound round to a maximum distance of 1,985 yards. (Two decades later, in the Vietnam War, fast patrol boats and smaller patrol craft would be fitted with a tandem-mounted 81-mm mortar/.50-caliber machine gun. This was a very potent combination.)

Late in the war, PT boats were fitted with launch rails for rockets. Early in 1944, PTs in the Mediterranean and New Guinea were experimentally armed with 4.5-inch rocket launchers, one 12-round launcher on each side, forward of the torpedo tubes. The rockets were highly destructive, but lacked accuracy. Subsequently, an eight-shot launcher for 5-inch, spin-stabilized rockets was provided in large numbers, with some boats carrying two launchers. This was an effective weapon, and the 5-inch rocket was widely used by the Navy for shore bombardment. These were relatively accurate, each rocket having the hitting power of a 5-inch gun round.

Opinions differed about the viability of rocket launchers: Some PT-boat officers didn't want them; others proposed removing all weapons except the

The *PT 564* was a 70-foot Higgins design that the firm dubbed "Hellcat." The craft was impressive, with the shorter length made possible by the Mark XIII torpedoes that did not require tubes. The design was not approved for series production. *U.S. Navy*

.50-caliber machine guns and mounting all the 5-inch rockets that could be fitted on the boats!

PT boats carried two or more depth charges for attacking submarines, while PTCs carried eight. These were generally Mark VI charges, steel casings weighing 420 pounds with a 300-pound TNT charge. These weapons were 27

The *PT 396* was one of the large number of Vosper 70-foot PT boats ordered by the U.S. Navy for Britain. These craft, with two torpedo tubes, were too small to carry the weapons needed for U.S. operations. The machine gun mounts (one visible) are covered with canvas, as are the torpedo tube openings. *James C. Fahey collection (USNI)*

inches long and 17 inches in diameter. They were rolled off the deck, hopefully over an enemy submarine whose periscope had been sighted. A PT boat could also release depth charges into its wake in an effort to discourage a pursuing enemy ship.

A few PT boats were also fitted with one or two "Mousetraps," short-range anti-submarine weapons. This was a diminutive version of the highly effective Hedgehog ASW weapon. A mousetrap was a spigot-mortar consisting of four or eight spigots aimed to fire over the bow of the PT boat; the spigots were slightly angled, so that the 70-pound projectiles, fired in salvo, would hit

A British Vosper at high speed. Built by the Annapolis Yacht Yard (Maryland) as the *BPT 66*, she was given the British pennant number 376. She is shown here in Chesapeake Bay in 1943, prior to being shipped overseas. *U.S. Navy*

The *PT 69* was an experimental design of the Huckins Yacht firm. The 72-foot craft was unsuccessful, but demonstrated the continuing efforts of the Navy and private yards to develop improved MTB designs. Two dummy torpedo tubes are mounted on the craft. *James C. Fahey collection/Electric Boat Co. (USNI)*

the sea some 230 yards ahead of the ship in a pattern. Each projectile was 7 inches in diameter with tail fins for stability in flight, and was filled with 30 pounds of the explosive Torpex. The launchers were reloaded by hand.

In addition, PT-boat crews were provided with a variety of individual weapons—M1 Garand .30-caliber rifles, M1 .30-caliber carbines, M1928 Thompson .45-caliber submachine guns ("Tommy" guns), and M1911 .45-caliber pistols. Hand grenades were also provided for close-in combat ashore.

PT boats were continually undergoing armament modification. While it is virtually impossible to cite a "standard" armament, by the latter stages of the war most of the PT boats appear to have carried a 37-mm cannon forward, one or two 20-mm cannon forward of the bridge, two mounts for twin .50-caliber machine guns, and another cannon aft, either a 20-mm or 40-mm weapon, along with four Mark XIII torpedoes. A few Elco boats operated as motor gunboats without torpedoes, carrying a 40-mm Bofors forward and aft plus several .50-caliber machine guns.

A few other weapons were tested, but not provided for combat use. This included flame-throwers and a 3.5-inch Bazooka mount with six launch tubes.

With the great variations in armament, the crews of the PT boats varied in size. The accommodations provided for the crews in the later years of the war were:

The Elco *BPT 47* making knots off Terminal Island (San Francisco), California. Transferred to Britain as the *MTB 305* upon completion in March 1943, she was seconded to the Indian Navy. *U.S. Navy*

A Mark VIII torpedo is loaded onto the *PT 65*, a 77-foot Elco boat, at Melville in 1942. The Mark VIII was the Navy's first 21-inch-diameter "long" torpedo. It was outdated when the war began and proved to have limited effectiveness. *U.S. Navy*

Elco type	3 officers + 14 enlisted men
Huckins type	2 officers + 10 enlisted men
Higgins type	3 officers + 14 enlisted men
Vosper type	3 officers + 9 enlisted men

The first PT-boat officers, as most U.S. Navy line officers in the 1930s, were Naval Academy graduates and regular naval officers. Almost all officers assigned to PT boats after the first couple of squadrons were commissioned were Naval Reserve officers.

With the mass production of PT boats, the Navy Department made the decision to establish a specialized training center. Initially, in the spring of 1941, Lieutenant William C. Specht took several PT boats and the tender *Niagara* to Newport, Rhode Island, site of the Naval Torpedo Station, to establish an MTB school aboard the tender.

This training program was short-lived (with the *Niagara* departing for the South Pacific at the end of August 1941). Meanwhile, MTB Squadron 4 under Lieutenant Commander Alan R. Mont-

The 78-foot *PT 95* was the first of a small series of MTBs produced by the Huckins Yacht firm. Twin .50-caliber machine guns are abaft the bridge and a 20-mm cannon is fitted aft; there are racks for eight depth charges in place of a second pair of torpedo tubes. These boats were produced in small numbers. *U.S. Navy*

Mark XIII torpedoes being produced at the American Can Company plant in Forest Park, Illinois. These "fish" are complete, except for warheads. This was a lightweight torpedo developed for aircraft use that was readily adaptable for MTBs, replacing the larger, heavier Mark VIII tube-launched weapons. *U.S. Navy*

A Mark XIII slides from the launching rack on a PT boat. Its contrarotating propellers are spinning and exhaust gas is escaping from the rear. These torpedoes were developed by the Navy for aircraft use. *U.S. Navy*

With warheads attached, these Mark XIII torpedoes are loaded onto a barge in a forward area. They will be launched against Japanese warships by aircraft or PT boats. Like most American torpedoes, they had low reliability, and PT boat crews were poorly trained in their use. *U.S. Navy*

A trio of PT boats maneuvers wildly during an exercise in the Canal Zone. MTBs were sent to the area to help defend the canal against enemy attack and for tropical training. The boat in the foreground has two torpedo tubes with eight depth charges fitted amidships. *U.S. Navy*

Even bazooka rocket launchers were tried on PT boats. This mount on the *PT 354* had three 2.36-inch (71-mm) launchers mounted on each side of the gunner. The bazooka's 3-pound rocket had a range of some 100 yards. The weapon was not used in combat on PT boats. *U.S. Navy*

A squadron of PT boats travel in formation during exercises off the Rhode Island coast. Melville became the training center for PT boat sailors and for repair specialists who would maintain the boats in forward areas. *U.S. Navy*

gomery was designated as the PT-boat training squadron. On February 17, 1942, the Secretary of the Navy directed the establishment of the MTB Squadrons Training Center at Melville, Rhode Island. Specht, who had been promoted to lieutenant commander, was relieved as Commander MTB Squadron 1 at Pearl Harbor and ordered to command the Melville center, which began operations in March 1942.

The center expanded rapidly, with Squadron 4 providing under-way training. By 1944 the center was capable of handling 90 student officers and 860 enlisted students. Initially the training curriculum was two months; it was increased to three months in 1943. The training center became the personnel control point for PT-boat crewmen, recommending assignments for PT boats and recommending

The *PTC 1*—the first motor boat submarine chaser—on speed trials. The PTC was an attempt to employ existing MTB production lines to produce a short-range ASW craft. They were not successful because of their small size and lack of sonar.

Detail of the *PTC 1* showing depth charge rails running along the craft's starboard side. The depth charges were pushed aft to the twin "Y" guns that simultaneously fired a charge to either side. Thus, a four-charge pattern could be fired plus charges rolled off the stern.

The *PTC 1* high and dry. She has six depth charges mounted on her port side. The hulls, superstructure, and .50-caliber Dewandre gun mounts of the Elco PTCs were identical to contemporary Elco PT boats. *U.S. Navy*

Close-up of the twin Y guns on a PTC. The cranks are visible for cranking the 300-pound depth charge from the side rails to the Y guns. There are two depth-charge racks fitted on the stern.

overall personnel procedures. Veterans came back to Melville as instructors and guest lecturers to impart their combat experience to trainees.

In March 1944 the Repair Training Unit was added to the center and in November 1944 a command course was established for perspective MTB squadron commanding officers.

By the time of its third anniversary, March 16, 1945, the center had trained 1,797 officers and 11,668 enlisted men. Those officers and enlisted men sailed the PT boats and tenders that were fighting around the world.

The *PTC 4* off the New York skyline. The Elco-built sub chaser and other PTCs were severely limited in effectiveness by their small size and lack of sonar for submarine detection. *U.S. Navy*

The *PTC 6* after her transfer in April 1941 to the Royal Navy for service as an MGB. These craft were often painted all white. The U.S. Navy heavily armed PT boats rather than develop separate fast MGBs. U.S. gunboats were developed to support amphibious operations.

The *PTC 62*, a Trumpy-built sub chaser. Her twin .50-caliber machine guns and single 20-mm cannon are covered by canvas. A Radio Direction Finding loop is just forward of the bridge and there are four depth charge racks on each side amidships. *U.S. Navy*

Chapter 5

War in the Pacific

Following the attack on Pearl Harbor and the ill-fated American defense of the Philippines, PT boats saw little action. MTB Squadron 2 was dispatched to the Panama Canal Zone to help provide the defense of that vital sea link between the Atlantic and Pacific against a possible German or Japanese attack. The squadron saw no combat.

The Japanese successes in the Pacific continued into the summer of 1942. Although its attempt to capture Port Moresby at the southeast corner of New Guinea was halted, the Japanese Navy had still not experienced a major defeat.

War in the Aleutians: This is the PT base at Finger Bay, Adak, Alaska, in 1944. The weather was arduous, the waters treacherous, and ice forming on (and inside) the boats was a constant danger during the long Arctic winter. The four MTBs at right are fitted with radar. *U.S. Navy*

That would occur the first week of June 1942 at the Battle of Midway.

Midway would become the turning point of the Pacific War, as the U.S. Navy, forewarned by codebreakers, was able to deploy three aircraft carriers to intercept the massive Japanese naval force intending to capture Midway. The Japanese viewed the capture of Midway as a means of extending their defensive perimeter and serving as a steppingstone for the neutralization and possible assault of Oahu with its vital airfields and naval base at Pearl Harbor.

In anticipation of the Japanese assault on Midway, Admiral Chester W. Nimitz, the Commander-in-Chief, Pacific Ocean Areas, poured reinforcements onto the small atoll—Marines, guns, light tanks, and Army, Navy, and Marine aircraft. Eleven PT boats of MTB Squadron 1—*PT 20* through *PT 30*—were sent to the island. Commanded by Lieutenant Clinton McKellar, Jr., the boats proceeded under their own power from Pearl Harbor to Midway, a distance of 1,385 miles. Refueling from patrol craft and a seaplane tender en route, they made the longest open-sea transit of American MTBs yet attempted. The only casualty was the *PT 23*, which broke a crankshaft and had to turn back on the first day. (The *PT 23* was repaired and then went out to Midway.) From Midway, two of these boats were sent on to the nearby islet of Kure.

Beginning at 6:30 A.M. (local time) a Japanese carrier strike force of 108 planes began

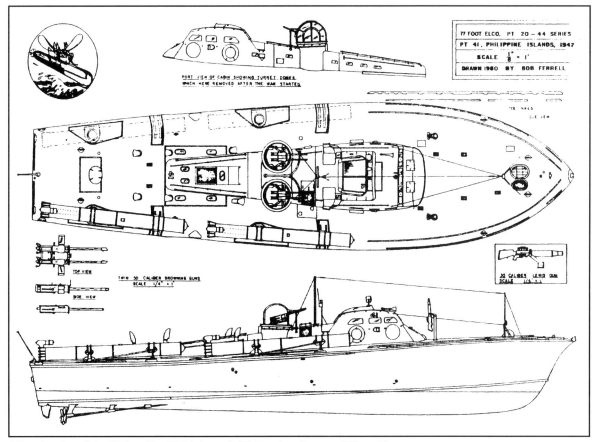

A line drawing of the 77-foot Elco PT 20 through PT 44 series. *Courtesy PT Boat Museum*

bombing the Midway atoll. Their bombs and bullets destroyed the Marine command post, mess hall, fuel tanks, and a seaplane hangar; set fire to the hospital and some storehouses; and seriously damaged the island's power-generating plant. Lieutenant McKellar's MTBs raced around the lagoon and the waters offshore, adding their .50-caliber machine guns to the massive anti-aircraft fire from the island's defenders. Zero fighters strafed the *PT 25*, wounding one of her officers and two enlisted men.

The PTs claimed credit for shooting down three Japanese aircraft. More important, they picked up several Midway-based fliers whose planes came down at sea because of battle damage or having run out of fuel.

After this single Japanese air attack on Midway, the scene of the historic battle shifted to an area 240 miles north of the island. There, the four Japanese fleet carriers were devastated by U.S. carrier-based dive bombers that sunk all four ships. The large number of planes based at Midway also participated in the battle but with little effect except for the ubiquitous PBY Catalina flying boats. During the early evening of June 4, all

11 PT boats set out to find the remnants of the Japanese fleet, including damaged carriers that were reported to still be afloat.

Throughout the night the PT boats cruised northward, traveling almost 200 miles from

The *PT 84* at Adak along the desolate Alaskan coast. Facilities to support MTBs were few and far between in these northern waters. It was a tribute to the boats' crews and the few support personnel available that they were able to keep the craft operational. *U.S. Navy*

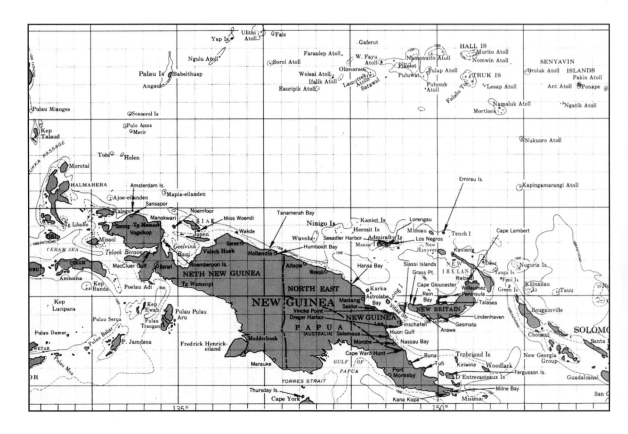

Midway. But they sighted no targets and returned to base the next day.

With the threat to Midway gone, MTB Squadron 1 returned to Pearl Harbor for rest and rehabilitation. In mid-July four boats departed for the Southwest Pacific (see below); four other boats, the *PTs 22, 24, 27*, and *28*, were sent to Alaska.

The Japanese advance toward Midway had entailed a diversionary carrier strike on U.S. installations in the Aleutians and occupation of two small islands, Attu and Kiska. The American response was to build up naval and air forces in the area. Four PT boats were sent to the area in the belief that under cover of perpetual fog they could easily attack enemy ships. The boats were designated MTB Division 1 and, under Lieutenant McKellar, they departed Pearl Harbor aboard a cargo ship on July 30. They arrived at Seattle, Washington, on August 11 and nine days later departed under their own power for the 2,500-mile voyage through the Alaska inland passage and gulf to Dutch Harbor. The four PTs arrived on September 1. There, the *PT 28* was fitted with an aircraft-type radar to help the MTBs navigate in the fog.

Shortly thereafter they pushed on to Adak, where they stood by to help repel additional Japanese landings. When none materialized, the Army employed the Navy-manned boats as scouting and supply craft, and used them to lay mines. Winter cold and moisture penetrated the thin sides and decks of the torpedo boats, with as much as 2 inches of frost forming on the inner surfaces, against which the tiny gasoline galley stoves—the only source of heat in the boats— made no headway. Spray and green water, freezing topside, weighed the boats down dangerously.

In a squall, the *PT 22* and *PT 24* collided and all four boats took refuge in a small cove. For four days they attempted to ride out a gale. Anchors dragged and cables parted, and the force of the wind blew three boats ashore. The *PT 27*, although damaged, tried to pull the others free. Her towlines parted and, when doubled up, jerked cleats out of the decks like loose teeth. With help from other craft, the three PT boats were pulled clear and taken in tow. The *PT 28* twice broke her tow and, on January 14, 1943, she was washed up on the rocks and destroyed. The damaged *PT 22* was to be shipped back to the United States on a cargo ship, but suffered irreparable damage when she was dropped while being loaded.

Meanwhile, additional PTs were being sent to Alaskan waters. MTB Squadron 13, the first with the 78-foot Higgins boats, was commissioned on September 13, 1942, with Lieutenant James B. Denny in command. After modifications, in part to

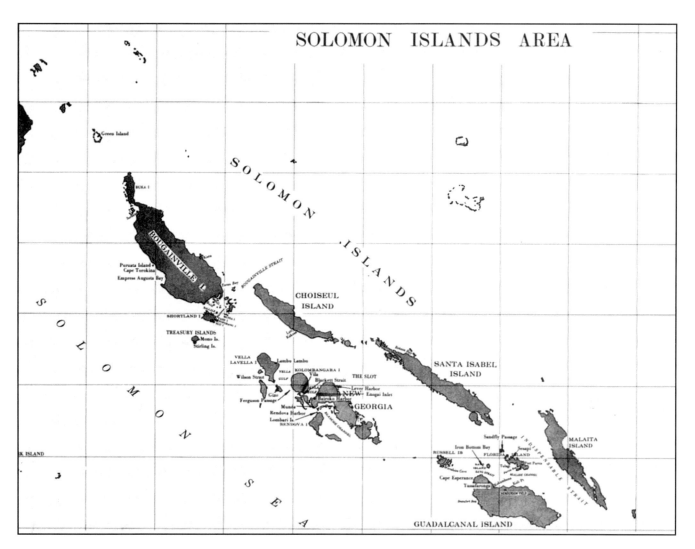

SOLOMON ISLANDS AREA

enable the boats to reach their designed 40-knot speed, the boats undertook a 2,500-mile voyage from the East Coast to the Canal Zone. The 12 boats arrived in December-January. After several weeks of training, the squadron was loaded aboard cargo ships and transported to Seattle.

Under their own power, the *PT 73* through *PT 76* departed for Adak, arriving on March 31. The second section, *PT 77* through *PT 80*, arrived on May 1, and the *PT 81* through *PT 84* on May 27. With these 12 boats available, Lieutenant McKellar turned over the repaired *PT 24* and *PT 27*, and returned to the United States. His two boats were soon sent back to Seattle (under their own power) where they were rebuilt and then

The 80-foot Elco *PT 103* comes alongside the seaplane tender *Pocomoke* for refueling off the U.S. Atlantic coast. Several sister MTBs keep formation, awaiting their turn at the fuel hose. In early 1943 these boats went to the Solomons. *U.S. Navy*

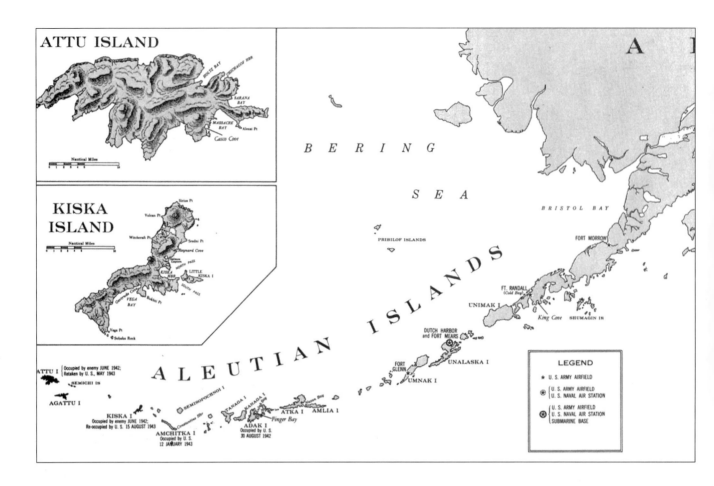

ATTU ISLAND

KISKA ISLAND

B E R I N G

S E A

BRISTOL BAY

A L E U T I A N   I S L A N D S

A L E U T I A N

ATTU I | Occupied by enemy JUNE 1942; | Retaken by U. S., MAY 1943

SEMICHI IS

AGATTU I

KISKA I
Occupied by enemy JUNE 1942;
Re-occupied by U. S. 15 AUGUST 1943

AMCHITKA I
Occupied by U. S.
12 JANUARY 1943

ADAK I
Occupied by U. S.
30 AUGUST 1942

PRIBILOF ISLANDS

FORT MORROW

FT. RANDALL
(Cold Bay)

UNIMAK I

King Cove   SHUMAGIN IS

DUTCH HARBOR
and FORT MEARS

UNALASKA I

FORT GLENN

UMNAK I

LEGEND

★ U. S. ARMY AIRFIELD

⊛ U. S. ARMY AIRFIELD
   U. S. NAVAL AIR STATION

⊛ U. S. ARMY AIRFIELD
   U. S. NAVAL AIR STATION
   SUBMARINE BASE

shipped out to Pearl Harbor. Meanwhile, a major MTB base was built at Adak. The Higgins boats were better suited for cold-weather operations than the Elcos, being more sturdily constructed and having motor-driven hot-air heaters.

There were no further Japanese attacks on the Aleutians, and in May 1943 the PTs supported the Army's recapture of Attu in the face of savage

The *PT 48* in the Solomons area with a Mark XIII torpedo being fitted into a lightweight torpedo launcher. This 77-foot Elco boat was one of the first to carry the Mark XIII torpedo.

Japanese resistance. The boats saw no action in the operation. Subsequently, another MTB base was established at Attu.

When the Army began bombing Japanese-held Kiska island, the PTs served as rescue boats (with one being strafed by an Army B-24 Liberator). While there was no action against the Japanese, the weather was a savage opponent. The boats were constantly battered by high winds and rough seas. After the MTB Squadron 16 with the *PT 219* through *PT 224* arrived in September 1943, the newly arrived *PT 219* was driven ashore by winds on September 14. Although pulled off the rocks, she was badly holed, and subsequently had to be scrapped.

The last "action" of the Aleutians campaign came in August 1943 when the Army assaulted Kiska. Five PTs joined the assault force—modified to look like landing craft. The torpedo boats closed the beach and attempted to draw Japanese fire. Despite their proximity to the beach and blasting away with their guns, there was no response. The Japanese had secretly evacuated the island.

The PTs continued to patrol the Aleutians. In May 1944 MTB Squadron 13 withdrew from Adak and Squadron 16 from Attu. Their boats

U.S. transports unload troops at Empress Augusta Bay, Bougainville, on November 20, 1943. The transports and landing craft were photographed from one of the PT boats standing by to help protect them from Japanese air attack. *U.S. Marine Corps*

The Solomons campaign cost the U.S. Navy several PT boats. The *PT 43* was shot up, run aground, and abandoned on Guadalcanal on February 16, 1943. The campaign for the Solomons was marked by intensive naval engagements involving battleships, aircraft carriers, cruisers, destroyers, and PT boats. *U.S. Marine Corps*

A PT boat on nocturnal prowl off the coast of New Guinea. The greatest value of U.S. PT boats in both the Southwest Pacific and the European-Mediterranean areas was in attacking enemy supply barges and small combat craft. *U.S. Navy*

returned to Seattle for overhaul in preparation for being sent to the Southwest Pacific.

Following the Battle of Midway, the Japanese were temporarily on the defensive in the Pacific. Admiral Nimitz took the opportunity to undertake a "limited offensive." With the 1st Marine Division available, he undertook an assault on the adjacent islands of Tulagi and Guadalcanal in the Solomon Islands. The Japanese were building a seaplane base on Tulagi and an airstrip on Guadalcanal to support a planned second effort to capture Port Moresby.

U.S. Marines stormed ashore at Tulagi and Guadalcanal on August 7, the first American offensive of the war. Even before the landings, MTB Squadron 2 in the Canal Zone was alerted for possible transfer to the South Pacific. The squadron, with 14 PT boats, was divided to form a new MTB Squadron 3, carrying on the designation of the "expendable" squadron. The new squadron was commissioned on July 27, 1942, with Lieutenant Commander Alan R. Montgomery in command. Two days later, the first division of the squadron's boats departed Panama aboard Navy oilers, arriving at Nouméa in New Caledonia. They were then towed to Espiritu Santo and then to a point 300 miles from Tulagi. There the *PTs 38, 46, 48, and 60*—all Elco boats—were cut loose and proceeded under their own power to Tulagi, arriving at dawn on October 12. The second division, consisting of the *PTs 37, 39, 45, and 61*, went to Nouméa by freighter, and then on to Tulagi, arriving on October 25. These eight boats were followed to Tulagi by MTB Squadron 2,

which was replaced at Panama by MTB Squadron 5. The six boats of MTB Squadron 2 were the *PT 109* through *114*, new 80-foot Elco boats, commanded by Lieutenant Rollin E. Westholm. They departed Panama aboard ship and reached Tulagi at the end of November. Thus, by the first of December 14 PT boats were available at Tulagi.

With more PTs en route to the South Pacific, the Navy would establish, on December 15, 1942, MTB Flotilla 1 under Commander Allen P. Calvert. With headquarters at Sesapi, Florida, a small island just north of Guadalcanal, the flotilla would be the largest MTB tactical organization of the war, intended to bring all squadrons in the area under a single command. However, tactical employment of the boats would remain with local naval base and squadron commanders. A short time later an administrative command, Commander MTB Squadrons South Pacific, was established under Captain M. M. Dupre, Jr., to provide

The Catalina was one of the most successful military seaplanes ever produced. The PBYs were invaluable for locating enemy warships for PT boats as well as other U.S. attack forces. The "Cats" could also carry bombs and torpedoes to make attacks themselves. There is a large radar housing above the cockpit of this PBY-5A. *U.S. Navy*

An 80-foot Elco PT boat in Tulagi Harbor in the Solomons. Canvas covers over the craft's guns indicate the area is "secure," with no threat of enemy air attack. Note the radar mast on this Elco boat; sun helmets were preferred to steel helmets when not in combat. *U.S. Navy*

better logistics support for the PTs. Heretofore, the boat squadrons had needed to scrounge from other commands; this "admin" command would improve their support. These commands also were recognition that PT boats had become a first-line component of the fleet.

The battle for Guadalcanal was a savage one as Japanese aircraft (flying mainly from Rabaul and at times from carriers) and major Japanese warships fought U.S. naval and air forces in the southern Solomons. In the predawn darkness of October 14, U.S. PT boats entered combat, led by Lieutenant Commander Montgomery. Four boats attacked Japanese warships in the channel between Tulagi and Guadalcanal. The *PT 60*—with Montgomery aboard—tangled with two destroyers, firing two torpedoes at one. Observers saw two explosions. The *PT 60* escaped the enemy gunfire but, while standing idle, was washed aground on a coral reef. The *PT 48* also engaged a destroyer, but could only score hits with her machine guns.

Three torpedoes were launched against Japanese ships that morning. The PT-boat sailors claimed a cruiser damaged and one possibly sunk. Again, postwar analysis found no evidence of major damage to Japanese warships. These were the first torpedoes fired in anger by U.S. MTBs since Bulkeley's April 8 attack on a Japanese cruiser.

The *PT 60* was pulled off the reef, but repairs in the primitive conditions at Tulagi took several weeks. Additional boats were arriving at a regular rate, however. The battle for Guadalcanal would rage for six months, in the island's jungles, along its coasts, and at sea where the U.S. and Japanese fleets fought several savage battles, some involving battleships and aircraft carriers as well as less-

er warships. PT boats sought to intercept both the periodic foray of Japanese warships trying to bombard the U.S. airfield on Guadalcanal, and the transports and destroyers bringing reinforcements and supplies for the Japanese soldiers fighting on Guadalcanal. A key battleground was "The Slot," the Allied term for the body of water between the major islands of the Solomons that the Japanese used to run their ships down to Guadalcanal; these runs by merchant ships and then troop- and supply-laden destroyers were called the "Tokyo Express" by the sailors that tried to stop them.

Almost every night the PT boats went into The Slot to hunt the enemy. These boats lacked radar, but so did most of the Japanese warships that they encountered. Once the battle was joined—often at distances too close to maneuver and launch torpedoes—the PT boats were heavily outgunned by their antagonists.

While nights were spent on patrol (U.S. aircraft could control the area by day), the PT-boat crews spent the daylight hours catching a few hours of sleep, eating, and, mostly, working to maintain their MTBs in the primitive Tulagi facilities. Beyond needing normal maintenance requirements, the boats were often damaged by enemy gunfire. On the night of November 8–9, a large-caliber shell hit the *PT 61*, blowing off her bow. Excellent ship handling by the crew and calm seas enabled the craft to return to Tulagi for repairs.

Early in December 1942, the Navy assigned several SOC biplanes, normally operating from cruisers and battleships, to scout for the PT boats. Their pilots had had little experience in night flying and several were lost, in part because of the bad weather. More suitable for working with the

PT boats were the PBY Catalina flying boats, which became available for that role in early January 1943. The night-flying "black cats" were fitted with radar, aiding in their navigation and their ability to locate nocturnal targets for the PT boats. And using bombs and even torpedoes the PBYs could themselves attack targets.

Although the PT boats turned back numerous Japanese ships coming down The Slot and damaged several, confirmed sinkings were few. The PTs were also a threat to Japanese submarines. One submarine commander, Zenji Orita, in his autobiographical *I-Boat Captain*, written with Joseph D. Harrington, recalled: "American PT boats turned out to be the unconquerable enemy of Japanese submarines. They were very small, which made them hard to see, either at sea or against a shoreline. It did no good to fire torpedoes at them, as the Model 95s passed well beneath them. And they had radar. While they could hide under the smallest cover cast by an overshadowing cloud or in a cove, they could still see us at a great distance with their electronic eyes. They could dart in and attack with machine guns, torpedoes or depth charges, then race away at high speed before a submarine could do anything."

The first major Japanese warship loss credited to PT boats in the Solomons was a submarine.

The sinking of the MTB tender *Niagara*. Damaged by Japanese air attacks on May 23, 1943, off Cape Surville, San Cristobal Island, in the Solomons, she was subsequently abandoned. Four PT boats are hovering around the stricken ship. The PTs rescued her entire crew. *James C. Fahey collection (USNI)*

The *I-3*, with a surface displacement of 2,135 tons, was sunk by the *PT 59* off Guadalcanal on the night of December 9. The submarine was being used to resupply troops ashore, and was unloaded by barge. That night the *PT 59* and *PT 44* opened fire on a barge sighted off Guadalcanal. Then Lieutenant (jg) Robert L. Searles in the *PT 59* sighted the submarine and quickly fired two

Awaiting nightfall, four PT boats rest in a cove along the New Guinea coast. The engine exhausts and mufflers are visible in their stern counters. Drying clothes are visible on some of these boats as crewmen take time for housekeeping chores between nighttime operations. *U.S. Navy*

torpedoes, one of which struck amidships. As many as three other Japanese submarines may have been sunk by PT boats (see below).

Two nights later the *PT 44* and *PT 110* sank the destroyer *Terutsuki* as they intercepted a force of three destroyers coming down The Slot. The *PT 44* was hit by enemy gunfire, began burning, and was abandoned. Only two men survived the sinking; nine others were lost.

By January 1943, the situation for the Japanese on Guadalcanal was becoming desperate. The first PTs of MTB Squadron 6 had arrived to join in the battle for Guadalcanal. On the night of January 10–11, nine Japanese destroyers made the run toward Guadalcanal. Forewarned, the Navy deployed 13 PT boats to intercept the Japanese ships. A furious firefight occurred when the two forces met. Probably three of the destroyers were damaged (with the *Hatsukaze* being holed on both sides by a single MTB torpedo hit). But two torpedo boats were sunk: The *PT 112* was hit by several shells, wrecked, and sunk; her entire crew survived. The *PT 43*, also shot up, was abandoned; three of her crewmen were lost. The Japanese towed her ashore but she was then destroyed by gunfire from a New Zealand ship.

The destroyers, unable to unload by barge, dumped overboard hundreds of steel drums filled with munitions and supplies, hoping that the tide would bring them ashore. The next morning the PTs sank more than 250 of the drums. The trickle of supplies being sent in by destroyers, submarines, and barges was not enough to keep the surviving Japanese troops fed. Captured Japanese diaries of this period reflect the writers' dire conditions. The troops stayed alive eating meager rice and soybean rations with grass, roots, ferns and even, on occasion, human flesh. The malaria rate was almost 100 percent as was the dysentery rate, the disease spreading by flies feeding on unburied corpses and exposed refuse.

Finally, most of the surviving Japanese troops were withdrawn in February 1943. On the afternoon of February 1, Allied intelligence reported up to 20 Japanese destroyers coming down The Slot. They were attacked by U.S. planes from Guadalcanal, but since the destroyers were supported by Japanese fighters, only one of them was seriously damaged. The next Allied move was an attempted night interception by three U.S. destroyers, which also failed to stop the oncoming flotilla.

Next the PT boats attacked—11 were deployed in the path of the destroyers. In the furious daylight engagement three PTs were lost and several others damaged by both destroyer gunfire and air attack. A shell hit the *PT 37*'s gasoline tanks and the craft exploded; there was only one survivor, an enlisted man. The *PT 111* was hit by gunfire, caught fire, and had to be abandoned. Her skipper survived with severe burns; two crewmen were lost. The *PT 123* was hit by a bomb and abandoned; four crewmen were lost. The total U.S. casualties were three MTBs with 15 killed and six injured.

The only Japanese casualty in this encounter was the destroyer *Makigumo*, sunk when she struck an American mine while evading PT boats. Historian Samuel Eliot Morison wrote, "This was the last and most violent PT boat action in the

A line of PT boats stand by to provide fire support for U.S. soldiers going ashore in the Admiralty Islands on March 30, 1944. The ability of the MTBs to close with the beach and provide pinpoint fire was useful in several small landings. *U.S. Navy*

PT boats provide close-in gunfire support at Biak Island on August 17, 1944. At left is a 20-mm Oerlikon cannon; a twin machine gun is mounted forward. The 20-mm was a drum-fed gun, found on numerous larger ships for close-in defense against aircraft. Helmets were issued, but rarely worn by PT boat sailors in the early period of the war. *U.S. Navy*

Most of the crew of the *PT 109*, somewhere in the Southwest Pacific. Kennedy stands at far right. This photo was heavily retouched; the PT boat's mast and the background have been taken out, probably for reasons of security. *U.S. Navy*

Guadalcanal campaign. As on other occasions, their valiant officers and men accomplished less than they had intended, or thought they had done; but they would have been pleased to have read Tokyo's lament in a special report devoted to the doings of [the PT boat crews]. 'The enemy has used PT boats aggressively. . . . On their account our naval ships have had many a bitter pill to swallow—there are many examples of their having rendered the transport of supplies exceptionally difficult.' The writer, urging Japan to develop a motor torpedo boat force, wisely observed, 'It is necessary to assign to the boats young men who are both robust and vigorous.' "

The next few months were relatively quiet in the Solomons, but not elsewhere. Six hundred miles to the west of Guadalcanal is New Guinea, one of the world's largest islands. The Japanese had landed on the northern coast in March 1942, while the allies held onto Port Moresby, south of the mountainous spine of the island. After building up a combined Australian-U.S. Army force in Australia, General MacArthur, in late 1942, began a drive to recapture the northern coast of New Guinea.

The long, drawn-out New Guinea campaign, like the Solomons, would provide productive hunting waters for U.S. PT boats. The first U.S. MTBs to arrive in New Guinea were four boats from MTB Squadron 1, which had been at Midway. After returning to Pearl Harbor, four boats designated as Division 2 under Lieutenant Jonathan F. Rice were dispatched to the Southwest Pacific. These were the *PTs 21, 23, 25,* and *26.* The MTB tender *Hilo* departed Pearl Harbor on July 15, 1942, towing two boats, while the other two traveled under their own power, refueling

A rare photo of the *PT 109*, shown here on board the cargo ship *Joseph Stanton* in preparation for being shipped to the Southwest Pacific. The "109" is painted on the pedestal for the after 20-mm cannon on the early 80-foot Elco MTB. *U.S. Navy*

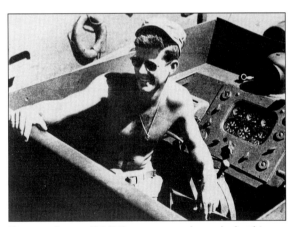

The most famous U.S. PT boat commander—who lost his boat in a surprise collision with a Japanese destroyer—was John F. Kennedy. This view shows the control panel and helm of an early Elco PT boat. *John F. Kennedy Library/U.S. Navy*

each morning from the tender. Midway to their destination the boats switched position. The crews of the boats being towed were far less comfortable to be aboard.

Their first destination was Palmyra Island, 1,100 miles southwest of Oahu. On October 25 the *Hilo* and PTs departed for the Ellice Islands, arriving on November 2. It was closer, but still not in the combat area. Operating out of the

MTB base at Funafuti in the Ellice Islands, the *PT 21* picked up a life raft with a sick American flier. He had been the pilot of the B-17 Flying Fortress in which World War I fighter ace Eddie Rickenbacker had been flying across the Pacific. Subsequently, a Navy floatplane sighted another raft on November 12 and came down near it. The pilot took aboard three men, including Rickenbacker, and began taxiing the 40 miles to Funafuti, being too heavy to take off. The *PT 26* rendezvoused with the plane and took aboard Rickenbacker and one survivor. The other survivor

The *PT 109* sinking—at least Hollywood's view of the historic event. The 1963 film *PT 109* starred Cliff Robertson as John F. Kennedy, shown at the lower right helping an injured crewman as the survivors abandoned the bow section of the smashed PT boat. *Warner Studios*

Bow aspect of the *PT 109* aboard the *Joseph Stanton* shortly after being loaded aboard at the Norfolk Navy Yard (Portsmouth), Virginia. *U.S. Navy*

was considered too ill to transfer to the PT boat. Rickenbacker and his colleagues had been on the raft for 21 days. (Three other survivors had waded ashore on another island.)

The *Hilo* was then ordered to lead six new Elco boats to Cairns, on the northern coast of Australia, to establish an MTB base. These were the *PTs 113, 114,* and *119-122,* a composite squadron under Lieutenant Daniel S. Baughman. Arriving on December 11, 1942, the force was then ordered to New Guinea. In anticipation of major MTB operations, Commander Task Group 50.1 under Commander Edgar T. Neale was established to control PT boat operations along the New Guinea coast; as in the Solomons, day-to-day operational control was vested at the base and squadron level. (TG 50.1 would be changed to TG 70.1 on March 15, 1943, when the Seventh Fleet was established as "MacArthur's Navy.")

Operating from an advance base at Porlock Harbor, the *PT 121* and *PT 122* made their first patrol in New Guinea waters on the night of December 18–19, 1942. They sighted a surfaced submarine and fired two torpedoes. No detonations were observed.

During the night of December 23–24 the *PT 122* attacked a large surfaced submarine and fired two torpedoes at 1,000 yards, then closed to fire another pair at 500 yards. The *PT 122* observed two explosions and reported the 2,135-ton submarine *I-22* being sunk. Postwar analysis, however, indicated that no Japanese submarine had been lost at that time or location. Ten minutes after that attack the crew of the *PT 122* detected four torpedoes racing toward them. The PT boat maneuvered to escape these missiles from an unseen attacker. (The *I-22* was probably an operational loss in the Solomons area.)

On the same night the *PT 114* and *PT 121* attacked two Japanese landing craft carrying troops. Subsequently the PTs regularly attacked the large number of Japanese small craft and barges that provided a steady traffic along the New Guinea coast. This became a most productive role for the craft, albeit employing primarily its .50-caliber machine guns and 20-mm Oerlikon cannon and not torpedoes.

Tufi, Milne Bay, Kana Kopa, Dreger Harbor, and, eventually, Mios Woendi became MTB bases. All were relatively primitive. Initially the ex-yacht *Hilo* served as a floating repair shop, and there was a small marine railway on the island of Sariba at the entrance to Milne Bay. Parts and equipment were in short supply; generators, radar sets, and other gear were removed from boats returning from a patrol and sent out on the next night's patrol in other boats. A boat being taken out of the water for maintenance would be stripped of parts for other boats. (The *PT 67* and *PT 119* would be destroyed by fire at Tufi on March 17 when fire devastated the facility; miraculously, there were no casualties.)

In late February 1943 more boats arrived in New Guinea, from MTB Squadron 7 under Lieutenant Commander John D. Bulkeley, and MTB Squadron 8 under Lieutenant Commander Barry K. Atkins. They arrived in time to attempt to participate in the Battle for the Bismarck Sea.

On March 1 a convoy of 16 Japanese cargo ships and transports and their escorts was spotted en route to Lae on the northeast coast of New Guinea. The convoy was carrying reinforcements for the Japanese garrisons. The following morning, U.S. Army B-17 Flying Fortress bombers attacked the ships, sinking one transport. Two Japanese destroyers, rescuing soldiers from the transport, were then attacked by more U.S. B-17s as well as other Australian and U.S. planes using new, low-level tactics bombing and strafing tactics. The two destroyers were sunk as was a third trying to join in the rescue. One of the destroyers, in her death throes, rammed another Japanese ship, which also sunk. A second Allied air attack in the afternoon sank a fourth destroyer.

Air attacks followed for three more days. On the afternoon of March 3, ten MTBs went to sea seeking survivors of the air strikes. Both the *PT 119* and *PT 132* struck submerged objects, probably logs, and turned back to base. The remaining eight MTBs made contact with Japanese ships late that night.

The *PT 143* and *PT 150* each fired a torpedo into the already-burning cargo ship *Oigawa Maru*, which sank rapidly in an explosion of flames. Although other boats fired torpedoes at "shadows," the dying cargo ship was the only ship sunk by MTBs. But in the following days many troop-filled Japanese boats from the convoy were encountered and sunk by machine gun and cannon fire. This distasteful task had to be performed to prevent the troops from reaching the shore and reinforcing the Japanese garrisons.

At daylight on March 5 the *PT 142* and *PT 150* caught a large I-boat on the surface, 25 miles off the New Guinea coast, with the submarine taking on troops from three boats. The PTs attacked, each firing a torpedo; that of the *PT 143* ran erratically while the *PT 150* torpedo missed the submarine. The PTs fired at the conning tower of the submarine as she dived to safety. They then sank the three boats.

A tank landing ship at Amsterdam Island off New Guinea became a PT-boat base. Here, a tank landing ship unloads Seabee construction personnel and material while PT boats hover around—their crews probably seeking provisions and hot showers. *U.S. Navy*

A pair of PT boats alongside a grounded landing craft at Amsterdam Island off New Guinea. Any quiet cove or beach, with a ship or landing craft to provide support, rapidly became an advanced base for PT boats. *U.S. Navy*

As MacArthur's troops moved from point to point along the northern coast of New Guinea—a procedure called "leap-frogging"—the PTs continued interdicting Japanese coastal barges. On the night of June 29–30 the *PTs 68, 120, 142,* and *143* each embarked some 70 troops of the Army's 41st Infantry Division. Screened by other PTs, they would join landing craft in putting troops ashore at Nassau Bay. Rough seas and rain made

A PT boat rests in a quiet cove somewhere along the jungle-covered coast of New Guinea. A camouflage net is stretched over the boat. The crew may be gathered on the forecastle for a briefing about the night's operation. *U.S. Navy*

the operation difficult, but there was no enemy opposition. The troop-carrying boats closed with the beach for landing craft to take the soldiers ashore. PT boats could thus add troop transport to their many roles. The PTs also carried scouts and reconnaissance teams, which were clandestinely put ashore behind Japanese lines. On a few occasions PT-boat crewmen accompanied them ashore.

Another submarine was sunk by MTBs on the night of May 13–14. Commander Morton C. Mumma, Jr., Commander TG 70.1, was riding the *PT 150* accompanied by Lieutenant Commander Atkins in the *PT 152*, patrolling off Lae. They sighted a surfaced submarine and attacked, each boat firing two torpedoes at 6,000 yards, a very long-range shot. The submarine crew stopped the vessel and the torpedoes passed ahead. The PTs closed to 4,000 yards and the *PT 150* fired a torpedo. The submarine cranked up her twin diesel engines and sped forward. The torpedo missed astern.

The submarine then crash dived. Moments later a torpedo passed under the *PT 150*. None of the antagonists was hurt in the encounter. The submarine was the 601-ton *RO-102*, which had departed Rabaul on May 2. She disappeared about this time, probably an operational loss—but possibly one of the PT torpedoes had damaged her, leading to the loss.

But most of the MTB targets were Japanese barges carrying troops and supplies along the coast. During most of 1943 about a dozen barges a month were destroyed. These MTBs became so expert at ferreting out barge convoys that one Japanese diarist at Finschhafen wrote thankfully that on August 29 he had made the only trip "when barges were not attacked by torpedo boats." But the PTs apparently got his barge on its return passage. In November 1943 the PTs found lucrative hunting off Morobe, claiming 45 barges destroyed plus several damaged.

That same month the *PT 147* and *PT 322* ran aground and had to be destroyed. While operating close inshore the PTs ran the risk of grounding; the benefits of closing with the barge traffic tended to outweigh the risks.

In March 1944 brought additional losses: The *PT 337* was smashed and sunk by Japanese shore batteries early on March 6 off Awar Point. Her surviving crewmen spent four days in a raft before U.S. Army planes dropped them food and medical supplies. The next day a PBY Catalina picked up the ten survivors. At least three of the crew were captured by the Japanese; they did not survive the war.

PT operations extended to New Britain, the large island to the northeast of New Guinea. On December 26, 1943, the 1st Marine Division landed at Cape Gloucester, at the western tip of New Britain, followed by other landings along the island coasts. Monsoons—16 inches of rain falling in a single day—and violent winds gave the invaders more opposition than enemy troops. Falling trees alone killed 25 Marines. Japanese attempts to repulse the landings failed. Torpedo boats supported the landings, and several were damaged by Japanese air attacks and suffered several casualties.

The next Japanese-held group of islands on General MacArthur's assault plan was the Admiralties, an island group at the head of the Solomons. U.S. Army troops assaulted Los Negros Island on March 2, 1944. Ten days later the MTB tender *Oyster Bay* entered Seeadler Harbor in company with MTB Squadrons 18 and 21. Japanese snipers still hid in the area, periodically taking potshots at the anchored PTs and their tender. The MTBs were to intercept any Japanese attempts to send troops from New Guinea, 150 miles away, and to support U.S. operations ashore.

The *PT 321* and *PT 369* tried to shoot up a Japanese installation at Loniu Village. When they failed to set fire to the buildings and the large canoes under them, the skippers of the two MTBs went ashore and used gasoline to set fire to the structures. Other PTs and the *Oyster Bay*, armed with two 5-inch guns, shelled Japanese installations. Some of the PTs were fitted with 60-mm mortars in addition to their machine guns and cannon.

In the spring of 1944 four PTs and 24 crewmen were lost to Allied aircraft. On March 27 the *PT 121* and *PT 353* were patrolling Bangula Bay, New Britain, when four Australian P-40 fighters and a twin-engine Beaufighter attacked the two boats, mistaking them for Japanese craft. (Another Beaufighter correctly identified the PTs and tried in vain to call off the attackers.)

After several strafing runs the PTs did fire a few rounds at the planes. Both PTs were hit, exploded, and sank. Four officers and four enlisted men were dead; another 12 crewmen were wounded.

A month later, on the morning of April 29, off Cape Pomas, New Britain, the *PT 350* was trying to pull the *PT 347* off a reef when two U.S. Marine F4U Corsairs attacked them. The PTs did not identify the planes correctly—despite their distinctive gull-wing configuration—and shot down one of their antagonists.

Three men on the *PT 350* were killed and the boat was damaged. The surviving F4U pilot called for reinforcements. More than a score of U.S. planes responded. When they arrived the *PT 346* was on the scene, attempting to aid the stranded *PT 347*. The planes rushed to the attack. The *PT 346*, in desperation, opened fire and shot down an F6F Hellcat. The other planes pressed home the attack. Both the *PT 346* and *PT 347* were destroyed. Eleven more PT crewmen died and 13 were injured. Two PTs and two aircraft were lost.

(Other torpedo boats lost in this period included the *PT 337*, lost to Japanese shore batteries in Hansa Bay on March 7, and the *PT 339*, grounded and destroyed near Pur Pur, New Guinea, on May 27; the *PT 301* was scrapped after an engine room explosion that killed two men at the Mios Woendi base on November 4.)

On several occasions, however, PTs did cooperate with aircraft—both U.S. and Australian—in several operations.

Combat operations for PT boats in the New Guinea area ended in November 1944. From the original six PT boats the force expanded to 14 squadrons and almost 180 boats. In *At Close Quarters*, historian Robert Bulkley wrote: "From first to last they met and overcame the bitterest opposition the enemy could mount against them; with relatively little damage to themselves they took terrible toll of the Japanese. Along the coastline was the wreckage of hundreds of blasted barges; the former enemy encampments were bodies of thousands of soldiers who died for lack of supplies."

After the conquest of Guadalcanal, U.S. forces rested and prepared to move up the Solomon Island chain—or "ladder"—at the top of which were New Britain and New Ireland. U.S. and Australian forces made amphibious landings on New Georgia, Vella Lavella, and Bougainville, the last in November 1943.

MTBs accompanied the amphibious forces in their northward thrusts, seeking out enemy ships and craft, and serving as escorts for landing craft. As plans were being made for the New Georgia landing in June 1943, the PT force in the Solomons was being built up. Still, in May six PTs of MTB Squadron 23 and the tender *Niagara* were dispatched from Tulagi to New Guinea.

Although the U.S. units took a circuitous route to keep them out of range of Japanese aircraft, just before noon on May 23 the ships were sighted by a Japanese reconnaissance plane. The plane attacked, dropping four bombs amidst a hail of anti-aircraft fire. The bombs were near misses on the *Niagara*, inflicting minor damage.

Half an hour later six twin-engine planes approached the ships. The planes were too high for even the 3-inch gun on the *Niagara* (a second 3-inch gun had been disabled in the first attack). The planes made a single pass, releasing between 12 and 18 bombs. One struck the *Niagara* forward and several near-misses caused further damage.

Holed below the water line, the ship began taking on water as fires spread. The PTs closed to take off the tender's crew—not a single member of which had been killed or even injured. The fuel-limited PTs returned to Tulagi, and an hour later a U.S. torpedo sank the *Niagara*. She was the only MTB tender lost in the war.

While the *Niagara* was being bombed, the freighter *Stanvac Manila* was approaching

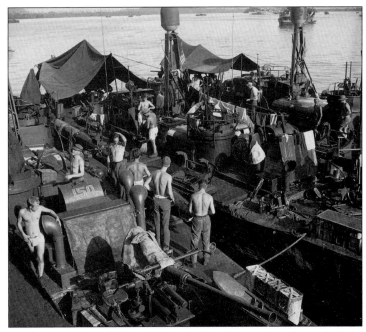

Another gathering of PT boats along the New Guinea coast shows their crews washing clothes and maintaining the boats. The *PT 150*, in the foreground, was involved in several attacks on Japanese submarines—an unexpected role for MTBs. *U.S. Navy*

A pair of 80-foot Elco PT boats on the forward deck of a large Navy oiler being transported to the Pacific war zone. These boats, from MTB Squadron 10, have zebra-stripe camouflage, intended to confuse enemy aircraft pilots and gunners. *U.S. Navy*

Nouméa when she was torpedoed by a Japanese submarine. On her deck, in cradles, were *PTs 165, 167,* and *171* through *174*. The torpedo struck when the ship was 100 miles south of Nouema. As the ship sunk, the PTs floated free. Two were damaged and sunk, the *PT 165* and *PT 173*. A U.S. destroyer arrived and towed the *PTs 167, 171,* and *174* to safety; the *PT 172* reached Nouméa under her own power. One PT crewman was lost in the sinkings.

Then, in another "blue-on-blue" mistake, PT boats sank the *USS McCawley*. The transport was attacked by Japanese planes on June 30 while preparing for the invasion of New Georgia. Japanese planes hit the *McCawley* with a torpedo that damaged the ship. Attempts to salvage the ship were under way when she was strafed by a Japanese plane.

Late that night, in the Blanche Channel, the *McCawley* was again torpedoed—by PT boats. She sank within seconds. There were no casualties from this mistake.

The following month, early on July 30, three PTs were attacked by a formation of U.S. Army B-25 twin-engine bombers. Again, the planes mistook the boats and attacked. A couple of MTB gunners returned fire. One B-25 crashed. All three boats were hit and the *PT 166* caught fire and exploded. The PTs suffered 11 wounded.

The Japanese inflicted more losses. On August 1 a formation of Japanese bombers struck the MTB base on Lumbari Island. The *PT 117* and *PT 164* were destroyed by a single bomb, with two men killed.

Another PT was sunk by a Japanese destroyer. On the night of August 1–2, five Japanese destroyers slid along the west coast of Kolombangara. Fifteen U.S. PTs in groups lay in wait for the enemy. The destroyers opened fire, and two MTBs fired six torpedoes but made no hits. The destroyers continued southward. Five additional MTBs each fired four torpedoes without effect. (Other PTs did not detect the destroyers until they were beyond torpedo range.)

Another trio of PTs lay in wait for the Japanese in Blackett Strait, the *PT 109, PT 169,* and *PT 162*. Suddenly, a lookout in *PT 109*, commanded by Lieutenant John F. Kennedy, yelled "Ship at two o'clock!" Every one looked out to starboard to see the Japanese destroyer *Amagiri* bearing down on them. The destroyer rammed the boat and split it in two. Of 13 crewmen, only two were missing.

The *PT 162* was almost run down while the *PT 169* fired torpedoes at a destroyer too close for the warheads to arm. The last shots of the battle were two torpedoes from *PT 157*, also misses. Thirty torpedoes had been launched by eight PTs that night, yet the only damage to the enemy was a dent in the *Amagiri*'s bow.

Kennedy and his crewmen, some on a portion of the hull that remained afloat, expected planes to come to their rescue in the morning but none showed up, and by mid-afternoon, with the half-hull of *PT 109* sinking, he decided to swim for it. Kennedy clenched between his teeth the tie-lines of the life jacket of his badly burned engineer and towed him. The others swam unaided to a small island. That night Kennedy donned a life jacket and with a salvaged battle lantern swam into Ferguson Passage to intercept the nightly PT patrol, but none came. The current pulled him into Blackett Strait, but in the morning returned him to where he had started, and he crawled ashore, exhausted.

Subsequently, with the help of friendly natives, Kennedy was able to reach Allied forces and return to rescue his surviving crewmen. Memorial services had already been held for the crew of *PT 109*.

As it was off New Guinea, the PT campaign in the Solomons was primarily one of barge hunting. But unlike the PTs operating off New Guinea, in the Solomons the torpedo boats periodically fought Japanese aircraft, mostly flying from Rabaul. On November 5, 1943, the *PT 167* was escorting a couple of landing craft when a dozen Japanese torpedo planes attacked the group. One plane came in so low that it struck the PT boat's antenna and crashed into the sea. The PT gunners kept up a lively fire, downing one of the attackers. During the battle the crew of the *PT 167* felt a "jolt," but there was no explosion. When the attack was over, it was found that a Japanese torpedo had passed completely through the bow of the *PT 167* without exploding.

The next PT boat to be sunk in the Solomons was the *PT 279*, sunk in collision during a rain squall on the night of February 11–12, 1944. She was rammed in the engine room by the *PT 282*. One crewman was lost. Two other boats were lost operationally on June 18 when the *PT 63* and *PT 107* refueled at a dock at Hamburg Bay, Emirau Island. When the *PT 107* started her engines, the exhaust ignited gasoline on the surface of the water. Both boats burned and sank. No men were lost.

Combat was also taking its toll. During a barge-busting mission on the night of February 25–26, the *PT 251* was hit by shore batteries and exploded; none of the crew of 13 was found. Another PT returned from the same mission with an unexploded 57-mm shell embedded in the warhead of a torpedo! Machine-gun fire from the beach exploded the gas tanks of the *PT 283* on the night of March 17–18; four crewmen were lost.

The Japanese, suffering from the MTBs' nocturnal operations, set a trap on the night of May 5–6. Three PTs entered the Rantan area. They sighted three barges and prepared to attack. As the PTs closed, additional barges were sighted, in all directions. The Japanese gun batteries on Bougainville and Rantan opened fire, while the barges blazed away with machine guns and cannon. The PTs returned fire. The *PT 247* was hit and set on fire. She sank with the loss of one officer.

On May 27–28, Charles Lindbergh went to sea in the *PT 178* of MTB Squadron 11, operating from New Ireland. Lindbergh's mission was to evaluate combat aircraft in the war zone. In his *Wartime Journals*, Lindbergh wrote: "The PT boats are built for stealth and striking power. They are so low and small that they leave very little silhouette. They are painted in grays and blacks to blend with the night. They can leap forward in an instant, throwing a smoke screen behind them to baffle enemy fire, and when a flash is seen on shore, they can spit back death from seven guns. . . ."

On May 1, 1944, the operational control of PT boats in the Solomons was given to Task Group 30.3 under Captain Edward J. Moran. Previously he had had the administrative title of Commander MTB Squadrons South Pacific. By this time there was an average of 24 PTs under way on the nightly patrols.

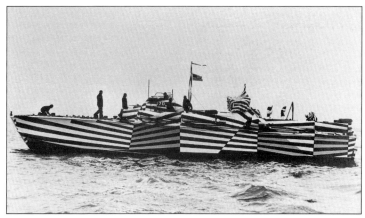

Yes, there is a PT boat beneath these zebra stripes—the *PT 170*. While zebra stripes did confuse the enemy—and sometimes Allied forces—they were difficult to paint and maintain, and this scheme of camouflage was not widely used.

A few PT boats were also painted with shark teeth and eyes. Like the "flying tiger" aircraft (which were also painted as sharks), they were intended to play on the Japanese fear of the watery denizens.

TG 30.3 was a component of the Third Fleet, under Vice Admiral William F. Halsey, part of Admiral Nimitz's Pacific Ocean Areas. In June 1944, jurisdiction of the area was shifted to General MacArthur as Commander Southwest Pacific Area. The PT command became TG 70.8 in MacArthur's Seventh Fleet. By that time the major combat in the Solomons area was ending. The PTs helped in mopping up operations and prepared for the invasion of the Philippines.

Chapter 6

Return to the Philippines

When General MacArthur reached Australia in March 1942, he explained at the Adelaide railroad station how he had been ordered to leave the Philippines and declared, ". . . I shall return." But in the spring of 1942 the Allies were virtually impotent, having lost the Philippines, Guam, Wake, Malaya, the Solomon islands, the Dutch East Indies, and most of Burma to Japanese assaults; Japanese naval and air forces controlled the western Pacific and eastern Indian Ocean. Indeed, even as MacArthur reached Australia, cities along the country's northern coast were being bombed by Japanese planes and there was a threat of invasion.

The PT 330 at speed in Subic Bay. The successors to ill-fated MTB Squadron 3, the PT 330 and her sister MTBs, came to the Philippines in larger numbers and came to stay. The 40-mm Bofors cannon at the stern is at full elevation. *U.S. Navy*

During the next two years the tide of war in the Pacific shifted. The offensive in the Pacific had advanced on two widely separated routes. Under the direction of Admiral William F. (Bull) Halsey and later MacArthur, Australian and U.S. forces moved northwest from Guadalcanal, through the Solomons, the Bismarck Archipelago, and along the northern coast of New Guinea. By the end of July 1944, U.S. troops had landed at the western end of New Guinea, just 600 miles from the Philippines. The other thrust, led by Admiral Raymond A. Spruance's Fifth Fleet, had advanced through the Gilberts, Marshalls, and recaptured the Mariana Islands.

The recapture of the Philippines was on-again, off-again, as the Navy and Army wrangled with each other. MacArthur did not have many friends and supporters, and the Navy was driving steadfastly toward Japan. Most Navy leaders wished to capture portions or all of Formosa and then an enclave on the coast for China, in preparation for the blockade and, if necessary, the invasion of Japan. But MacArthur prevailed in a private meeting with President Roosevelt and Admiral Nimitz in Hawaii in July 1944, at which Roosevelt personally gave approval for the recapture of the Philippines.

On October 20, 1944, using some 500 ships of his Seventh Fleet, MacArthur began landing more than 200,000 troops on Leyte, the central main island of the Philippines. The Third Fleet, commanded by Admiral Halsey, provided carrier-based aircraft to

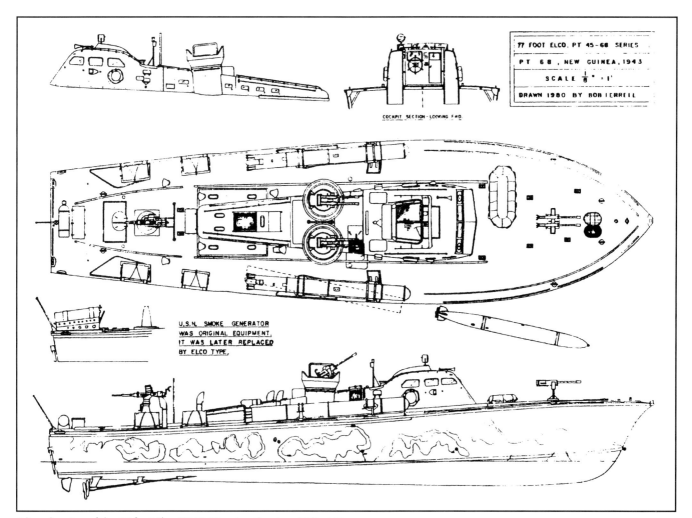

A line drawing of the 77-foot Elco PT 45-68 series. *Courtesy PT Boat Museum*

protect the Leyte landings and intercept any Japanese attempt to interfere with the assault.

Early planning for the Philippines operation identified a need for PT boats to patrol the coast of Leyte and innumerable adjacent islands. The planning was under Commander Selman S. Bowling, Commander MTB Squadrons Seventh Fleet. The nearest U.S. base from which PT boats could depart for Leyte was Mios Woendi at the northwestern end of New Guinea; the distance was some 1,200 miles, believed by many planners to be too far for the small craft, even with escort ships.

On October 13, Lieutenant Commander Robert Leeson led 45 PT boats to sea on a northerly course toward Leyte. These consisted of:

MTB Squadron 7 with 9 boats
MTB Squadron 12 with 10 boats
MTB Squadron 21 with 11 boats
MTB Squadron 33 with 10 boats
MTB Squadron 36 with 5 boats

Accompanying the diminutive warships were three PT-boat tenders, the *Oyster Bay, Willoughby,* and *Wachapreague,* and the small seaplane tender *Half Moon.* The PT boats refueled from their consorts off the Palau islands while the tenders, in turn, refueled from Navy oilers. Subsequently, the PT boats refueled again at sea and began arriving in Leyte Gulf on the morning of October 21. The first units to arrive were immediately ready to begin patrols.

The last boats arrived on the 23rd. The eight-day voyage was the largest and longest mass movement ever undertaken by MTBs. All 45 boats made the trip successfully, without breakdowns. They began nocturnal patrols on the 22nd, and immediately began intercepting and destroying Japanese barge traffic that was attempting to move troops and supplies into the Leyte area to counter the U.S. assault.

Meanwhile, the Japanese high command reacted to the landings. Four separate Japanese forces were under way to destroy the U.S. transports and landing ships. One force—known by the Japanese as "C" Force—was steaming through the Mindanao Sea and would attempt to enter Leyte Gulf via Surigao Strait in the early hours of the 25th. The U.S. Navy was ready and

The *PT 596* in the Philippines poses to show off her armament. The multiple 5-inch rocket launchers forward of the bridge are "cranked" outboard to their firing position. Note the OS3 radar antenna. *U.S. Navy*

The *PT 194* refuels from the MTB tender *Wachapreague* as she and three other tenders accompanied the transit of 45 PT boats from the Palau Islands to Leyte Gulf in October 1944. MTBs demonstrated an unexpected long-range transit capability during the war. *U.S. Navy*

waiting. The ensuing battle would be history's last dreadnought-versus-dreadnought encounter, and would see PT boats battling battleships.

U.S. Navy carrier planes found the "C" Force—under Vice Admiral Shoji Nishimura—consisting of two battleships, the *Fuso* and *Yamashiro*, one heavy cruiser, and four destroyers. The carriers' scout bombers scored hits on one battleship and a destroyer before the planes were called off to help strike a larger Japanese force in the Sibuyan Sea. Behind the "C" Force came a second force under Vice Admiral Kiyohide Shima, consisting of three cruisers and four destroyers that were also headed toward Surigao Strait. Onward came the 14 Japanese warships through the darkness.

Thus forewarned, Vice Admiral Kinkaid, commanding the Seventh Fleet off Leyte, prepared a trap at Surigao Strait. First he deployed the 39 available PT boats, then a screen of destroyers, then four heavy and four light cruisers, and then six old battleships—five of them survivors of the Pearl Harbor attack.

In the darkness the Japanese ships entered the 12-mile-wide channel. Nishimura planned to arrive off the Leyte landing beaches early on the morning of the 25th, where his guns would destroy American transports and supply ships. If he encountered U.S. warships en route, according to Commander Shigeru Nishino, the commanding officer of the destroyer *Shigure*, the admiral was "the sort of fellow who would prefer to fight a night battle." The Japanese Navy had long excelled in night combat. He probably believed that his best opportunity of penetrating to Leyte Gulf lay under cover of darkness, since he had no air support and American carrier-based aircraft controlled the skies during daylight hours.

After the war Commander Nishino told American interrogators that Admiral Nishimura had emphasized the need for spiritual readiness as much as combat readiness. His attitude permeated the ranks, and his men went along with him willingly on this obviously suicidal mission.

The PT-boat sailors had been longing for such an action: To attack enemy warships, especially cruisers and battleships. Shooting up barges and coastal craft was not what they perceived to be their real mission in life. But the 39 boats converging in the Surigao Strait had little or no experience in torpedo attacks since the struggle for Guadalcanal and the action in Blackett Strait on August 2, 1943. The only "fish" that most of them had fired in the last year and a half had been relatively rare practice shots.

Lieutenant Commander Leeson deployed his boats in 13 sections of three boats each. As they reached their night stations the boats lay to avoid leaving a wake and provide best conditions for radar and radio operation. The sea in the strait was smooth and glassy. The night was clear until a quartering moon set shortly after midnight; then the sky became partly overcast and the night pitch-black. The PT boats awaiting battle were:

PT 127	PT 192	PT 331
PT 128	PT 194	PT 489
PT 129	PT 195	PT 490
PT 130	PT 196	PT 491
PT 131	PT 320	PT 492
PT 132	PT 321	PT 493
PT 134	PT 322	PT 494
PT 137	PT 323	PT 495
PT 146	PT 324	PT 497
PT 150	PT 326	PT 523
PT 151	PT 327	PT 524
PT 152	PT 328	PT 526
PT 190	PT 329	
PT 191	PT 330	

Farther east the destroyers, the cruisers, and finally the old battleships steamed slowly back and forth. Above the straits PBY Catalina flying boats used radar and their crews' eyes to seek out the approaching Japanese ships in the darkness.

At 10:36 P.M. Ensign Peter Gadd commanding the *PT 131*, operating off Bohol, picked up Admiral Nishimura's lead ships on radar. His section of three PT boats opened up to 24 knots and closed to attack. At 10:50 they visually sighted the enemy at a distance of 3 miles. Two minutes later the destroyer *Shigure* sighted them.

Admiral Nishimura ordered an emergency turn to starboard, toward the PT boats. At 10:56, as the boats were radioing their contacts to Rear Admiral Jesse B. Oldendorf, the U. S. tactical commander in the Strait. They were illuminated by searchlights and taken under gunfire by the *Shigure*'s 4.7-inch main battery. The *PT 152* received a direct hit that blew up her 37-mm gun, killed one man and wounded three of her crew of 15. A shell passed through the *PT 130* while she was making smoke to cover the *PT 152*. Although the shell did not explode, it shattered a torpedo warhead and the concussion knocked out all of her radios. As soon as the action broke off the *PT 130* made speed to close the next section to get off her contact report. It was relayed from the *PT 127* and reached Admiral Oldendorf at 0026 on October 25.

PT boats maneuver off Leyte in October 1944 as Japanese aircraft attack U.S. transports unloading troops and supplies. The PT boats could make only a limited contribution to the defense of larger ships from air attacks. *U.S. Navy*

BATTLE OF SURIGAO STRAIT
2200 24—0300 25 OCTOBER 1944
MOTOR TORPEDO BOAT PATROL LINES
AND ATTACKS ON ADVANCING SOUTHERN FORCE

○ Attacks by Motor Torpedo Boats
○ Central Point and Number of PT Sections
---- Track of Enemy Ships and Times Sighted

0   5   10   15
Nautical Miles

The *PT 131* in a nest of MTBs alongside the tender *Wachapreague* in the Leyte Gulf area. There are several "extra" machine guns and 20-mm Oerlikon cannon on this boat; two hedgehog/mousetrap ASW projectile launchers are mounted forward of the torpedoes with locally installed blast shields to protect the torpedo warheads. *U.S. Navy*

By this time additional torpedo boats were entering battle against both Japanese groups. Admiral Nishimura radioed the other Japanese forces closing on Leyte: "Advancing as scheduled while destroying enemy torpedo boats."

Now the PT boats were buzzing around the Japanese warships like hornets, darting on, being fired on, responding with their small-caliber guns and trying to launch torpedoes. Each succeeding torpedo boat section along the Japanese course observed gun flashes from the previous fight, made contact itself, attempted to get off its report (and sometimes did), and then raced in to attack.

Nishimura was well pleased with the way in which his ships were dealing with these nuisances. Indeed, the PT boats, each launching up to four torpedoes, and blazing away with their 37-mm, 20-mm, and .50-caliber guns, were inflicting virtually no damage on the Japanese ships.

A shell hit the *PT 490*—the PT boat in the very center of the strait. She had launched all four of her torpedoes before being caught in the glare of Japanese searchlights that darted across the water, seeking out their antagonists. The *PT 493*, with a torpedo hung up in the rack, covered the retirement of *PT 490* with smoke and in so doing sustained three 4.7-inch hits that shot away the charthouse, punched a large hole in the bottom, killed two men and wounded five. Machinist's Mate 1st Class Albert W. Brunelle, described by a shipmate as "a

slight, sissified-looking boy whom no one expected to be of any use in combat," saved the boat by stuffing a life jacket into the hole, slowing the inflow of water enough to enable the boat's skipper, Lieutenant (jg) John M. McElfresh, to beach on Panaon Island. (The *PT 493* subsequently would slide off the beach at high tide and sink in deep water; the entire crew was rescued.)

In all, 10 of the 34 boats were hit by gunfire but only the *PT 493* was lost. The Allies' total casualties were three killed and ten wounded.

The Nishimura force continued through the strait. Now Admiral Oldendorf's forces were fully alert to the progress of the Japanese forces and a savage night battle ensued. The Japanese were first hit by gunfire and torpedoes from the destroyers, and then Oldendorf's cruisers and battleships "crossed the T"—their massive broadsides pounding the Japanese ships while the latter could bring only their forward guns to bear on the American ships. Beyond the early warning provided by the PT boats and their tactical position, the U.S. warships were aided by radar, which was far superior to the few sets carried in the Japanese ships.

The U.S. guns and torpedoes sank both of Nishimura's battleships and two destroyers; his heavy cruiser and another destroyer were damaged. The single unscathed destroyer, the *Shigure*, reversed course and raced back through the strait, followed at a distance by the two damaged warships.

Vice Admiral Shima, now passing through the strait with his three cruisers and four destroyers, knew that Admiral Nishimura had encountered PT boats, and he was advancing with caution.

The destroyer that sped past him identified herself, but said nothing of the ambush, indicating only that the ship had a rudder problem.

Admiral Shima realized there was trouble ahead when the *PT 137*, commanded by Lieutenant (jg) I. M. Kovar, attacked his force, scoring a torpedo hit on the light cruiser *Abukuma*. The explosion killed about 30 men and slowed the cruiser to ten knots. She fell out of the formation.

In response, Shima ordered his ships to fire a spread of torpedoes at what were believed to be U.S. ships in the darkness ahead and then, at 4:25 A.M. on October 25, he directed a withdrawal. During the retreat one of his heavy cruisers, the *Nachi*, collided with the damaged cruiser *Mogami* from Admiral Nishimura's force, which slowed the withdrawal of the combined force to 18 knots, the *Nachi*'s best speed. The surface fight in the strait ended at 4:55 when the destroyer *Shigure* was attacked by three of the PT boats. The destroyer was unhurt and inflicted minor damage on the *PT 321*.

The Japanese had two battleships and two destroyers sunk, and suffered damage to four other warships. U.S. casualties were one destroyer badly damaged—primarily by friendly gunfire—and ten PT boats shot up, with the *PT 493* lost.

(The next morning U.S. ships tried to catch up with the fleeing survivors of the night surface fight and succeeded in finishing off the damaged destroyer. The Japanese ships were then hit by aircraft from U.S. escort carriers that further damaged the already-smoking cruiser *Mogami*; a Japanese destroyer took off her crew and sent the *Mogami* to the bottom. On the morning of October 26, Army bombers finished off the damaged light cruiser *Abukuma* from Admiral Shima's force.)

The MTB phase of the Battle of Surigao Strait was a mixed success. Thirty of the 39 boats had engaged the enemy. All together, they fired 34 torpedoes, all but two of which ran "hot, straight and normal," but obtained only the single hit on the light cruiser *Abukuma*. The massive PT boat attacks on Nishimura's ships neither stopped nor confused the enemy, and were chased off by gunfire. The attacks on Shima's smaller force did contribute to his decision to withdraw. Historian Samuel Eliot Morison wrote of the PT boats: ". . . they performed an indispensable service through their contact reports which, in addition to the fireworks that they produced from the enemy, alerted Admiral Oldendorf's forces. Under the battle conditions in which the MTBs operated, their reporting was good; anything approaching it in Guadalcanal days would have saved the Navy several ships and

hundreds of lives. The 'Peter Tare' boys showed determination in closing for attack, and cool courage in their snakelike retirement under fire. And they proved to be surprisingly tough."

The night engagement in Surigao Strait was one of three fought in what became known as the Battle of Leyte. The battle marked the final defeat of the Japanese fleet—never again would major Japanese naval forces go to sea. The PT boats had but a small role in the battle, but continued to conduct nocturnal and sometimes daylight patrols around Leyte, seeking out and destroying Japanese coastal shipping. They also escorted landing craft carrying troops to seize adjacent islands.

And PT boats provided liaison with Filipino guerrilla groups on those islands still under Japanese control, landing arms, radios, and Army liaison officers. On one occasion, PT boats under Lieutenant Commander N. Burt Davis were maintaining contact with guerrillas at Batangas Bay, Luzon, who reported that the area was full of Japanese suicide boats. As senior Navy commanders were skeptical of their existence, Davis organized a raid with two of his boats, with two Army planes as air cover. Davis himself with a couple of sailors landed at Batangas, captured a suicide boat, and took it in tow. On their way back to Mindoro both the PT boat and tow were attacked by friendly planes, and the captive craft swamped; but the Seventh Fleet's staff accepted the evidence of the existence of suicide boats and due precautions were taken.

While the PT boats controlled much of the water around the Philippines at night, during

The *PT 287* helps rescue survivors from an LST struck by a Japanese kamikaze during operations off Mindoro in December 1944. Crewmen still man the craft's guns, ready to repel attackers—although the primary target of the suiciders were landing ships and troop ships. *U.S. Navy*

The wreckage of the *PT 323* after she was hit by a Japanese kamikaze. She was sunk in Leyte Gulf on December 10, 1944. One of her Mark XIII torpedoes is visible at far right. *U.S. Navy*

daylight hours U.S. aircraft had supremacy. Initially U.S. aircraft carriers had battled and then swept away the Japanese land-based fighters and attack planes, and, after airfields were established ashore, mainly U.S. Army Air Forces planes provided control of the air. These manifestations of U.S. military power did not always mix.

For example, after U.S. troops landed at San José on the island of Mindoro on December 15, the Japanese dispatched a force of two cruisers and six destroyers to bombard the beachhead and destroy the transports. This force steamed from Camranh Bay in Indochina across the South China Sea without being detected until, in the afternoon of December 26, a Leyte-based U.S. Navy PB4Y-1 Liberator sighted the Japanese ships. At their speed of advance the Japanese force, commanded by Rear Admiral Masanori Kimura, would reach the beachhead that night.

No major U.S. warships could reach a position to intercept Kimura's ships. But the entire available strength of Army Air Forces on Mindoro airfields—92 fighter planes, 13 B-25 Mitchell bombers, and a number of night-fighting P-61 Black Widows—took off to meet the enemy. Kimura's ships were next sighted at 8:30 p.m. on the 26th by another Navy Liberator, now some 50 miles northwest of San José. About a half-hour later the air-surface battle began.

The only U.S. "warships" near the San José beachhead were motor MTBs. Eleven PTs under Lieutenant Commander Davis were deployed to provide warning of the approach of the Japanese ships and to intercept them. All the boats were in poor material condition after 12 days of continuous operations, with hull or engine problems.

Lieutenant Commander Alvin W. Fargo's *PT 80* was the first to detect the enemy, by radar, at 8:48 on December 26. At 9:55, when about six miles off shore, the *PT 80* and three other boats were taken under gunfire by the Japanese. Fargo's boats increased speed to 30 knots, zigzagged, and laid small diversionary smoke-puffs, escaping damage as they shadowed the Japanese movements and made radio reports.

But the greater danger to the PTs came from Army aircraft shuttling between the Japanese ships and Mindoro airfields. Fargo's men, knowing that these planes were friendly, made vain efforts to signal them, and refrained from firing at them. The PT boats were strafed and rocked by near-misses. At 10:05 a bomb exploded close aboard the *PT 77*, badly damaging her and wounding almost every crewman. Fargo detailed the *PT 84* to escort her to safety, while the two remaining boats laid smoke to cover their retirement.

The Japanese ships kept coming down the coast. Rear Admiral Kimura stayed well outside the PT patrol line until 10:40 when he turned his column shoreward. While under continual air attack, he bombarded San José town and airfield and the U.S. beachhead for about 30 minutes. A few Japanese planes based on Luzon turned up at the same time and attempted to bomb and strafe the town and airstrip, but these attacks were not pressed home, while the naval bombardment was also ineffective. Only superficial damage was inflicted on the airfield and there were no casualties.

Kimura's ships reversed course shortly before midnight and retired to get beyond the range of land-based craft. Several of the ships had been hit, with damage to fire-control equipment affecting the effectiveness of their fire. A single U.S. cargo ship was taken under gunfire by the Japanese ships, hit, and set afire. Fargo saw a B-25 flying low over the merchant ship and later investigation of the ship, which had beached, revealed evidence of aircraft strafing and bombing, whether enemy or friendly was never ascertained. Even after the Japanese reversed course, the tale of confusion in Ilin Strait was not exhausted.

At 0050 two PT boats found themselves two miles abeam of the Japanese ships, one of which illuminated the *PT 221* with a searchlight and opened accurate gunfire. The PT boat retired shoreward at 25 knots on a zigzag course, pursued by Japanese salvos. In the meantime the skipper of *PT 223*, Lieutenant (jg) Harry E. Griffin, closed to attack and at 1:05 A.M. he fired two torpedoes at a range under 4,000 yards. Three or four minutes later a flame shot up from a Japanese destroyer and she was observed to go dead in the water. This was the 2,100-ton *Kiyoshimo*, one of the newest and most powerful destroyers in the Japanese Navy. According to survivors she had already been damaged by air attack, but a torpedo sank her.

At dawn on December 27 several PTs were searching for survivors of the night's action, or for evidence of an enemy landing. Five survivors of the *Kiyoshimo* were taken aboard. One Japanese destroyer had been sunk by a PT boat and almost every enemy ship sustained damage from air attacks—as did several PT boats. Two PT boats ran aground on a coral reef. Both were salvaged. (Twenty-six U.S. Army planes were lost, some by anti-aircraft fire, but most in crash landings; most of the pilots and crewmen were rescued, and no appreciable damage was done to the airfield or to installations by the Japanese bombardment.)

Major fighting on the main island of Leyte continued until Christmas 1944, when General MacArthur declared the island secure. The next target for the Army-Navy forces under MacArthur was Luzon, the principal island in the Philippine archipelago. But when the first of 200,000 U.S. troops stormed ashore at Lingayen Gulf in western Luzon on January 9, 1945, the enemy did not appear in any strength, and U.S. commanders uneasily wondered why. The answer: A new Japanese tactic allowed an amphibious landing to take place uncontested, thereby sparing the defenders a punishing bombardment. Inland, the Americans found an intricate defense system of caves, tunnels, and pillboxes. The U.S. troops fought determined defenders who saw resistance here as a way to deflect an American invasion of the home islands.

A key objective of the U.S. forces was the fortified island of Corregidor—popularly called The Rock—at the entrance to Manila Bay. The harbor and port could not be used until Corregidor was captured or at least neutralized; because of the mass of tunnels built on the island by U.S. forces in the 1930s it would have to be seized. (When the Japanese had assaulted the Philippines in 1941–1942, U.S. troops on Corregidor had held out until April 9.) Because of the rocky coastline of The Rock and the massive number of protected positions for small guns as well as large artillery, the Allies decided to seize Corregidor by a combined airborne and amphibious assault. Two small areas, each only a few hundred yards across, were available as parachute drop zones—the rubble-strewn parade ground and the bomb-cratered, nine-hole golf course. Some 6,000 Japanese defenders, provided with food and munitions, stood ready to resist the assault.

For 25 days Army planes bombarded the island, dropping 3,125 tons of bombs on the 2.7 square miles of Corregidor in one of the most concentrated attacks of the war. Navy cruisers, destroyers, and smaller ships closed to add the voice of their guns to the crescendo.

Then, at 8:30 A.M. on February 16, moments after 70 A-20 Havoc light bombers strafed and bombed anti-aircraft positions, two streams of C-47

General MacArthur had a special affinity for PT boats. Here he and his aides ride the *PT 490* from Negros Island to Panay Island after his return to the Philippines. Mark XIII torpedoes are fitted to the boat's forward launchers; none of her guns are manned. *U.S. Army*

A hive of mosquito boats alongside a tender at Leyte. The twin .50-caliber guns in the foreground have flash-suppressers on their muzzles; steel helmets abound in this view. These boats fought Japanese battleships during the Battle of Surigao Strait in October 1944. *U.S. Navy*

The MTB tender *Oyster Bay* tends PT boats in the Leyte Gulf area in the fall of 1944. The Navy's 19 AGPs provided repairs and munitions to the PT boats, and food, medical care, and—in some respects most important—hot showers to the PT crews. *U.S. Navy*

Dakota transports roared over the island at 550 feet. One thousand Army paratroopers began jumping over the island. Two hours later 25 LCM landing craft touched down on the south side of the island, disgorging another thousand troops plus light artillery and M4 Sherman tanks. The initial airborne assault was followed up by another thousand-man drop. In all, 20 paratroopers were killed by the withering Japanese fire as they landed; another 260 paratroopers were wounded or injured in the drop—a relatively small casualty rate for a combat drop in very difficult circumstances. (One C-47 transport suffered engine trouble; it dropped its 25 troopers over nearby Bataan and then landed safely.)

Many paratroopers missed the island and fell into the sea as a 20-plus knot wind blew over Corregidor at the time of the drop. PT boats were there to rescue them, moving into the shallow waters off Corregidor, often under fire from Japanese guns on The Rock. The *PT 376*, commanded by Lieutenant John A. Mapp, spotted several paratroopers caught on the face of the cliff and under fire from Japanese snipers. The *PT 376* moved in close, and put a rubber boat into the water which, manned by Lieutenant Raymond P. Shafer and Lieutenant (jg) Charles Adams, twice was paddled to shore to bring off 17 paratroopers and put them ashore elsewhere. Other PT boats picked up paratroopers from the water.

The savage battle for Corregidor continued for 12 days. MacArthur's intelligence staff had badly underestimated the number of defenders. Most estimates were that 850 combat troops—not the actual 6,000—were on the island. Most survived the intensive bombings; and most were killed by the U.S. soldiers who assaulted from the sky and the sea. As the Americans took control of most of Corregidor, some Japanese tried to swim the 3 miles to the mainland. Some were picked up by PT boats, with one swimmer shooting at an approaching boat. Few Japanese surrendered (the last on January 1, 1946, when 20 well-fed, shaved, and clothed Japanese soldiers emerged from a hidden tunnel!).

General MacArthur returned to Corregidor on March 2, 1945, traveling to the battered island with several senior officers aboard the *PT 373*. Three other PTs carried additional officers and newsmen. MacArthur had left the island, in darkness, on March 11, 1942, on the *PT 41*. In the bright light of day, with 336 troops of the 503rd Parachute Infantry Regiment and 34th Infantry Regiment standing at attention, wearing brand-new fatigues that had been brought out to them for the occasion, the American flag was again raised over Corregidor. MacArthur made a brief speech, with the newsmen taking down his words and snapping his picture. It began, ". . . the capture of Corregidor is one of the most brilliant military operations in history."

MacArthur announced on June 30 that most of the Philippines was liberated, but the fighting went on. General Tomoyuki Yamashita led about 65,000 Japanese troops into Luzon's hills and held out until the end of the war, a more effective resistance than MacArthur had been able to offer against the Japanese three years earlier.

Smaller pockets of Japanese resistance along the coasts of the Philippines were assaulted from the sea, with landing craft being protected by the PT boats, which often provided covering fire for the troops. Support by the motor torpedo boats was indispensable to the American mopping-up operations in the Philippines. As Major General J.R. Hodge, commander of the Army's XXIV Corps, stated, ". . . wholehearted cooperation by the PT boats provided invaluable support to elements of the XXIV Corps. Operating primarily at night, boats of the PT squadrons located at Ormoc [on Leyte Island] sortied continuously to the east coast of Cebu and north along the western coast of Leyte. Many Japanese barges, at least two sizable freighters and several schooners, many of which were loaded with Japanese troops or equipment, were sunk by PT boats.

"During these attacks the boat crews were often fired upon by shore batteries and by weapons mounted in Japanese vessels. The eagerness of the PTs to close with the enemy and furnish aid to our ground operations was outstanding throughout their support of the XXIV Corps."

PT boats continued to operate in the Philippines until the end of the war. Invariably the PT boats confronted larger enemy warships and at times Japanese aircraft (as well as U.S. Army aircraft). On only one occasion did the PTs encounter Japanese torpedo boats—but not in a sea battle. On May 14 the *PT 335* and *PT 343*, working with small LCI-type gunboats, patrolled the northeastern part of the Davao Gulf. About noon, following up a report of a Japanese motor torpedo boat hideout near Piso Point opposite Davao, the two PTs set course for the location and found a concealed channel leading through mangroves into a cove where six enemy PTs were so cleverly camouflaged that at one hundred yards they could be seen only with the aid of binoculars.

The two PT boats opened fire with their 40-mm guns at point-blank range, blew the camouflage off one enemy boat, exploded its fuel tanks, and fired some fuel drums ashore. The fires spread to an ammunition dump, which exploded with a tremendous blast, throwing debris 300 feet into

the air and destroying another Japanese torpedo boat. The remaining four enemy craft were strafed by Marine aircraft and severely damaged before the U.S. boats retired, their crews pleased with the day's work.

The next morning two other boats, the *PT 332* and *PT 334*, returning from night patrol, heard explosions near Piso Point and concluded that the Japanese were destroying their base. Two hours later, Lieutenant Commander Edgar D. Hogland, Commander MTB Squadron 24, in the *PT 106* with the *PT 341* rendezvoused with the destroyer escort *Key* off Piso Point. After the *PT 106* closed to within 400 yards of Piso Point she came under fire from heavy automatic weapons. With the *PT 106* indicating targets, the destroyer escort fired 252 rounds of 5-inch ammunition, set for impact and air bursts, and 1,072 rounds of 40-mm ammunition at the anchorage. Three large fires were ignited, and one explosion was heard. Two LCI gunboats arrived on the scene and used their 3-inch guns to set more fires. Two U.S. PTs then entered the cove and at 75 yards shelled the four Japanese boats, which had been damaged the day before. Three of them caught fire and exploded, and the fourth, which was already partly burned out, was shelled again. A fifth boat, heavily camouflaged, was discovered and set afire by shellfire from the PTs.

PT boats continued to operate in Philippine waters until the end of the war, carrying out the vast variety of combat and support functions that had become the hallmark of 'Peter Tares.'

In the aftermath of the battle in Surigaro Strait the *PT 321* takes aboard Japanese survivors from sunken ships. U.S. troops were always wary of Japanese subterfuge, as this sailor at right standing ready with a carbine indicates. Prisoners were important for intelligence interrogations. *U.S. Navy*

General MacArthur returns to Corregidor aboard the *PT 373*—the same means by which he had departed the island in March 1942. PT boats had played a significant, albeit secondary, role in the American recapture of "The Rock" from its determined Japanese defenders. *U.S. Navy*

Chapter 7

War in the Mediterranean

The first U.S. MTBs to reach European waters arrived at Gibraltar on April 13, 1943. U.S. naval forces had been engaged in the Battle of the Atlantic from 1941, and U.S. Army aircraft began striking German-held areas of Europe in August 1942.

U.S. ground forces entered combat—against Vichy French forces—with the invasion of North Africa on November 8, 1942. Subsequently,

German forces entered the battle for North Africa, but U.S. and British forces from the west, and British forces from the east, were able to successfully advance against the Germans.

MTB Squadron 15 had been commissioned on January 20, 1943, under Lieutenant Commander Stanley M. Barnes. When orders came for duty in European waters, six additional PTs were added to the squadron, bringing its strength to 18 boats—*PT 201* through *218*. These were 78-foot Higgins boats.

In early April 1943 the fleet oilers *Enoree* and *Housatonic* departed Norfolk, each carrying four MTBs. The *Housatonic* arrived at Gibraltar on April 13 and the next day the *PT 205* through *PT 208* were put in the water. The *Enoree* arrived at Gibraltar on the 22nd, where her boats, the *PT 201* through *PT 204* were unloaded that day and the next. The MTBs then proceeded to the port of Bône, near the eastern border of Tunisia, where they were attached to the British Inshore Forces. The British already operated torpedo boats and motor gunboats from Bône, their MTBs being 70- and 77-foot Elco boats built in the United States.

The American PT boats made their first patrol in the direction of the German-held North African coast on the night of April 27–28. The Anglo-American MTBs and motor gun boats patrolled in anticipation of interdicting enemy shipping when the Germans attempted to withdraw their surviving troops from North Africa. Low on fuel, ammunition, and food, the Germans had pulled back to

Racing in for an attack—for the benefit of the cameraman—this Elco PT boat has all guns manned and ready. The use of Mark XIII torpedoes permitted the deletion of torpedo tubes in favor of launch devices, making more space and weight available for other weapons. *U.S. Navy*

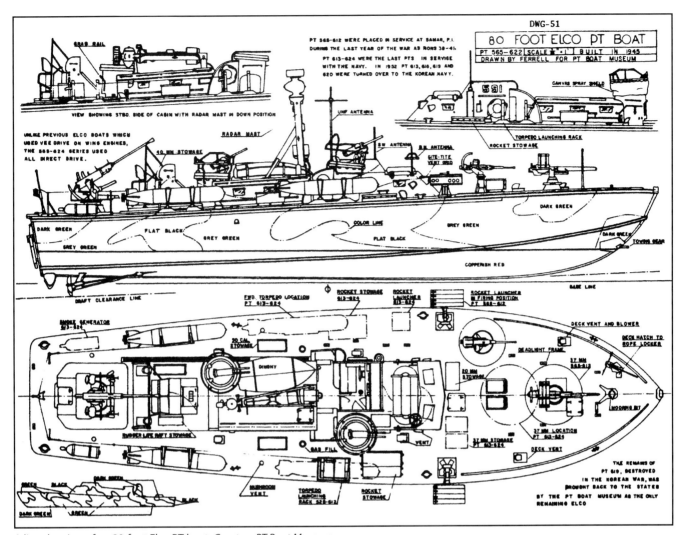

A line drawing of an 80-foot Elco PT boat. *Courtesy PT Boat Museum*

a bridgehead encompassing Bizerte, Tunis, and the Cape Bon Peninsula.

The nightly patrols by U.S. PT boats resulted in no action until the night of May 8–9, when Lieutenant Commander Barnes in the *PT 206* in company with three British MTBs were patrolling the eastern side of Cape Bon. The *PT 203* was patrolling an adjacent area to the south in company with two British MTBs.

Two of the British boats with Barnes entered Ras Idda Bay, where they discovered several German ships. Advised of the find, Barnes took the *PT 206* and third British boat into the harbor. Unfortunately, the two craft then became separated. The U.S. boat fired a single torpedo at a shadowy target, resulting in an explosion. But no more targets were found and the PT returned to sea—where she was promptly attacked by her British colleague, which fired two torpedoes, both of which passed under the PT.

To the south, one of the British MTBs in the second group ran aground and was intentionally destroyed. The *PT 203* picked up her entire crew with German small arms fire coming from the beach.

It was an eventful night. Two German tankers were reportedly sunk in the area, probably one going down to the torpedo from the *PT 206*.

Only two nights later the *PT 202*, *PT 204*, and *PT 205* were in action—against the British. After patrolling off Cape Bon, the PTs were returning to base when they were taken under fire by two British destroyers. The PTs fired recognition flares and increased speed. Moments later two German E-boats—large torpedo craft— opened fire on the PTs. (The term E-boat originated with the Royal Navy, probably indicating "enemy" motor torpedo boat. The German designation was S-boat, for *Schnellboot* or fast boat.)

The British destroyers continued to fire at both the E-boats and PT boats. The *PT 204* was able to blast away at one E-boat with her guns before continuing, with the *PT 202*, to escape from the pursuing destroyers. Separated from the other boats, the *PT 205*, running low on fuel, entered the Allied-held port of Bizerte, where she was promptly fired upon by shore batteries. The three U.S. boats suffered only machine-gun hits during the engagements. The British destroyers had come under fire from the E-boats as they had sighted the PTs and concluded that the American flares were tracer rounds and assumed that they, too, were E-boats and blasted away at everyone.

Another exciting night.

All German resistance ended on May 13. The Allies totally controlled the coast of North Africa, from Tangier in the west to Port Said in the east. A second U.S. PT base was set up at Bizerte, 100 miles east of Cape Bon, with MTB Squadron 15 being brought up to its full strength of 18 PT boats.

With North Africa secure, the Allies immediately began planning for the assault of Sicily, the large island south of the Italian "toe." Garrisoned by German and Italian troops, Sicily-based aircraft and torpedo boats would interfere with Allied use of the Mediterranean.

The southwestern coast of Sicily was 100 miles from Bizerte and the PT boats and their British cousins were soon operating off the coast of Sicily. In addition to hunting German shipping, the MTBs were also employed to land agents on deserted coastal areas of Sicily and other enemy-held islands. The U.S. boats carried agents of the Office of Strategic Services, comprising personnel from all of the U.S. military services. For these long-range missions the PT boats had additional fuel in rubber tanks and the familiar 55-gallon gasoline drums.

On June 11, 1943, Allied troops landed on Pantelleria, a small island between Cape Bon and Sicily. The Italian garrison, having been subjected to intensive aerial bombardment, surrendered as the Allied troops came ashore. Immediately, U.S. and British boats were directed to patrol between Pantelleria and Sicily, 60 miles away, to prevent any of the garrison from escaping by sea.

German aircraft attacked the PT boats that night, with an estimated eight planes dropping 30 to 40 bombs. The *PT 203* was riddled by shrapnel, which killed one sailor.

The invasion of Sicily began on July 10, 1943. The night before, the 17 available PT boats patrolled the western flank of the massive Anglo-American assault force. No German E-boats in

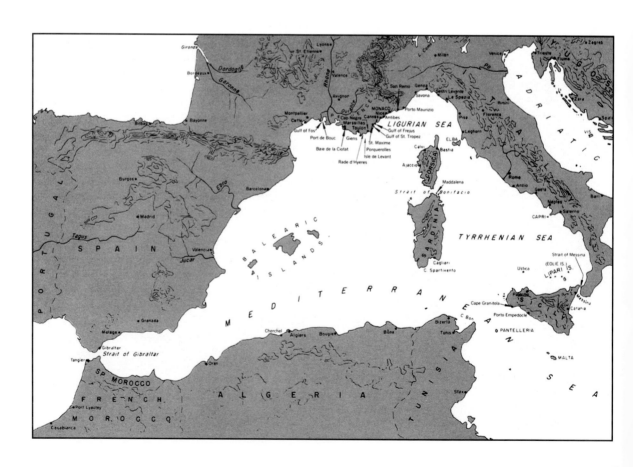

the area and the PT boats were employed for search-and-rescue, diversionary actions (such as pretending they were landing craft, as at Kiska).

On the 14th the PT boats were directed to operate between Sicily and Italy, to intercept enemy surface craft attempting to reinforce the German-Italian troops on Sicily. The Sicilian port of Palermo fell on July 23, and an advance PT base was immediately established. On her first mission from Palermo on the night of July 24–25 the *PT 216* encountered a tug towing the 8,800-ton Italian merchant ship *Viminale*. The PT boat fired a single torpedo that sank the merchant ship, then used gunfire to sink the tug. During the encounter the *PT 216* was being fired on by shore batteries.

Subsequently the PTs began seeking out German supply barges, known as MFPs for *Marine-Fahrprahme*, literally "naval perambulators," but called F-lighters by the Allies. These craft had larger gun batteries than the PT boats, carrying 88-mm guns and smaller weapons, while the PTs mounted only 40-mm and 20-mm cannon in addition to their machine guns. The first engagement of PT boats with F-lighters took place off the volcanic island of Stromboli on the night of July 26–27. The PTs fired six torpedoes and thought that two of their adversaries exploded; but German sources indicate that all torpedoes missed, and the ensuing gunfire duel resulted in slight damage to both sides. On the night of July 28–29, three PT boats attacked what were believed to be three F-lighters off Cape Orlando, but they turned out to be Italian MAS boats—MTBs somewhat smaller than U.S. PT boats. Again, torpedoes that ran hot, straight, and normal slid under the enemy craft without exploding. In a brisk exchange of gunfire the *PT 218* was punctured in some 60 places, one engine was disabled, and three officers were badly wounded; but she was able to return to Palermo with all hands alive and 18 inches of water in her hull.

At times torpedoes also were fired at the F-lighters, but generally without effect because of the shallow draft of those craft.

Nocturnal firefights were fast and furious. Several PTs suffered damage as they shot up and sank their opponents. While the F-lighters were more heavily armed, the German E-boats tended to be faster than the PT boats, in part because the American craft suffered from being overloaded, in need of overhauls, and saddled with engines that could not provide full performance in the Mediterranean heat. Major repairs could only be undertaken at Bizerte.

The *PT 211* was typical of the 78-foot Higgins boats that fought in the Mediterranean. This boat had four mousetrap ASW projectile launchers mounted forward. U.S. and British MTBs made a major contribution to the Allied campaign in the Mediterranean. *James C. Fahey collection (USNI)*

M4 Sherman tanks roll past a Higgins-type PT boat as they are loaded onto LSTs at Bizerte, Tunisia, probably for the July 1943 invasion of Sicily. The PT boat is high and dry, undergoing repairs. *U.S. Navy*

In their fights with the heavily gunned F-lighters, MTB Squadron 15 experimented with using rockets. This was discontinued after two encounters with the barges because of the rockets' lack of accuracy and their illumination, upon ignition, of PT boats in nighttime engagements.

Seventeen PTs participated in the first landing on the Italian mainland, which took place at Salerno on September 8, 1943. That day the Italian government surrendered to the Allies, after having made a secret agreement to do so several days earlier. But strong German forces remained in Italy, supported by some fascist Italian units, and the battle for Italy would continue until May 1945.

A 78-foot Higgins boat lays a smoke screen off the Salerno beachhead during the Allied landings in September 1943, seeking to hide larger ships from German air attacks. These 78-foot Higgins boats had short forecastles. *James C. Fahey collection (USNI)*

The PTs supported the Salerno assault by patrolling against interference by German E-boats. No E-boats were encountered, but German planes attacking the beachhead periodically released a bomb or two on the PT boats. The *PT 211* suffered a near miss by a bomb from an Me 109 fighter that bent the boat's rudders. She retaliated by shooting down the plane. The PTs also laid smoke screens in an effort to hide landing ships from air attack.

To the west of Italy, Anglo-American torpedo boat bases were established on the large islands of Sardinia (Maddalena) and Corsica (Bastia), enabling the boats to operate in the western Mediterranean. Again, the PT bases were primitive. When a British LST struck a mine and was severely damaged, the PTs picked up survivors in rough seas. The PT crews then stripped the LST's galley of pots, pans, plates, and cutlery for their own austere base.

The PT targets continued to be E-boats, F-lighters, and coastal shipping in the area (the southern coast of France being occupied by the Germans). And the U.S. boats continued to operate in conjunction with their British counterparts. Robert J. Bulkley in *At Close Quarters* wrote: ". . . Lieutenant Commander Barnes realized that the PTs, because they were equipped with radar and the British boats were not, were superior to the British boats in the matter of finding enemy vessels and in executing the necessary maneuvers for a sneak attack. He also realized the [British] MTBs were superior to the PTs in the matter of torpedoes—the British torpedoes were more reliable than the [U.S.] Mark VIIIs, were faster, and carried a heavier explosive charge—and that the MGBs [Motor Gunboats] were superior to the PTs in the matter of firepower—their guns included ancient but powerful 6-pounders. Barnes proposed [to the British] that a PT accompany each group of British boats to serve as a scout and tracker."

The ungainly appearance of the German MFB L-lighter is evident in this captured one. Heavily armed, these lighters were important to the Germans for moving troops and supplies along the Mediterranean coasts. *U.S. Army*

The first definite score for MTB Squadron 15 in the Salerno operation occurred during the night of October 22–23, south of Giglio Island. Three PTs made an undetected torpedo attack on a small cargo ship escorted by four German torpedo or gunboats. One of four PT torpedoes hit the ship, which disintegrated in a violent explosion. Between Giglio and Elba on the night of November 2–3, two PTs torpedoed a small tanker of about 4,000 tons, which, before sinking, fired at her attackers, putting an incendiary bullet through a gasoline tank of the *PT 207* and into the officers' spaces. The explosion blew open a hatch, and flames shot up to the top of the radar mast. A quick-witted sailor grabbed a fire extinguisher, opened its nozzle, threw it below, and slammed shut the hatch cover; another sailor blanketed the fuel tank compartment with CO_2, and the flames were smothered.

On many winter nights the boats could not go out because of heavy seas. On the evening of November 29 the *PT 204* and *PT 211* began a patrol from the base at Bastia. Two hours later the heavy seas, 35-knot winds, and visibility of less than 100 yards forced them to curtail their patrol. The boats became separated, and when the *PT 204* was three miles from Bastia, four German E-boats and minesweepers appeared about 75 yards away on an opposite course; then a fifth showed up, crossing the PT's bow. Lieutenant (jg) Eugene S.A. Clifford, the PT-boat skipper, called for hard left rudder, but was unable to avoid a glancing collision with a minesweeper. As they sheered off, the opposing craft exchanged machine-gun fire at about ten yards' range. The *PT 204* was riddled with more than 100 bullet holes, all of which missed the gasoline tanks, and the engines, although hit, kept running. Not a man was scratched.

By December 1943 the PT boats were also engaging destroyer-type ships. These were Italian ships manned by Germans, operating from Genoa. The first encounter was inconclusive when two PT boats, with their radars inoperative, were surprised by two destroyers on the night of December 11–12. The destroyers gave chase for a few minutes.

On the night of December 16–17 two destroyers steamed down to Bastia and shelled the town for 15 minutes. Because of heavy seas no effort was made by the PT boats based at Bastia to go to sea. Two nights later, two groups went to sea to intercept any attempt by the destroyers to again bombard Bastia. The first group consisted of the *PT 209* plus a British MTB and two motor gunboats; the second consisted of the *PT 206, PT 208, PT 210*, and *PT 214*.

Early on December 19 American forces sighted two German destroyers steaming toward Bastia. The destroyers first confronted the four U.S. PT boats. Two boats fired seven (of their eight) torpedoes but without effect. The *PT 206* and *PT 208* were then told to return to their base. The other PT boats continued after the destroyers as they encountered the second group of Allied craft.

The *PT 209* and the British MTB each fired two torpedoes at the Germans, while the *PT 210* and *PT 214* now closed, each firing four torpedoes. The night exchange, with some PTs laying smoke, the German ships firing, and shore batteries from German-held Elba also joining in, made for a confusing encounter.

The U.S. and British torpedo boats had put 19 torpedoes into the water. None had struck a target. None of the torpedo boats suffered damage. Forewarned, the Germans did not make another destroyer foray toward Bastia until mid-February (when there was another, less-complicated night encounter, again without any torpedo hits).

The year 1944 began in the Mediterranean with an amphibious "end run" to overcome the stalemate of the Italian campaign. The U.S. and British armies fighting toward Rome had been completely stopped by the German defenses. Early on January 22, U.S. troops came ashore at Anzio, 37 miles south of Rome.

A major antagonist of Allied MTBs in the Mediterranean and European waters were German E-boats. The German torpedo boats were larger but had about the same speed as the U.S. PT boats; however, the U.S. MTBs were often more heavily armed. *U.S. Army*

The *PT 552* on the prowl in the Mediterranean. There was plenty of action for U.S. and British MTBs and motor gunboats in the "central sea." After combat in the Mediterranean, the *PT 552* was transferred to the Soviet Union in April 1945. *James C. Fahey collection (USNI)*

These wounded soldiers were carried by PT boat out to a transport standing offshore during the Allied landings on the southern coast of France in August 1944. Their hospital garb shows they had already been treated at a medical facility ashore. *U.S. Navy*

That morning Lieutenant General Mark Clark, Commanding General of the U.S. Fifth Army, arrived at the beachhead aboard a PT boat and was then taken ashore by a landing craft. Clark had two PT boats—not always the same units—continuously assigned to him through March to transport him and his staff between Naples and Anzio. Occasionally, these two PTs were also employed in intelligence and rescue missions.

Meanwhile, in an effort to interdict the German small craft traffic in the western Mediterranean, the Allies established a joint British-American attack group. Called Operation Gun, the effort consisted of teaming three British gunboats (LCG), fitted with two 4.7-inch guns and two 40-mm guns and manned by Royal Marines, with a close escort of three British MTBs to protect against E-boat attack, and a scouting group of two U.S. torpedo boats, the *PT 212* and *PT 214*. Finally, there was a control group consisting of the *PT 208* and *PT 218*. Riding in the *PT 218* was Commander Robert A. Allan, a Royal Navy officer commanding the force.

The force arrived off San Vincenzo early in the evening of March 27. Late that night the scouting group detected six F-lighters proceeding south along the Italian coast. A short time later two German destroyers were reported as a seaward defense for the barges.

The two PT boats of the scouting group attacked the destroyers, firing three torpedoes at a range of less than 400 yards, and they returned behind a smoke screen. Heavy fire from the German ship hit the *PT 214*, causing minor damage and wounding two crewmen. She continued operations. The two destroyers fled northward.

Now Commander Allan ordered the LCG to open fire. First, starshells illuminated the German F-lighters. These were followed by high-explosive shells as the Marine gunners quickly found the range. One F-lighter blew up with a tremendous explosion. Within ten minutes three others were on fire. Two barges attempting to withdraw were also caught by the LCGs. All six were sunk by gunfire.

The action was repeated on the night of April 24–25 when Commander Allan, again embarked in the *PT 218*, attacked a convoy of a tug and several F-lighters, some of which had been provided with additional guns to defend against air attacks. In this engagement the PT boats launched four torpedoes that blew up two lighters. The score was three F-lighters and two "flak" lighters sunk as well as a tug.

The LCG-MTB-PT boat team was an unqualified success. Significantly, attempts to coordinate U.S. PT boats with destroyers was a failure. Historian Samuel Eliot Morison wrote, "Efforts to arrange joint operations between PTs and DDs [destroyers] were unsuccessful. On one occasion, when they tried a joint patrol, the destroyers fired on the PTs and spattered their decks in the first salvo. Since the PTs were 5 knots slower than the DDs, they actually ran for protection under enemy shore batteries on Cape Rasocolmo, which fired on the DDs and drove them seaward!"

Beginning in late April 1944 additional PT boats arrived in the Mediterranean, the first boats of MTB Squadron 22 with Higgins boats under Lieutenant Commander Richard J. Dressling, and MTB Squadron 29 with Elco boats under Lieutenant Commander S. Stephen Daunis. Squadron 22 was based at Bastia and Squadron 29 was established at Calvi on Corsica. The long-serving Higgins boats of MTB Squadron 15 operated from both bases. Lieutenant Commander Barnes became the operational commander of all three squadrons as Commander Boat Squadrons Eighth Fleet. With the new boats came new torpedoes, the more effective Mark XIII type launched from racks rather than heavier torpedo tubes; also, the newer boats were faster. And during overhauls these new Squadron 15 boats were given even more powerful engines, raising their speed to more than 40 knots.

With more boats and more-capable torpedoes, the PT boats operated in MTB groups and as part of Allan's "battle group." One of the latter engagements—an Operation Gun sortie with Commander Allan embarked in the *PT 217*—was highly successful. This engagement, however, was fought entirely by the scouting group, comprised of the *PT 202*, *PT 213*, and *PT 218*. The trio launched 11 torpedoes at two German corvettes. Two torpedoes hit and sank one corvette; the second turned tail and ran.

Commander Allan directed that the *PT 302*, *PT 303*, and *PT 304* make a radar-directed, long-range (1-1/2 mile) attack against the fleeing corvette. Six torpedoes were launched; one torpedo hit. The *PT 218* then joined the foray with her last torpedo, but the stricken corvette escaped. She managed to reach Leghorn, where she was stripped and abandoned.

Two more German corvettes were taken under attack by three PT boats on the night of June 14–15. The *PT 552*, *PT 558*, and *PT 559* each launched two torpedoes. One corvette exploded and sank. Observers then saw an explosion on the second corvette; a short time later, she sank.

Two days later saw the largest PT boat operation in the Mediterranean. Thirty-seven MTBs took part in the invasion of Elba. The Germans had laid mines to prevent large landing ships from approaching the island. The PTs were assigned to land French and British commandos (in rubber landing craft), escort gunboats and landing craft, cause a diversion, and attack any German ships that attempted to interfere with the operation.

A zebra-striped Higgins PT boat in the Mediterranean. One squadron in the Mediterranean and one in the Pacific had these 18-inch black-and-white stripes. Note the fixed angle of the boat's 21-inch torpedo tubes. *U.S. Navy*

Late on the night of June 17, Lieutenant (jg) Howard J. Nugent commanding the *PT 210* sighted what he believed was a part of the multi-national Elba invasion group. He pulled the PT alongside one of the ships, removed his helmet, and hailed the ship with his megaphone. Quoted in *At Close Quarters*, Nugent recalled, "The answer I received was one I shall never forget. First there was a string of guttural words followed immediately by a broadside from the ship's two 88-mm guns and five or six 20-mm guns. The first blast carried the megaphone away and tore off the right side of a pair of binoculars that I was wearing around my neck. It also tore through the bridge of the boat, jamming the helm, knocking out the bridge engine controls, and scored a direct hit on the three engine emergency cut-off switches (Higgins boat) which stopped the engines."

The *PT 210*—dead in the water—opened fire against her more heavily armed antagonist. The enemy E-boats and F-lighters withdrew. The *PT 210* was badly damaged, but, remarkably, none of her crew had been hit. The nearby *PT 209* had also been hit, with one man killed. The *PT 211* was also damaged when she engaged an F-lighter.

During the next few nights the PTs worked with British MTBs to damage a corvette, sink an F-lighter, and damage several other enemy craft. The conquest of Elba—"invasion by PT boat"—was a complete success.

Shortly after the operation, on the night of June 29–30, the *PT 308* and *PT 309* were on patrol when they sighted two Italian torpedo boats. The U.S. craft gave chase. One of the fleeing Ital-

ian boats slowed and then stopped. As the PTs drew alongside, they found that the craft's 14-man crew—including an Italian flotilla commander—had gone into a rubber boat. The Italian craft appeared to be burning so the PTs picked up the prisoners and departed. The next morning an aircraft reported the craft was still afloat. The *PT 306* located it, put out the fire, and towed the prize into Bastia.

On August 1, 1944, all PT boats were withdrawn from Mediterranean operations in preparation for the invasion of southern France. The original Allied plans called for an invasion of the French Riviera—Operation Anvil-Dragoon—at the same time as the landings in Normandy, but the southern France operation was postponed in order to devote full attention to Normandy and because of the shortages in landing ships and craft, especially LSTs. The invasion began on August 15, when U.S. and Free French forces made three major landings on the French Mediterranean coast between Cannes and Toulon.

The night before, PT boats were assigned to diversionary activities, to protect the main transport areas from enemy surface attack, and to support the landings of several hundred troops coming ashore in rubber boats some six hours before the main landings.

The only PTs to see action against enemy ships during the landings were the *PT 553* and *PT 554*. Two German corvettes came on the scene and were quickly overwhelmed by U.S. and British warships, with each PT firing a single torpedo in the face of heavy gunfire. The U.S. destroyer *Endicott* also fired two torpedoes at the corvettes, all without effect. It was gunfire from the Allied ships, especially 40-mm and 20-mm fire from the destroyer, that devastated the two corvettes, which finally sank under the pounding.

While these two PT boats escaped damage, the *PT 202* hit a mine on the evening of August 16, which blew off her stern. The *PT 218* attempted to help and suffered the same fate. Despite horrendous damage, only one man was killed and six were injured in the two boats. As the boats were sinking, the survivors took to rubber rafts and came ashore on a deserted beach after dark. The next morning they were found by a U.S. Army patrol.

The *PT 555* was also mined on August 24. Two men were killed and several injured. With the boat slowly sinking, the crew members jettisoned guns and other equipment as they bailed. The boat was towed into port and sank at the dock.

Meanwhile, the boats continued to support

The *PT 559* fitted with a six-gun Thunderbolt mount fitted aft. The *PT 559* saw combat in the Mediterranean. Several PTs carried the Thunderbolt mount during operations in the Mediterranean.

the landing operations and consolidation of Allied positions along the coast. Within days, the Allied invaders secured 40 miles of beach and the southern ports that would prove vital to the movement of men and material for the Allied drive into Germany. By August 28, aided by French guerrillas, the Allies had liberated Toulon and Marseilles. Nice fell by the end of the month. Heavy casualties were inflicted on the Germans, with the Allied forces suffering relatively few losses. The PTs were involved in patrolling the coast, transporting senior officers, delivering blood and other high-priority cargo, and seeking out enemy ships and small craft. The latter included small, explosive-laden boats, some manned by a single operator who was to jump overboard before the craft hit a target, and drone, radio-controlled boats.

The PTs attacked several groups of these explosive craft and contributed to their failure to damage any Allied ships in the invasion of Southern France. But F-lighters and corvette-type ships were still a threat. On the night of September 13–14 the *PT 559* was among MTBs attacking a convoy of F-lighters. After the action began the *PT 559* was the only torpedo boat still carrying torpedoes. A corvette appeared on the scene and the *PT 559* fired a torpedo that hit and sunk the warship. She then fired her last torpedo at the F-lighters and sped off under fire from several German ships.

With the Allies in control of the French coastline, the Germans were left with only a stretch of the Italian coast for naval operations. Accordingly, MTB Squadron 15 was decommissioned at Malta on October 17, 1944. The squadron's 16 boats were transferred to the Royal Navy.

The remaining PT boats moved to bases on the French coast at St. Maxime and then to Gulf Juan, and to Leghorn, Italy. The Leghorn-based *PT 311* struck a mine on the morning of November 18. Ten of her crew died. The survivors—five men who had been in their bunks at the time—were picked up off the boat's bow by other PT boats.

As the war was ending, the PT boats were employed in an unusual manner: to attack German-held harbors with torpedoes. During March and April several PTs approached harbors to fire long-range Mark VIII torpedoes, generally from a range of about 2 miles. Fifteen torpedoes were expended in this manner; several caused major secondary explosions, indicating they had struck ships in the harbors.

Swashbuckling actor Douglas Fairbanks, Jr., a U.S. Naval Reserve officer, led a force of PT boats to the northern side of Elba in August 1944 as part of an Allied deception operation. He saw extensive action in World War II. *Douglas Fairbanks, Jr. collection courtesy James E. Wise*

U.S. PT boats carried out their last combat patrols of the Mediterranean on the night of April 28–29, 1945. In *At Close Quarters* historian Bulkley summed up the nation's two years of combat operations in the Mediterranean, "Their losses were 4 boats destroyed by mines; 5 officers and 19 [enlisted] men killed in action; 7 officers and 28 men wounded in action. They fired 354 torpedoes and claimed to have sunk 38 vessels totaling 23,700 tons and to have damaged 49, totaling 22,600 tons; and in joint patrols with British boats to have sunk 15 vessels totaling 13,000 tons and to have damaged 17, totaling 5,650 tons."

From 1940 onward the Mediterranean was the scene of savage naval battles between the British and Italian navies, involving battleships, aircraft carriers, cruisers, destroyers, and submarines. Subsequently, German land-based aircraft, U-boats, and small combat craft entered the fray. By the time of the Allied invasion (Italy surrendered in September 1943), the Germans had only small craft and a few corvettes and destroyers in the Mediterranean. Against these were arrayed mainly U.S. and British torpedo boats and British gunboats. It was largely a "small boys" conflict at sea and, as in the Pacific, the U.S. PT boats proved to be an effective weapon.

Chapter 8

The Invasion of Europe

The Battle of the Atlantic began on September 3, 1939, the day that the European war began. U.S. naval forces—under the aegis of a Neutrality Patrol—entered the battle early in 1941. After December 1941, American naval forces were fully engaged in the Atlantic.

While the British employed coastal forces—motor gunboats and motor torpedo boats—on a large scale along the Atlantic coast of France, there was no role for U.S. PT boats until the

spring of 1944, when the Allied invasion of France was being planned. The first U.S. PT boats arrived in the theater at the behest of the Office of Strategic Services (OSS), which controlled American intelligence agents in the European theater.

The Navy established MTB Squadron 2 on March 23, 1944, at Glenwood Landing on Long Island, New York. (The previous MTB Squadron 2 had been decommissioned in the Solomons on November 11, 1943.) Intended specifically for the European theater, the squadron was led by Lieutenant Commander John D. Bulkeley and consisted of just three MTBs—*PT 71, PT 72,* and *PT 199,* all Higgins boats. The three had been employed for almost two years as training boats at Melville, Rhode Island. With the large MTB commitments to the Pacific and Mediterranean theaters, these were the only units immediately available for operations out of Britain.

After being overhauled, the three PT boats were shipped to England, arriving at Dartmouth on April 24. There they were fitted with improved navigation equipment for operations off the French coast, and the crews were trained in handling small boats to put agents ashore and then retrieve them.

The first mission to German-occupied France occurred on the night of May 19–20 when the *PT 71* set out from England with several OSS agents and considerable equipment. The boat successfully transited the English Channel, passed through offshore German naval patrols and

A 78-foot Higgins PT boat at high speed. The first U.S. PT boats to operate under the American flag in the English Channel area were Higgins boats. These and the Elco boats proved highly durable for such fragile craft. *U.S. Navy*

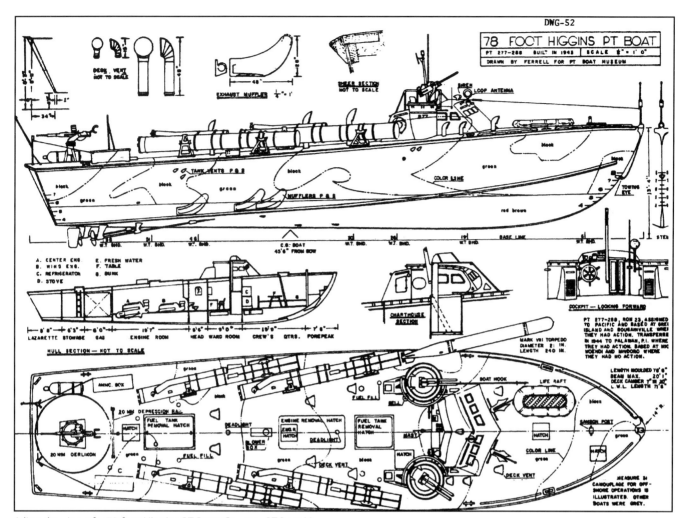

A line drawing of a 78-foot Higgins PT Boat. *Courtesy PT Boat Museum*

minefields, and anchored some 500 yards off the beach. The OSS agents and their gear were landed without incident and the *PT 71* successfully transited the obstacles to return safely to England. In all, these PTs carried out 19 such missions for the OSS to the French coast through November 1944.

Historian Samuel Eliot Morison related the story of one of Bulkeley's PT missions in support of the Normandy landings: ". . . they were told to bring in a few buckets of sand from each of the Omaha beaches. That was a risky job and it seemed to make no sense. . . . it made plenty of sense. Long after the beaches had been selected, a scientist who claimed local knowledge came up with the alarming statement that these beaches consisted largely of peat, with only a thin covering of sand; and if that were true, our thousands of vehicles would bog down before reaching dry land. Fortunately, the reconnaissance parties found that it was completely false."

Meanwhile, the Navy was shipping additional PT boats to England. Three squadrons followed Bulkeley's MTB Squadron 2 although only one, MTB Squadron 34 under Lieutenant Allen H. Harris, arrived in time to participate in the D-day landings on June 6, 1944. This unit was followed by MTB Squadron 35 under Lieutenant Commander Richard Davis, Jr., which arrived in England on June 4 and MTB Squadron 30 under Lieutenant Robert L. Searles, on June 7. The first two squadrons each had 12 Elco boats; Squadron 30 had six Higgins craft. Thus, including Bulkeley's squadron, there were 33 U.S. Navy MTBs available in England in early June. Also, in June, Bulkeley was designated as the task group commander in charge of all PT-boat operations for the Normandy landings.

The PT boats of MTB Squadrons 2 and 34 saw considerable action on D-day. The three Higgins boats were parceled out to major flagships—the *PT 71* accompanied the cruiser *Augusta*, flagship of

A PT boat turns at high speed, showing off its maneuverability. Although press reports often overestimated their speed—some articles claimed they went up to 60 knots—the boats were relatively fast and hence difficult targets when they were under way. *U.S. Navy*

the Western Naval Task Force and Lieutenant General Omar N. Bradley, commander of the First U.S. Army; the *PT 72* was with the command ship *Ancon*, flagship of the Omaha Beach assault force; and the *PT 199* sailed with the transport *Bayfield*, flagship of the Utah Beach assault force. The PT boats were to carry Army commanders to the beach. On D-day the *PT 199*, after carrying officers to Utah Beach, rescued 61 survivors from the U.S. destroyer *Corry*, which had struck a German mine and sunk.

The 12 Elco boats, now under Lieutenant Robert R. Read, were assigned to support the Utah assault by escorting minesweepers and then keeping sea lanes open for transports and landing ships, primarily by providing protection against German torpedo boats. At the time there were perhaps a score of E-boats based at the ports of Boulogne, Dieppe, and Le Havre.

The German high command, caught by surprise and overwhelmed by the Allied air and surface escorts, was unable to either effectively attack the assault forces steaming for Normandy or prevent the initial landings. During the initial assault, the only action involving PT boats came on the night of June 5–6, when the U.S. minesweeper *Osprey* struck a mine and sank. The *PT 505* and *PT 506* picked up six of the survivors.

Things changed the next day. On the evening of June 7, the *PT 505* sighted what was believed to be a U-boat periscope. The PT boat gave chase and, when about to drop depth charges,

struck a mine. The boat was heavily damaged with two crewmen injured.

The *PT 507* came alongside and took off the radar and radio equipment from the sinking boat, while the crew jettisoned torpedoes and other gear. The *PT 507* then helped keep the stricken craft afloat until the next morning, when two LCM landing craft towed the *PT 505* to the beach. While high and dry for six hours her hull was patched and, on June 11, the *PT 507* towed the *PT 505* through heavy seas to Portland, England. (The craft was repaired and later transferred to the Soviet Union.)

On June 8 the U.S. destroyer *Glennon* struck a mine and began sinking. The destroyer escort *Rich* and a pair of minesweepers attempted to assist the stricken ship. Another mine detonated nearby. Then a mine explosion blew off the stern of the *Rich*. Drifting out of control, the ship hit another mine three minutes later.

The *PT 502*, *PT 504*, and *PT 506* and a British motor launch tried to assist the stricken warships. The PTs took off 69 wounded men before the *Rich* sank.

Meanwhile, the three PTs assigned to carry senior officers between their flagships and the Normandy beachhead were having a busy time of it. On June 12 the *PT 71* carried an unprecedented boatload of VIPs: Admirals Ernest J. King, the Chief of Naval Operations; Harold Stark, Commander U.S. Naval Forces Europe; and Alan G. Kirk, Commander Western Naval Task Force; and Generals George C. Marshall, Chief of Staff U.S. Army; Dwight D. Eisenhower, Supreme Allied Commander Europe; H.H. Arnold, Commander U.S. Army Air Forces; and Bradley, as well as several lesser flag and general officers. On the 17th the three Higgins boats that were carrying senior officers between their flagships and the Normandy beachhead were relieved by Elco boats, with the older craft returning to Portland for upkeep and to resume their missions for the OSS.

The German Navy and Air Force were unable to significantly interfere with the Normandy landings. Although a few U-boats and E-boats made attacks, their scores were few. Indeed, mines were the most efficient German weapon against the invasion forces.

The PT boats had escaped damage during the first two weeks of Operation Neptune, except for the *PT 505*, which had been heavily damaged by a mine. Several boats were damaged during the massive storm that pounded the Normandy coast from June 19 to 22 as 21 PTs rode out the heavy weather.

With the beachheads secure by the beginning of August, preparations were in hand for withdrawing the PT boats. John D. Bulkeley, promoted to commander, departed his beloved PT boats to take command of the destroyer *Endicott*. He was replaced as the commander of PT boats in the English Channel by Lieutenant Harris, who had earlier been relieved by Lieutenant Read as Commander MTB Squadron 34.

Upon their withdrawal from the Normandy area, nine PTs were assigned to Portsmouth to work with British MTBs and motor gun boats to patrol off the French port of Le Havre, and 18 were assigned to Cherbourg, replacing British coastal forces to interdict German shipping between the Channel Islands and the remaining German positions on the coast of France.

The first PT boat action for the craft enforcing a blockade of German-held Le Havre came on the night of August 6–7 when the British frigate *Thornborough* vectored the *PT 510, PT 512*, and

PT 514 to intercept three E-boats coming out of Le Havre. The PTs attacked them with gunfire, scoring several hits, and forcing the E-boats to return to port.

On the night of August 8–9 three PTs attacked a German auxiliary ship escorted by five minesweepers off Cap d'Antifer. German shore batteries illuminated the ships before they could make a torpedo attack, so the PTs closed to attack with gunfire. Again the German firepower was impressive, damaging the *PT 520* and *PT 521*. These boats retired behind a smoke screen laid down by the *PT 511*. More inconclusive attacks followed until the Germans began to evacuate Le Havre on August 23. Beginning the following night the PTs regularly engaged German forces. In a gunnery engagement with four E-boats the *PT 511, PT 514*, and *PT 520* severely damaged the torpedo boat *S-91*, which was abandoned and blown up.

Until Le Havre was sealed off by Canadian troops on September 1, the nocturnal firefights

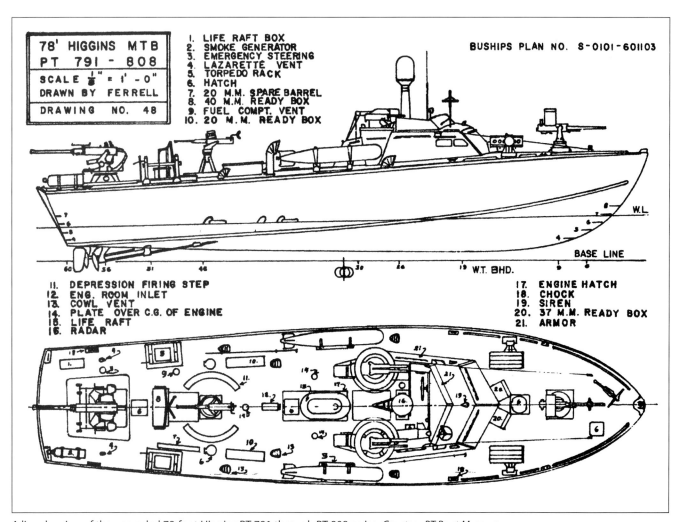

A line drawing of the upgraded 78-foot Higgins PT 791 through PT 808 series. *Courtesy PT Boat Museum*

The *PT 509* and the minesweeper *Pheasant* stand by the minesweeper *Tide*, sinking off Omaha Beach, Normandy, after striking a mine on June 7, 1944. Mines, which sank more ships than any other weapon in World War II, destroyed four U.S. torpedo boats. *U.S. Navy*

continued, with the PTs inflicting damage on numerous small craft, and preventing many vessels from escaping from Le Havre.

In another action on August 21, the *PT 502* and *PT 504* were sent to reconnoiter Morlaix, a small port on the northern shore of Brittany, which had been bypassed by the Army. Entering at daybreak, the two boats moved slowly over the mudflats and through a minefield indicated on a captured German chart. The PT crewmen were startled by a fusillade of small-arms fire from the shore. The PTs broke out their largest American flags, at the same time sounding their foghorns, while everyone topside waved his arms vigorously and bellowed "Americans! Amis!"

This demonstration had its effect: The firing ceased and a small boat put out from shore, almost concealed under the folds of a large French flag. As the boat came alongside, the Mayor of Morlaix, resplendent in top hat and frock coat, emerged from under the tricolor and offered a profuse and apologetic welcome. A pilot guided the

PT 502 and *PT 504* upriver to the town, where officers and men were entertained around the clock with lobster and champagne and all the embellishments. Two days later British minesweepers cleared the approaches to the port, and on the 25th the first Allied convoy arrived. But, as historian Morison wrote, ". . . the pioneer PTs had all the glory—and the gravy—of liberating Morlaix."

In the Channel Islands operations, the PTs conducted night raids against German ships. They teamed up with a destroyer escort that could provide longer-range radar, command and control, and fire support for the PTs.

On the night of August 8–9 the U.S. destroyer escort *Maloy* patrolled west of the German-held Island of Jersey in company with the *PTs 500, 503, 507, 508,* and *509.* Early on the 9th the *Maloy*—in a heavy fog—vectored the three northern MTBs to fire torpedoes at a group of six German minesweepers. Their torpedoes missed.

The *Maloy* then vectored the three southern PTs to attack. They fired several torpedoes, again with no results. In this engagement the *PT 509* disappeared.

When the *PT 503* and *PT 507* searched for their missing colleague in the fog-shrouded area, they came across a German minesweeper. The *PT 503* fired a single torpedo and both PT boats and the minesweeper exchanged heavy gunfire. All three craft took numerous hits. Two sailors were killed and four wounded aboard the *PT 503*; one crewman was wounded on the *PT 507*.

A day later an Allied aircraft sighted wreckage of the *PT 509* and the body of one of her crewmen. After the war ended, Radarman's Mate 2nd Class John L. Page of the *PT 509* was liberated from a German prisoner of war camp on the Island of Jersey. He related that the *PT 509* had fired a torpedo based on radar bearings, and then closed with an enemy minesweeper to engage her with gunfire. A shell exploded in the chart house of *PT 509*'s deck, but Lieutenant Harry Crist, a veteran of the Pacific War, steered a course to ram and struck one of the minesweepers with such force that the bow of his burning craft was jammed into her side. The German crew worked frantically with crowbars to clear the flaming PT boat. As the PT drifted away she exploded and disappeared.

When Page had reached the deck he found his PT boat in flames and smashed against a 180-foot German minesweeper. The Germans were pouring gunfire down into the PT boat and lobbing hand grenades. They rescued Page, who had suffered a broken arm and leg and 37 wounds.

Page was given medical attention aboard the damaged minesweeper. He recalled counting 15 German dead as well as several wounded. He was the only survivor of the *PT 509*. The 204-foot German minesweeper survived the encounter.

Before mid-August there were two more brushes—both inconclusive—between American PTs and German minesweepers. Thereafter, for several months the German craft kept in port, but German gun batteries in the Channel Islands continued to harass Allied convoys and vessels passing along the coast, despite frequent attempts by Allied destroyers and even by the British battleship *Rodney* to silence them. But after the night encounters of August 11–12 and August 13–14, there was no further PT boat action in this sector; the Channel Islands held out until the end of the European War.

With most of the French coast under Allied control, the PTs of MTB Squadron 2 were left without a mission as the OSS dispensed with using PTs to land agents and supplies. One final operation was planned: A volunteer crew led by Lieutenant William M. Snelling was to man the *PT 72* to carry arms and ammunition through German-controlled waters to resistance fighters in Denmark. The *PT 72* was fitted with extra gasoline tanks and loaded with her cargo. However, on her final check-out run, she developed engine trouble and the mission was canceled.

The three Higgins boats of MTB Squadron 2 were loaded aboard ship and returned to New York. The Elco boats of MTB Squadrons 34 and 35 (less the mine- and rough-sea damaged *PT 505*) sailed to Roseneath, Scotland, and, after several delays, they were transferred to the Soviet Navy. The *PT 505* was sent back to the United States and sent to the MTB training center at Melville.

MTB Squadron 30 remained at Cherbourg until the spring of 1945, employed to help protect Allied shipping along the French coast. The squadron engaged only small craft. With the end of the war in early May 1945, the squadron was packed up and shipped back to the United States in June. The boats were to be rehabilitated and then shipped to the Pacific. They were still in New York when the Pacific War came to an end.

Chapter 9

Victory and Defeat

MTB Squadron 40, being placed in commission at the New York Navy Yard on April 26, 1945. This was the last squadron to be shipped to the Pacific, but the 80-foot Elco boats arrived in the Philippines too late to see combat. The squadron commander, Lieutenant George E. Cox, Jr., had served in MTB Squadron 3 in the Philippines at the start of the war. *James C. Fahey collection (USNI)*

Preliminary American planning for the defeat of Japan was begun in August 1942 by a team within the U.S. Joint Chiefs of Staff. This effort led to a working paper, produced in April 1943, which declared that "achieving the unconditional surrender of Japan might require actual invasion of the Japanese homeland." By early 1945 plans were being readied for an invasion of the southern island of Kyushu in November 1945 (Operation Olympic), to be followed in the spring of 1946 by an invasion of the main island of Honshu (Operation Coronet) and a subsequent land campaign to capture Tokyo.

Each of the two invasions of the Japanese home islands were to be larger than the Allied landings at Normandy on D-day. In these final assaults of the war, PT boats would be invaluable for protecting amphibious ships and landing craft from the Japanese suicide boats and swimmers that were being massed to inflict enormous casualties on the American soldiers and Marines of the assault forces.

In early August 1945, B-29 Superfortress bombers flying from Tinian in the Mariana Islands dropped atomic bombs on Hiroshima and then Nagasaki. A few days later Japan surrendered. There was no need for the invasions.

By mid-August 1945 there were 30 squadrons of PT boats in commission. Nineteen squadrons were in the Seventh Fleet (which was being transferred from General MacArthur's command to Admiral Nimitz for the assaults on Japan), six were in Nimitz's Pacific Fleet, four were in the United States being prepared for the Pacific War, and one was employed in the training role at Melville. One additional unit, MTB Squadron 42, was placed in commission in New York on September 17, 1945—the last PT squadron to be formed. In all, there were some 370 PT boats in these squadrons.

Historian Robert J. Bulkley observed that with the end of the war, "The Navy Department properly

The *PT 810* was the Bath Iron Works entry in the post–World War II PT boat design competition. There is a 40-mm ammunition magazine forward of the bridge structure. These boats never carried torpedoes. *U.S. Navy*

got rid of most of its PTs. Their job was done, and because of their light wooden construction, they could not be stored away against future need as the steel-hulled ships of the fleet. Indeed, many of the older boats which had been kept running because of combat necessity, were no longer worth saving for any purpose. All the boats in the western Pacific were carefully surveyed. It was found that 118 hulls were defective because of broken frames, worms and dry rot, broken keels, cracked longitudinals, or battle damage. These boats were stripped of all salvageable material and the bare hulls were burned on the beach at Samar."

Their funeral pyre on Samar was a victory fire. The PT boats had performed exemplary wartime service, usually against difficult odds, often confronting enemy cruisers and destroyers as well as torpedo boats and gunboats. While their torpedoes and guns sank far fewer enemy ships than were credited to them during the war, their tonnage of their victims still exceeded the tonnage of the entire PT boat force.

In return, 69 PT boats were lost during the war:

Enemy gunfire:	5 (*PTs 37, 44, 111, 112, 493*)
Rammed by enemy ship:	1 (*PT 109*)
Ramming enemy ship:	1 (*PT 509*)
Strafed by enemy aircraft:	1 (*PT 34*)
Bombed by enemy aircraft:	4 (*PTs 117, 123, 164, 320*)
Aerial suicide attack:	2 (*PTs 300, 323*)
Enemy shore batteries:	5 (*PTs 133, 247, 251, 337, 363*)
Enemy mines:	4 (*PTs 202, 218, 311, 555*)
Grounded and destroyed:	19 (*PTs 31, 38, 43, 68, 73, 118, 135, 136, 145, 147, 153, 158, 172, 193, 321, 322, 339, 368, 371*)
Lost in sinking of carrying cargo ship:	2 (*PTs 165, 173*)
Destroyed to prevent capture:	3 (*PTs 32, 35, 41*)
Accidental loss to U.S. aircraft:	3 (*PTs 166, 346, 347*)
Accidental loss to Australian aircraft:	2 (*PTs 121, 353*)
Accidental loss to U.S. surface ships:	2 (*PTs 77, 79*)
Loss to enemy shore fire or U.S. surface ship:	1 (*PT 283*)
Storms or accidental grounding:	5 (*PTs 22, 28, 113, 219, 338*)
Fire or explosion in port:	5 (*PTs 63, 67, 107, 239, 301*)
PT boat collision:	3 (*PTs 110, 200, 279*)

By a large margin, most PT boats were lost when they ran aground in enemy waters and were destroyed to prevent their capture. Grounding was a continuous threat to PT boats as they sped through coastal waters, making an attack or attempting to escape after one. Accidents also took a major toll on PT boats; their highly volatile fuel (100-octane gasoline) made the boats vulnerable to enemy gunfire as well as to mishaps.

After the war the Navy initially retained three squadrons for training: MTB Squadrons 4, 41, and 42. However, in early 1946 the Navy Department decided to keep only four boats for experimental work, the *PTs 613, 616, 619,* and *620,* all newly completed Elco boats. With the last squadron decommissioned in April 1946, these four boats were assigned to the Operational Test and Development Force. The hundreds of other boats were broken up or sold for commercial use.

Shortly after the war the Navy initiated the design of a new series of PT boats. Reminiscent of the late 1930s design competition, the Navy ordered four PTs with different characteristics from four yards. All would have aluminum hulls and would be powered by four Packard engines (in place of three Packards of lesser horsepower in war-built boats). All were to carry 40-mm and 20-mm guns and have four torpedo launchers. These boats were:

PT 809—built by the Electric Boat Company in Groton, Connecticut—featured a riveted hull 98 feet in length.

PT 810—built by Bath Iron Works, Bath, Maine—with a hull partially riveted and partially welded, 89 feet in length.

PT 811—built by John Trumpy and Sons, Annapolis, Maryland—an all-welded boat 94 feet in length.

PT 812—built at the Philadelphia Naval Shipyard—with an all-welded hull, configured specifically for rough seas, 105 feet in length. The *PT 812* subsequently had her four Packard engines replaced by a pair of Metropolitan Vickers gas turbines on her outboard shafts with two smaller diesel engines being fitted to her inboard shafts, the latter to provide speeds up to 18 knots. This early U.S. Navy experiment with aircraft-type turbine engines was unsuccessful.

The four were completed in 1950–1951. After their initial trials, these boats operated from 1954 to 1959 as MTB Squadron 1 under the Navy's Operational Development Force. (U.S. MTB hull numbers reached *PT 822,* with the *PT 813* through *PT 822* built in Denmark with U.S. funds under the Military Defense Assistance Program.)

No PT boats operated under the American flag during the Korean War (1950–1953). The four surviving Elco boats were transferred to the South Korean Navy in 1952. The four competitive prototypes were not considered suitable for an overseas deployment in a combat environment. But they all had active careers.

The *PT 809* was transferred to the White House in late 1959 for use by the Secret Service as a "chase" boat for the presidential yacht. Assigned the name *Guardian,* she was based at the Washington Navy Yard. About 1965 she was transferred to the Central Intelligence Agency for classified work. In 1974 the craft was returned to the Navy and modified for use as a drone recovery boat, being renamed *Retriever* and designated *DR 1.* Through 1986 she supported Navy operations with remote-control aircraft, operating out of Little Creek (Norfolk), Virginia. She was then retired after 35 years of service!

Another view of the *PT 810,* racing at high speed in Chesapeake Bay. There is a twin 20-mm mount in a gun tub on the starboard side and a second twin 20-mm mount between the superstructure and the after 40-mm gun. A small boat is stowed forward of the lattice mast. *U.S. Navy*

The *PT 809*, produced by the Electric Boat Company, shows the sleek lines that reflect the earlier Elco PT boats of World War II. All four postwar PT boats carried single 40-mm cannon. There were provisions for four torpedo launchers for Mark XIII torpedoes. *James C. Fahey collection (USNI)*

The *PT 812* was transferred to the U.S. Army in 1959 and, in 1968, to the South Korean Navy.

The *PT 809* and *PT 810* were stricken from the Naval Vessel Register in late 1959. However, with the escalation of U.S. military operations in Vietnam, the craft were placed back in service in January 1963, and reclassified as *PTF 1* and *PTF 2*, respectively. PTF—for fast patrol boat—reflected their new role.

Beginning in 1961, U.S. and American-trained South Vietnamese Navy commandos carried out raids and delivered agents into North Vietnam. The commandos initially employed motorized junks. While these craft had the advantage of being able to hide among the thousands of junks that plied Vietnam coastal waters, they were slow and vulnerable.

In an effort to provide more capability to the commandos, on October 6, 1962, the Department of Defense directed the Chief of Naval Operations, Admiral David McDonald, to provide any suitable craft that could be used in South Vietnam. The *PTF 1* and *PTF 2* were reactivated; their Packard engines were overhauled and quieting features were provided. The PTFs were armed with single 40-mm cannon forward and aft and two twin 20-mm cannon. No torpedo gear was fitted. A Navy press release noted that the PTFs ". . . will be used for special operations with the Navy's Sea-Air-Land Teams."

The Sea-Air-Land Teams, better known as SEAL teams, are Navy units trained to conduct unconventional paramilitary operations and to train personnel of allied nations in these techniques.

After being used in the United States to train SEALs, these first two PTFs were shipped to the U.S. base at Da Nang, South Vietnam. U.S. Navy crews operated the PTFs under the control of Special Operations Group (later Studies and Operations Group) 34. This unit, with headquarters in Saigon, was under the U.S. Military Assistance Command Vietnam, the principal U.S. command

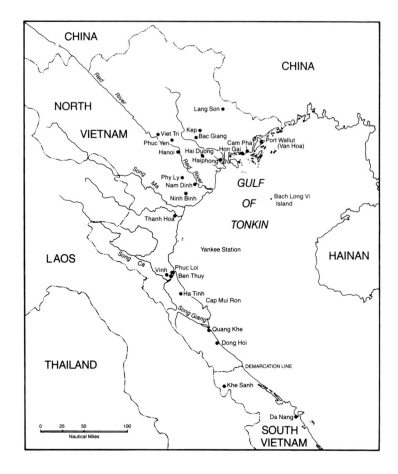

The *PT 811* barely under way. Built by John Trumpy and Sons in Annapolis, a veteran yacht builder, the *PT 811* was in some respects the least successful of the four prototypes. Note the twin 20-mm gun mounts fitted in addition to 40-mm guns. *U.S. Navy*

in South Vietnam. The maritime operations of SOG 34 had the code name 34A.

More fast patrol boats were needed to expand 34A operations. The decision was made to acquire Norwegian-built "Nasty" torpedo boats. The Norwegian design was considered one of the most advanced craft available, and while the Norwegian Navy had a long and successful history of operating with the U.S. Navy.

The Nasty design had been developed as a private-venture MTB by the firm Norwegian Boat Services (Båtservice Verft) and built in 1958. The Norwegian Navy adopted the design for series production, with the first boat, the *Tjeld*, being commissioned in June 1960.

The Nastys were built of double-layer mahogany sandwiching a layer of fiberglass, with laminated ash and oak for her keel and frames. They were just over 80 feet in length and were driven by two British-produced, Napier-Deltic diesel engines, and could drive the boats at about 45 knots. They were designed to carry four 21-inch torpedo tubes in addition to two 40-mm guns. Two 20-mm mounts were also installed. With the deletion of the torpedoes they could carry more personnel, rubber raiding craft, and other equipment.

The Navy installed PTF armament and electronic equipment in the United States, and all were shipped to South Vietnam. Upon arrival "in country," U.S. Navy small boat specialists and SEALs additionally fitted 81-mm mortars, 4.5-inch rockets, and 57-mm recoilless rifles to the boats. For a brief period flame throwers were tested on the craft. Later virtually all PTFs were fitted with a tandem-mounted .50-caliber machine gun/81-mm mortar, which proved to be a particularly effective weapon.

All PTFs would be capable of carrying torpedo launch racks and mines, but none of these weapons were ever fitted.

Under the tutelage of the U.S. Navy, South Vietnamese naval commandos accelerated their 34A operations. The first large-scale raid began on the night of July 30, 1964, when six boats were available. That night the *PTFs 2, 3, 5,* and *6* departed Da Nang to assault the North Vietnamese offshore islands of Hon Me and Hon Nieu. Just after midnight on July 31 the *PTF 3* and *PTF 6* closed with Hon Me to land sabotage teams. Without warning coastal gun batteries opened fire. The *PTF 6* was hit and four South Vietnamese were injured.

As the boats began to withdraw, a Chinese-built Swatow torpedo boat approached. The PTFs bombarded shore facilities for several minutes before fleeing southward, outracing the Swatow.

The *PTF 2* and *PTF 5* successfully bombarded facilities on Hon Nieu island, and then raced back to Da Nang.

The 34A operations continued, but with limited success. Meanwhile, the U.S. Navy had begun

The *PT 812* on trials with her 40-mm cannon forward and aft covered with canvas. After being evaluated for gas turbine propulsion, the *PT 812* was transferred to the U.S. Army and, subsequently, to South Korea. *U.S. Navy*

the so-called Desoto patrols, cruises by destroyers into the Gulf of Tonkin to carry out electronic surveillance missions. These periodic forays—in international waters—sought out and recorded North Vietnamese radar emissions and radio transmissions. Senior U.S. Navy commanders suggested that the destroyers on Desoto patrols could be employed to coordinate the 34A operations by PTFs. General William C. Westmoreland, the U.S. military commander in Vietnam, rejected the proposal, hoping to continue the deniability of U.S. involvement in the 34A operations, which were penetrating the three-mile territorial waters of North Vietnam, and actually putting agents and saboteurs ashore.

The Navy commanders agreed and steps were taken to prevent interference and direct mutual support of the two operations. Thus the scene was set for the night of August 3–4, 1964, when PTFs again attacked two North Vietnamese islands in the Tonkin Gulf. This time the *PTFs 1, 2, 5,* and *6* bombarded the North Vietnamese radar installation at Vinh Son and a security post on the banks of the nearby Ron River, about 90 miles north of the demilitarized zone between North and South Vietnam.

The *PTF 2* had engine problems and turned back. The *PTF 1* and *5* closed to the shore and bombarded the radar station before turning south for their base at Danang. The *PTF 6* attacked the security station and, although it encountered a Swatow MTB, the PTF was easily able to escape back south.

Meanwhile, the U.S. destroyer *Maddox* had commenced a Desoto patrol on July 31. On the morning of August 4, shortly after the South Vietnamese PTF attack, the *Maddox* steamed into the northern end of the gulf. The *Maddox* was passing off the coast of Hon Me Island, 30 miles south of the North Vietnamese MTB base at Loc Chao, which South Vietnamese commandos had raided the night before, when the destroyer's radar detected the approach of three unidentified high-speed craft, obviously North Vietnamese MTBs. The North Vietnamese craft were sent out to attack the destroyer in the belief that she was directly supporting the PTF operation.

The onrushing MTBs headed straight for the *Maddox*. Three 5-inch rounds fired by the *Maddox* failed to deter them. At a range of nearly 3 miles, two of the Communist boats each launched an 18-inch torpedo; both missed the

A Norwegian-built PTF leads the *PTFs 1* through *4* during trials off the Virginia Capes in May 1963. At the time the boats were assigned to Commander Amphibious Force, U.S. Atlantic Fleet, which controlled SEALs and other special operations in the Atlantic area. *U.S. Navy*

Maddox, which was taking evasive action. The MTBs continued the attack, launching all six of their torpedoes. The U.S. destroyer returned the fire and reported that one North Vietnamese MTB was hit.

While this engagement was in progress, four F-8E Crusader fighters, launched earlier from the U.S. aircraft carrier *Ticonderoga* on a training mission, were vectored to the area. Upon establishing contact with the *Maddox* and the embarked destroyer division commander, the Crusaders were ordered to attack the torpedo boats as they retired to the North. Armed with 20-mm cannon and Zuni unguided rockets, the fighters swung in over the North Vietnamese craft and made several attacks. The fliers reported that they had sunk a torpedo boat. Approximately three hours had passed from the initial contact by the *Maddox's* radar to the retirement of the American destroyer. U.S. estimates were that one MTB was sunk and two others heavily damaged. (Of the three Soviet-built P-4 MTBs that made the attack on the *Maddox,* the *T-333,* the command unit, was undamaged; the *T-336* was slightly damaged with her commander killed; and the *T-339* was damaged and dead in the water with her engines stopped but later restarted. The two damaged boats were beached to prevent sinking; all were repaired and returned to service.)

By presidential order, the *Maddox* was joined by the destroyer *Turner Joy.* The carrier *Constellation* was routed to the Tonkin Gulf while planes from *Ticonderoga* maintained a daylight watch;

The *PTF 1* and *PTF 2* were the reactivated *PT 810* and *PT 811*, respectively. They underwent little change from their original configuration for the PTF role until they arrived in the Far East. An AN/SPS-10 radar is fitted to the tripod mast of the *PTF 1* seen at Little Creek (Norfolk), Virginia, in March 1963. *U.S. Navy*

The *PT 812* after her modification to test gas turbine propulsion. She retains a single 40-mm gun aft. The U.S. Navy was late to adopt gas turbines for large surface warships. The test was unsuccessful, in part because of the "gas-guzzling" characteristics of gas turbine engines. *U.S. Navy*

Norwegian MTBs of the Nasty design in formation. The design, developed as a private venture, provided a most versatile combat craft that was readily adaptable to the special operations role in Vietnamese waters. *Båtservice Verft*

during the night, the destroyers would retire to about 100 miles offshore to reduce the danger of night torpedo-boat attack. But on the night of August 4–5 the *Maddox* picked up five high-speed radar contacts, again identified as North Vietnamese torpedo boats. In the bad weather that covered the area, the U.S. destroyers never had visual contact with enemy PT-boats. There were

radar contacts and then sonar contacts that were identified as torpedoes in the water.

The *Ticonderoga* launched two A-1 Skyraider attack planes to provide air cover, but by midnight the torpedo boats had vanished from the radar screens. Several hundred rounds of 5-inch and 3-inch ammunition had been fired by the destroyers at unseen assailants. The senior officer

The *PTF 4* operating in the Pearl Harbor area while en route to South Vietnam in October 1963. The craft has been fitted with single 40-mm guns forward and amidships (the Norwegian design provided for a 20-mm gun forward); single 20-mm guns are on each side of the bridge. Torpedo tubes have been deleted. *U.S. Navy*

A Nasty PTF at high speed. The forward 40-mm gun has been replaced by a combination .50-caliber machine gun/81-mm mortar. The single 20-mm guns on each side of the bridge cannot be seen clearly in this view. *U.S. Navy*

One of the most effective weapons carried by PTFs and other patrol craft during the Vietnam War was the tandem-mounted .50-caliber machine gun/81-mm mortar. Here a sailor drop-loads the mortar while the gunner steadies the weapon. *U.S. Navy*

The *PTF 13* fitted with an experimental gun system forward and a 40-mm gun with a splinter shield amidships. There are 20-mm guns, without shields, on each side of the bridge. A variety of weapons were tried on the PTFs. *U.S. Navy*

embarked in the destroyers urged caution on senior U.S. commanders in Hawaii and Washington: "Freak weather effects on radar and overeager sonar men may have accounted for many reports. No actual visual sightings by the *Maddox*. Suggest complete evaluation before any further action taken." In reality, there was no North Vietnamese attack on the night of August 4–5; no North Vietnamese MTBs were at sea.

Still, with reports of two unprovoked attacks on American men-of-war in international waters, the time for retaliatory action had come. President Johnson went on television to announce the actions he intended to take. He had planned the American response carefully. Johnson said, "Our response for the present will be limited and fitting. . . . We will seek no wider war. . . ." His remarks had been in coordination with the ongoing attack half a world away. "That reply is given as I speak to you tonight. Air action is now in execution against gunboats and certain supporting facilities in North Vietnam which have been used in these hostile operations."

An hour before the President spoke the *Constellation* and *Ticonderoga* began launching 64 aircraft to strike four North Vietnamese torpedo-boat bases. The area of coverage ranged from a small base at Quang Khe, 50 miles north of the demarcation line between North and South Vietnam, to the large base at Hon Gay in the north. The carrier planes began attacking their targets about 1 P.M. local time.

The attacking planes had damaged facilities at all four bases and destroyed or damaged an estimated 25 MTBs and gunboats—

The *PTF 23*, the lead craft of the Osprey design. These boats were to be the successors of the Nasty PTFs, but the PTF development program ceased when the Vietnam War ended. The *PTF 23* has the standard 40-mm and .50-caliber/81-mm gun arrangement plus 20-mm guns. *U.S. Navy*

A pair of PTFs assigned to the Naval Reserve Force on a high-speed run in Chesapeake Bay after the Vietnam War. Several hundred U.S. small craft were turned over to the South Vietnamese in the early 1970s; a few were retained by the U.S. Navy as a training cadre for U.S. coastal-riverine forces. *U.S. Navy*

more than half of the North Vietnamese naval force. The cost was two aircraft shot down and two others damaged, with one pilot dead and one captured.

The Gulf of Tonkin attacks—real and imagined—on the U.S. destroyers and the retaliatory raids against MTB bases became a key entry on the timeline of the Vietnam War.

With the escalation of the conflict, the PTF missions into enemy waters continued. Details of their operations are still classified. Five of the boats were sunk in the combat operations, the *PTFs 8, 9, 14, 15,* and *16,* all in 1966. (The veteran *PTF 1* was intentionally sunk as a target in 1966 by a U.S. submarine torpedo, while the *PTF 2* was sunk as a target by U.S. gunfire.)

Back in the United States additional PTFs were being procured. The John Trumpy yacht yard in Annapolis, Maryland, which had built the prototype *PT 811* (and which saw less service than any of the postwar prototypes) built the *PTF 17* through *PTF 22.* Delivered in 1968–1969, the Trumpy PTFs were near-duplicates of the Nasty design, all capable of about 45 knots. Simultaneously, the Stewart Seacraft yard in Berwick, Louisiana, which built offshore oil-rig support craft, produced the *PTF 23* through *PTF 26.* These boats, completed in 1968, had aluminum hulls almost 95 feet long. They were also fitted with Napier-Deltic engines, which drove them at about 40 knots. Their commercial name "Osprey" was often used by the Navy.

A total of 26 PTFs were delivered to the U.S. Navy in the 1960s, primarily for use by commandos and in gunfire attack missions in the Vietnam War. Of those, 2 were former aluminum-hull PT boats, 14 were Nasty-class MTBs built in Norway, 6 were Trumpy-built Nastys, and the final 4 were Seacraft-built boats. Most saw combat.

The political impact of the PTFs was significant—the 34A operations by PTFs in August 1964 led to major U.S. involvement in the Vietnam War; but, unlike their World War II predecessors, the PTFs had virtually no military impact on the war, a conflict that was lost by the

The Osprey design *PTF 24* showing the large, open decks of small craft when torpedoes are not carried. Several fuel drums are being carried, and there is a life raft canister visible on the port side of the craft. *U.S. Navy*

A close-up of a Nasty PTF, easily identified by its distinctive bridge design. The officer in service dress khaki on the bridge indicates that the boat is not operating in Vietnam waters. Note the bar-type radar antenna mounted above the bridge. *U.S. Navy*

The *PT 809* as a target drone retriever, named *Retriever* and designated DR 1. This craft earlier served as an escort craft for presidential yachts, operated by the Secret Service and named *Guardian*. *Giorgio Arra*

United States from both political and military viewpoints.

After the Vietnam War, 13 of the U.S. and Norwegian Nastys and the 4 Seacraft Ospreys were assigned to the Naval Reserve Force, the Navy's "weekend warriors." These PTFs were used by the reserves into the late 1970s.

One final "torpedo boat" was built for the U.S. Navy—the CPIC or coastal patrol and interdiction craft. This 100-foot craft was built as a prototype successor for the PT/PTF-type small combatant. The Tacoma Boatbuilding firm in the State of Washington launched the craft in 1974. The U.S. Navy carried out extensive trials. Among the CPIC's special features was a modular weapons configuration to permit rapid changeover to guns, rockets, missiles, torpedoes, and mines. Total weapons payload was ten tons (on a full load displacement of about 75 tons). The craft was propelled by two aircraft-type Avco Lycoming gas turbine engines with an auxiliary diesel; maximum speed was in excess of 40 knots.

After U.S. Navy trials, on August 1, 1975, the CPIC was transferred to South Korea. Additional craft of this type were constructed in South Korea.

The CPIC was the last U.S. small combatant built with a torpedo capability—the last PT boat. Anti-ship missiles, which could be carried by relatively small ships as well as large warships, aircraft, and even submarines, had replaced the torpedo.

The last U.S. small combatant designed to carry torpedoes was the coastal patrol and interdiction craft referred to as CPIC. Shown here on U.S. trials, the craft has a Mark 74 30-mm twin gun mount forward. After U.S. trials the craft was transferred to the South Korean Navy. *U.S. Navy*

Appendix A

U.S. Motor Torpedo Boats

[Hull numbers in parentheses ( ) were reclassified to another "PT" type or canceled.]

Hull Numbers	Class Name	Program Year	Boats Built For:			Total Built	Contract Canceled	Program Total
			US	USSR	UK			
PT 1–9*	Experimental	1940	18	––	––	18	––	18
PT 10–19	Elco 70 foot	1940	10	––	––	10	––	10
PT 20–68	Elco 77 foot	1941	39	––	10	49	––	49
PT 69	Huckins 70 foot	1941	1	––	––	1	––	1
PT 70	Higgins 76 foot	1941	1	––	––	1	––	1
PT 71–94	Higgins 78 foot	1942	14	4	6	24	––	24
PT 95–102	Huckins 78 foot	1942	8	––	––	8	––	8
PT 103–196	Elco 80 foot	1942	94	––	––	94	––	94
PT 197–254	Higgins 78 foot	1943	56	1	1	58	––	58
PT 255–264	Huckins 78 foot	1943	10	––	––	10	––	10
PT 265–313	Higgins 78 foot	1943	31	18	––	49	––	49
PT 314–367	Elco 80 foot	1943	54	––	––	54	––	54
PT 372–383	Elco 80 foot	1943	12	––	––	12	––	12
PT 384–449	Vosper 70 foot	1943	––	50	16	66	––	66
PT 450–485	Higgins 78 foot	1944	36	––	––	36	––	36
PT 486–563	Elco 80 foot	1944	78	––	––	78	––	78
PT 564	Higgins 70 foot	1944	1	––	––	1	––	1
PT 565–624	Elco 80 foot	1945	58	––	––	58	2	60
PT 625–660	Higgins 78 foot	1945	9	23	––	32	4	36
PT 661–730	Vosper 70 foot	1945	––	32	––	32	38	70
PT 731–790	Elco 80 foot	1945	––	30	––	30	30	60
PT 791–802	Higgins 78 foot	1945	––	––	––	––	12	12
PT 803–808	Elco 80 foot	1945	––	––	––	––	6	6
none	Vosper 70 foot	1945	––	8	40	48	––	48
PT 809–812	Experimental	1951	4	––	––	4	––	4
			535	**166**	**73**	**774**	**92**	**866**

Foreign-Built

Class	Hull No.	Country Built
Scott-Paine	PT 6	Britain
Vosper 70 foot	PT 368-371	Canada
Flyvefisken	PT 813-822	Denmark

Motor Torpedo Boat Chasers

Class	Hull No.
Elco 77-foot	PTC 1–12, (13–36)**
Trumpy 63-foot	PTC 37–66

British Motor Torpedo Boats

Class	Hull No.
Elco 77-foot	BPT 1–10, (11–20)
Vosper 70-foot	BPT 21–68

Fast Patrol Boats

Class	Hull No.	Country Built
PTF 1 Class	PTF 1–2	United States
PTF 3 Class	PTF 3–16	Norway
PTF 17 Class	PTF 17–22	United States
PTF 23 Class	PTF 23–26	United States

Notes:

* The PT 9 was built in Britain; two U.S.-built boats were designated PT 6.

** PTC 13–36 were completed as torpedo boats designated PT 33–44 and PT 57–68.

U.S. PT boats were built to several designs and sub-types. All war production boats for the U.S. Navy were capable of carrying four torpedo tubes and a minimum gun armament of four .50-caliber Browning M2 machine guns. They were all powered by three Packard gasoline engines. *U.S. Navy*

PT Boat Characteristics

Notes: Armament: Designed armament is listed; the gun, rocket, and mortar installations varied greatly.
After entering service, the torpedo tubes on all Higgins and 80-foot Elco PT boats were replaced by lightweight torpedo launch racks.

Table 1: Hull/Propulsion Characteristics

Type	Displacement Light tons	Full Load tons	Length Overall ft (m)	Max. Beam ft (m)	Max. Draft ft (m)	Propulsion/Total Horsepower	Shafts	Max. Speed (knots)	Endurance (nm)	Manning Off.	Enl.
PT 1, 2	–	33.6	58 (18.0)	16 (4.9)	4'3" (1.3)	2 supercharged Vimalert gasoline engines; 2,400 shp (PT 1), 4,500 shp (PT 2)	2	32	–	4	8
PT 3, 4	–	33.0	58 (18.0)	16 (4.9)	4'3" (1.3)	2 Packard 4–M2500 diesel engines; 2,700 bhp (PT 3), 4,700 bhp (PT 4)	2	32	–	4	8
PT 5, 6	35	53.4	81'3" (24.8)	15'3" (4.7)	4'6" (1.4)	PT 5: 3 supercharged Vimalert gasoline engines; 3,600 shp PT 6: 3 Packard 4–M2500 diesel engines; 3,600 shp	3	PT 5: 31 PT 6: 36	–	2	10
PT 6 (No. 2)	–	35.0	81 (24.7)	15'3" (4.7)	4'6" (1.4)	3 supercharged Vimalert gasoline engines; 4,050 shp	3	35	–	2	10
PT 7, 8	–	57.3 (PT 7) 54.4 (PT 8)	80'7" (24.6)	15'6" (4.7)	3'3" (1.0)	PT 7: 4 Hall-Scott Defender diesel engines; 3,600 bhp PT 8: Allison V-12 engines; 4,000 bhp and 1 Hall-Scott Defender diesel engine; 500 bhp	2	PT 7: 36 PT 8: 30	–	–	–
PT 9	–	40	70 (21.3)	19'9" (6.1)	4 (1.2)	3 Rolls-Royce Merlin diesel engines; 3,300 bhp	3	44.5	–	2	12
Elco 70-foot	33.0	40	70 (21.3)	19'9" (6.1)	4'6" (1.4)	3 Packard V-12 gasoline engines; 3,600 shp	3	45	–	2	15

| Type | Displacement | | Length | Max. | Max. | Propulsion/Total | Shafts | Max. | Endurance | Manning | |
	Light tons	Full Load tons	Overall ft (m)	Beam ft (m)	Draft ft (m)	Horsepower		Speed (knots)	(nm)	Off.	Enl.
Elco 77-foot (PT, BPT 1-10)	33.0	46	77 (23.5)	19'9" (6.1)	5'3" (1.6)	3 Packard 4-M2500 gasoline engines; 3,600 shp	3	41	259 nm @41 358 nm @35 (sust.); 1,050 nm @11 (one engine)	2	10
PT 69	35	–	72 (21.9)	16 (4.9)	3'2" (est.) (1.9)	4 Packard gasoline engines; 5,000 shp	3	40	–	–	–
PT 70	–	–	76 (23.2)	–	–	3 Packard W-14 M2500 gasoline engines; unknown	–	–	–	–	–

The 70-foot Elco *PT 19* on trials in early 1941. Her .50-caliber machine gun turrets are under canvas covers. Five ventilators are fitted amidships. Note her lengthened deck structure between the torpedo tubes. *U.S. Navy*

The *PT 20* at high speed on trials. Her .50-caliber twin gun mounts are pointing forward. The enclosed, aircraft-type turret was soon discarded. The four 21-inch torpedo tubes are covered with canvas. *U.S. Navy*

The 78-foot Huckins *PT 96* at high speed. She served with MTB Squadron 4, the training unit at Melville, Rhode Island, from her completion in August 1943 until the end of the war. There are .50-caliber gun mounts at the after end of the bridge and a 20-mm gun mount aft. *U.S. Navy*

Type	Displacement Light tons	Full Load tons	Length Overall ft (m)	Max. Beam ft (m)	Max. Draft ft (m)	Propulsion/Total Horsepower	Shafts	Max. Speed (knots)	Endurance (nm)	Manning Off.	Enl.
Higgins	43	48	Note: 1	20'1" (6.1)	PT 71-94: 6 (1.8) Others: 5'3" (1.6)	3 Packard 4-M2500 gasoline engines; 4,050 shp (except PT 791–802: 4,500 shp)	3	41	259 nm @2–3 41; 358 nm @ 35 (sust.); 1,050 nm @ 11 (one engine)	9–14	
Huckins	–	48	78 (23.7)	19'6" (5.9)	PT 95-102: 4 (1.2) Others: 5 (1.5)	3 Packard 4-M2500 gasoline engines; 4,050 shp	3	41	259 nm @ 41; 358 nm @ 35.0 (sust.); 1,050 nm @ 11 (one engine)	2	9
Elco 80-foot	–	51	80 (24.4)	20'8" (6.3)	5'3" (1.6)	3 Packard 4-M2500 gasoline engines; 3,600 shp (except PT 565–624. 761–790, 803–808: 4,500 shp)	3	Note: 2	550 nm on 3 engines at max.; 400 nm @30 (3 engines); 1,600 nm @ 6 (3 eng.)	2–3 9–14	
Scott Paine (PT, PTC (1-12))	––	38 (stand.)	70 (21.3)	19'10" (5.8)	5'3" (1.6)	3 Packard W-14 M2500 gasoline engines; 4,500 shp	3	41	–	2	10
Vosper 70-foot (PT)	–	38 (stand.)	72'6" (21.3)	19 (5.8)	4'8" (1.5)	3 Packard W-14 M2500 gasoline engines; 4,500 shp	3	41	–	2	11
PT 564	–	24 (stand.)	63 (19.2)	15'3" (4.5)	3'8" (1.2)	2 Hall-Scott Defender gasoline engines; 1,300 shp	2	28	–	2	8

Type	Displacement Light tons	Full Load tons	Length Overall ft (m)	Max. Beam ft (m)	Max. Draft ft (m)	Propulsion/Total Horsepower	Shafts	Max. Speed (knots)	Endurance (nm)	Manning Off.	Enl.
PT 809	59.6	93.7	98'7" (30.1)	25'9" (7.9)	5'10" (1.8)	4 Packard 1M-3300/ W-100 gasoline engines; 10,000 shp	4	52.4 (est.)	464 nm @ 40; 7,200 nm @15	4	16
PT 810	–	91	89'5" (26.0)	24'1" (7.3)	6'6" (2.0)	4 Packard 1M-3300/ W-100 gasoline engines; 10,000 shp	4	46	488 nm @ 40; 7,380 nm @ 15 .	3	15
PT 811	–	86.5	95 (29.0)	24'11" (7.4)	6'4" (1.9)	4 Packard 1M-3300/ W-100 gasoline engines; 10,000 shp	4	47.7 (trials)	497 nm @ 40; 7,200 nm @ 15	4	18
PT 812	–	100	105 (32.0)	22'6" (6.9)	5'10" (1.8)	4 Packard 1M-3300/ W-100 gasoline engines; 10,000 shp	4	45	707 nm @ 27; 7,149 nm @ 15	4	18

The *PT 105* was an early 80-foot Elco boat. She saw service in the Southwest Pacific area. *U.S. Navy*

The *PT 107* was another early 80-foot Elco boat. Her after torpedo tubes have been replaced by three depth charges, port and starboard, and boxes of ammunition for her after 20-mm Oerlikon cannon. *James C. Fahey collection (USNI)*

Bow-on view of the 80-foot Elco *PT 117* before delivery to the Navy and still operated by Elco personnel. *Electric Boat Co.*

A stern view of the *PT 117* showing the engine exhausts in her stern counter. There are compressed air flasks mounted above the torpedo tubes. *Electric Boat Co.*

Type	Displacement Light tons	Full Load tons	Length Overall ft (m)	Max. Beam ft (m)	Max. Draft ft (m)	Propulsion/Total Horsepower	Shafts	Max Speed (knots)	Endurance (nm)	Manning Off.	Enl.
PT 813	–	110 (stand.)	120'2" (36.6)	18 (5.5)	5'11" (1.8)	3 Mercedes Benz diesels; 7,500 shp	3	40	–	–	22 (tot.)
PT 819	–	119 (stand.)	118 (36.0)	17'8" (5.4)	6 (1.8)	3 MTU diesels; 9,000 shp	3	40	–	–	22 (tot.)
Trumpy 63-foot (PTC 37)	–	24 (stand.)	63 (19.2)	15'3" (4.5)	3'7" (1.2)	2 Hall-Scott Defender gasoline engines; 1,300 shp	2	28	–	2	8
Vosper 70-foot (BPT)	–	47	70'1" (21.7)	19'3" (5.9)	8 (2.4)	3 Packard/M2500/W-14 gasoline engines; 3,600 shp	3	34	–	–	–
PTF 1	53.9	89.5	89'5" (27.3)	24'1" (7.3)	6'6" (2.0)	4 Packard 1M-3300/ W-100 gasoline engines; 10,000 shp	4	45	550 nm @ 23	3	17
PTF 3	–	85	80'4" (24.5)	24'6" (7.5)	6'7" (2.0)	2 British Napier-Deltic T-18-37 diesels; 6,200 bhp	2	44	Note: 3	3	16
PTF 17	–	85	80'5" (24.5)	24'6" (7.5)	7 (2.1)	2 British Napier-Deltic T-18-37 diesels; 6,200 bhp	2	45	–	3	16
PTF 23	–	105	94'8" (28.9)	23'2" (7.1)	7 (2.1)	2 British Napier-Deltic T-18-37 diesels; 6,200 bhp	2	38	–	4	15

The 80-foot Elco *PT 141* at high speed. She was also assigned to MTB Squadron 4, the PT boat training unit and saw no combat during the war. *U.S. Navy*

The one-of-a-kind 70-foot Higgins "Hellcat." There is a twin machine gun mount on the bow; this photo was taken before installation of her mast and radome. *U.S. Navy*

The *PT 578*, a late 80-foot Elco boat in the camouflage typical of PT boats in the Pacific theaters. She was in MTB Squadron 39, which reached the Philippines in July 1945, too late to see action. *James C. Fahey collection (USNI)*

Table II: Armament

Type	Armament
PT 1, 2	2 stern-firing 18" torpedo tubes; 2 .50-cal. machine-guns
PT 3, 4	2 stern-firing 18" torpedo tubes; 2 .50-cal. machine-guns
PT 5, 6 (No. 1)	2 stern-firing 21" torpedo tubes; 2 .50-cal. machine-guns
PT 6 (No. 2)	2 stern-firing 21" torpedo tubes; 2 .50-cal. machine-guns
PT 7, 8	2 21" torpedo tubes; 2 .50-cal. machine-guns
PT 9	2 21" torpedo tubes or 4 18" torpedo tubes; 2 twin .30-cal. machine-guns
Elco 70 foot	4 18" torpedo tubes; 2 twin .50-cal. machine-guns
Elco 77 foot (PT, BPT 1-10)	PT 20-44: 4-21" torpedo tubes; 2 twin .50-cal. machine-guns, 2 .30-cal. Lewis machine-guns
	PT 45-48, 59-68: 4-21" torpedo tubes; 1 single 20-mm (Mark IV) gun; 2 twin .50-cal. machine-guns
	PT 49-58: 4-21" torpedo tubes; 1 single 20-mm (Mark IV) gun; 2 twin Vickers .50-cal. (Mark IV) machine-guns; 2 .30-cal. Lewis machine-guns
PT 69	2 single torpedo tubes; 8 depth charge racks for 300 lb. depth charges; 2 twin .50-cal. machine-guns
PT 70	4 21" torpedo tubes; 3 twin .50-cal. machine-guns
Higgins	PT 71/94: 4 21" torpedo tubes; 1 single Army 40-mm or 1 single 37-mm gun; 2 single 20-mm guns; 2 twin .50-cal. machine-guns
	PT 197 up: 4 21" torpedo tubes; 1 single 40-mm gun or none; 2 single 20-mm guns; 2 twin .50-cal. machine-guns
Huckins	4 21" torpedo tubes; 1 single Army 40-mm gun; 2 single 20-mm guns; 2 twin .50-cal. machine-guns
Elco 80 foot	4 21" torpedo tubes (except from PT 486 up: 4 lightweight torpedo launching racks); 2 single 20-mm guns; 2 twin .50-cal. machine-guns
Scott-Paine (PT & PTC 1-12)	PTs: 2 21" torpedo tubes (Mark 18); 2 twin .50-cal. machine-guns
	PTCs: 4 Y-guns firing 300 pd. depth charges; 2 stern depth charge racks each carrying 3 300 pd. depth charges; 2 twin .50-cal. machine-guns
Vosper 70 foot (PT)	2 21" torpedo tubes (Mark 18); 1 single 20-mm gun; 2 twin .50-cal. machine-guns
PT 564	4 lightweight torpedo launching racks; 1 single Army 37-mm gun; 2 twin .50-cal. machine-guns
PT 809	4 lightweight torpedo launching racks (Mark 2, Mod. 1 or 2) for Mark 16 torpedoes (fitted to carry, but never installed); 2 single 40-mm guns; 2 twin Oerlikon 20-mm guns; 1 81-mm mortar
PT 810	4 lightweight torpedo launching racks (Mark 2, Mod. 2) for Mark 16 torpedoes (fitted to carry, but never installed); 2 single 40-mm guns; 2 twin Oerlikon 20-mm guns; 1 81-mm mortar
PT 811	4 lightweight torpedo launching racks (Mark 2, Mod. 2) for Mark 16 torpedoes (fitted to carry, but never installed); 2 single 40-mm guns; 2 twin Oerlikon 20-mm guns; 1 81-mm mortar
PT 812	4 lightweight torpedo launching racks (Mark 2, Mod. 2) for Mark 16 torpedoes (fitted to carry, but never installed); 1 single 40-mm gun; 2 twin Oerlikon 20-mm guns; 1 Mark 107 rocket launcher
PT 813	2 21" torpedo tubes; 1 single 40-mm gun; 1 twin 20-mm gun
PT 819	4 21" torpedo tubes; 1 single 40-mm gun; 1 twin 20-mm gun
Trumpy 63 foot) (PTC 37–66)	8 single side-launching depth charge racks (4 per side) firing 300 pd. depth charges; 1 single 20-mm gun
Vosper 70 foot (BPT)	4 21" torpedo tubes (Mark 18) firing Mark 8 torpedoes; 1 single 20-mm gun; 2 twin .50-cal. machine-guns
PTF 1	2 single 40-mm (Mark 3, mod. 4) guns; 2 twin 20-mm guns (fitted to carry 4 torpedo tubes, but never installed)
PTF 3	1 single 40-mm gun; 2 twin 20-mm guns; 1 single .50-cal. machine-gun/81-mm mortar (PTF 3/9: fitted to carry 4 torpedo tubes, but never installed)

| PTF 17 | 1 single 40-mm gun; 2 twin 20-mm guns; 1 single .50-cal. machine-gun/81-mm mortar |
| PTF 23 | 1 single 40-mm gun; 2 twin 20-mm guns; 1 single .50-cal. machine-gun/81-mm mortar |

Notes:

General: PT 1 through the second PT 6 mounted stern-firing torpedo tubes. From PT 7 all boats fired their torpedoes over the bow.

1. The length overall of the various boats of the Higgins type is as follows:

PT 71-94, 197-258:	78 feet (23.7 meters)
PT 265-313, 450-485:	78'6" (23.9 meters)
PT 791-802:	78'8" (24.0 meters)

2. Max. Speed for the Elco 80-foot type was 43 knots for PT 103-196, 314-367, 486-563) and 41 knots for the remaining units of the class.

3. The PTF 3 Type was divided into two subclasses, PTF 3-8 and 9-16. PTF 3-8 had the following endurance: 450 nm @ 41 knots; 600 nm @ 25 knots. On the other hand PTF 9/16 had an endurance of 900 nm @ 35 knots due to larger fuel tanks. In addition, their engines were 50% quieter than those in PTF 3-8.

The *PT 791* was a late 78-foot Higgins boat. The craft mounts two torpedo tubes, unusual in that most late MTBs had torpedo-launching racks in lieu of tubes. The Higgins boats could carry four tubes. *U.S. Navy*

PT Boat Order of Battle

In the detailed listing of the vessels that follows each builder listed has been designated by a single name. The number of boats built by each yard follows the builder in parentheses.

Bath: Bath Iron Works, Bath, Maine (1)
British: British Power Boat Co., Hythe, Southampton, England (1)
Canadian: Canadian Power Boat Co., Montreal, Quebec, Canada (4) (NOTE: Modified with Elco fittings by Fyfe's Shipyard, Glenwood Landing, Long Island New York before entering USN service.)
Copenhagen: Frederikssund Vaerft, Copenhagen, Denmark (3)
Denmark: Royal Dockyard, Copenhagen, Denmark (7)
Elco A: Elco Works, Electric Boat Co., Bayonne, New Jersey (391)
Elco B: Harbor Boat Building Co., Terminal Island, California (12)
Fisher: Fisher Boat Works, Detroit, Michigan (2)
Groton: Electric Boat Co., Groton, Connecticut (1)
Higgins: Higgins Industries Inc., New Orleans, Louisiana (211)
Huckins: Huckins Yacht Corp., Jacksonville, Florida (20)
Miami: Miami Shipbuilding Corp., Miami, Florida (2)
Norway-A: Båtservice, Norway (7 PTFs)
Norway-B: Westermoen Hydro A/S, Mandal, Norway (7 PTFs)
Phil.: Philadelphia Naval Shipyard, Philadelphia, Pennsylvania (2)
Sewart: Teledyne Inc., Sewart Seacraft Div., Berwick, Louisiana (4)
Trumpy-A: John Trumpy and Sons Inc., Annapolis, Maryland (1 PT and 6 PTFs)
Trumpy-G: John Trumpy and Sons Inc., Gloucester, New Jersey (30)
Vosper-A: Robert Jacob Inc., City Island, New York (22)
Vosper-B: Annapolis Yacht Yard Inc., Annapolis, Maryland (128)
Vosper-C: Herreshoff Manufacturing Co., Bristol, Rhode Island (28)

Hull Number	Design/ Builder	Completed	Comments
PT 1	Miami	Nov. 20, 1941	Reclass. small boat "C 6083" on Dec. 24, 1941. Sold in 1947. Converted to a fishing boat. Disposition unknown.
PT 2	Miami	Nov. 20, 1941	Reclass. small boat "C 6084" on Dec. 24, 1941. Disposition unknown.

Hull Number	Design/ Builder	Completed	Comments
PT 3	Fisher	June 20, 1940	Lend-lease to UK Apr. 19, 1941 as MTB 273. Later renumbered B 119. Returned Apr. 21, 1945. Sold May 2, 1946. Converted to a commercial vessel. Still in existence as of Sept. 1996.
PT 4	Fisher	June 20, 1940	Lend-lease to UK Apr. 19, 1941, as MTB 274. Later renumbered B 120. Returned June 14, 1945. Sold Oct. 10, 1946. Converted to a commercial vessel. Last reported as still in existence in 1951.
PT 5	Higgins	Mar. 1, 1941	Lend-lease to UK Apr. 19, 1941, as MTB 269. Later renumbered B 117. Returned Mar. 28, 1945. Sold Aug. 29, 1946. Converted to a commercial vessel. Last reported as still in existence in 1956.
PT 6 (No. 1)	Higgins	Aug. 14, 1940	Trans. Finland in 1940. Sold to UK on June 21, 1940 as MGB 68. Sold in 1944. Disposition unknown.
PT 6 (No. 2)	Higgins	Feb. 3, 1941	Lend-lease to UK July 29, 1941, as MTB 270. Later renumbered B 123. Returned Mar. 20, 1945. Reclass. as small boat "C 104340" June 1, 1945. Out of service Dec. 14, 1945.

These 80-foot Elco PT boats are being loaded aboard a Navy oiler for shipment to an overseas port. Most U.S. PT boats went to war this way, six per oiler, transported to forward bases where they were formed into MTB squadrons. *James C. Fahey collection (USNI)*

Hull Number	Design/ Builder	Completed	Comments
PT 7	Philadelphia	Feb. 25, 1941	Lend-lease to UK Apr. 19, 1941, as MTB 271. Later renumbered B 118. Returned Mar. 10, 1945. Sunk as a target in Apr. 1945.
PT 8	Philadelphia	Feb. 25, 1941	Was to have been lend-leased to UK as MTB 272, but boat was retained. Reclass. YP-110 on Oct. 14, 1941, Reclass. as "floating equipment" Dec. 10, 1945. Sold 1947. Still in existence, owned by Mr. Ray Tyler, Franklin, La.
PT 9	British	June 17, 1940	Lend-lease to UK Apr. 11, 1941, as MTB 258. Re-transferred to Canada as SO-9 shortly after. Returned June 28, 1945. Sold Oct. 29, 1946.

(Note on PT 3–7, 9: These boats never reached England. They were trans. by the UK to Canada and employed as air-sea rescue boats, except PT 9, which operated in an ASW role.)

Hull Number	Design/ Builder	Completed	Comments
PT 10	Elco-A	Nov. 4, 1940	Lend-lease to UK Apr. 11, 1941, as MTB 259. Foundered in a storm on June 14, 1942, while under tow.
PT 11	Elco-A	Nov. 8, 1940	Lend-lease to UK Apr. 11, 1941, as MTB 260. Returned Mar. 16, 1946. Sold Dec. 1946.
PT 12	Elco-A	Dec. 11, 1940	Lend-lease to UK Apr. 11, 1941, as MTB 261. Destroyed in Sept. 1945, after sinking on Aug. 26, 1945. Her hulk became an obstruction to harbor traffic.
PT 13	Elco-A	Nov. 15, 1940	Lend-lease to UK Apr. 11, 1941, as MTB 262. Sunk Feb. 24, 1943, by German aircraft.
PT 14	Elco-A	Nov. 22, 1940	Lend-lease to UK Apr. 11, 1941, as MTB 263. Returned Mar. 16, 1946. Sold in Dec. 1946.
PT 15	Elco-A	Dec. 5, 1940	Lend-lease to UK Apr. 11, 1941, as MTB 264. Sunk by mine May 10, 1943.
PT 16	Elco-A	Dec. 20, 1940	Lend-lease to UK Apr. 11, 1941, as MTB 265. Returned Mar. 16, 1946. Sold in Aug. 1946.
PT 17	Elco-A	Dec. 12, 1940	Lend-lease to UK Apr. 11, 1941, as MTB 266. Irreparably damaged by Italian naval gunfire in the Mediterranean. Written off as a constructive total loss and destroyed Apr. 17, 1944.
PT 18	Elco-A	Dec. 17, 1940	Lend-lease to UK Apr. 11, 1941, as MTB 267. Severely damaged by heavy weather. Sunk by depth charges and gunfire from HMS *MTB 13* on Apr. 2, 1943.
PT 19	Elco-A	Dec. 23, 1940	Lend-lease to UK Apr. 11, 1941, as MTB 268. Returned Mar. 16, 1946. Sold in Aug. 1946.
PT 20	Elco-A	June 9, 1941	Scrapped.
PT 21	Elco-A	June 13, 1941	Scrapped.
PT 22	Elco-A	June 24, 1941	Badly damaged during storm off of Adak, Aleutian Islands on June 11, 1943. Beached and abandoned.
PT 23	Elco-A	June 25, 1941	Reclass. as small boat "C 55047" Oct. 6, 1943.
PT 24	Elco-A	June 26, 1941	Reclass. as small boat on Dec. 9, 1941, for tests.
PT 25	Elco-A	June 11, 1941	Reclass. as small boat "C 55048" Oct. 6, 1943.
PT 26	Elco-A	June 18, 1941	Reclass. as small boat "C 55049" Oct. 6, 1943.
PT 27	Elco-A	June 27, 1941	Reclass. as small boat Dec. 9, 1944.
PT 28	Elco-A	June 30, 1941	Wrecked in a storm while moored in Dora Harbor, Alaska, Dec. 1, 1943.
PT 29	Elco-A	Feb. 28, 1941	Scrapped.
PT 30	Elco-A	July 3, 1941	Sold Jan. 3, 1947.

Hull Number	Design/ Builder	Completed	Comments
PT 31	Elco-A	July 8, 1941	Severely damaged by grounding in Subic Bay, Philippines. Sunk by U.S. forces Jan. 20, 1942. Posit.: Long. 14° 45.0' North, Lat. 120° 13.0' East.
PT 32	Elco-A	July 10, 1941	Sunk Mar. 13, 1942, by gunfire from *USS Permit* (SS–178). Posit.: Long. 10° 58.0' North, Lat. 121° 12.0' East.
PT 33	Elco-A	July 11, 1941	Ex PTC 13. Reclass. PT 33 Mar. 24, 1941. Sunk by U.S. forces Dec. 15, 1941. Posit.: Long. 13° 46.0' North, Lat. 120° 40.0' East.
PT 34	Elco-A	July 12, 1941	Ex PTC 14. Reclass. PT 34 Mar. 24, 1941. Damaged by hit from Jap. bomber Apr. 9, 1942. Beached to avoid sinking. Posit.: Long. 10° 16.0' North, Lat. 123° 52.0' East. Destroyed by further attacks from Jap. aircraft the same date.
PT 35	Elco-A	July 16, 1941	Ex PTC 15. Reclass. PT 35 Mar. 24, 1941. Destroyed by burning Apr. 12, 1942 at Cebu City, Philippines, to prevent capture. Posit: Long. 10° 18.0' North, Lat. 123° 35.0' East.
PT 36	Elco-A	Aug. 27, 1941	Ex PTC 16. Reclass. PT 36 Mar. 24, 1941. Reclass. as small boat "C 73994" Apr. 15, 1944.
PT 37	Elco-A	July 18, 1941	Ex PTC 17. Reclass. PT 37 Mar. 24, 1941. Sunk by naval gunfire from Japanese destroyer *Kawakaze* Feb. 1, 1943.
PT 38	Elco-A	July 18, 1941	Ex PTC 18. Reclass. PT 38 Mar. 24, 1941. Reclass. as small boat "C 68730" Feb. 6, 1944.
PT 39	Elco-A	July 21, 1941	Ex PTC 19. Reclass. PT 39 Mar. 24, 1941. Reclass. as small boat Oct. 20, 1944. Destroyed in tests by the Bureau of Ordnance in Jan. 1945.
PT 40	Elco-A	July 22, 1941	Ex PTC 20. Reclass. PT 40 Mar. 24, 1941. Reclass. as small boat "C 73995" Apr. 15, 1944. Sold for commercial service. Last known to be in existence in 1970.
PT 41	Elco-A	July 23, 1941	Ex PTC 21. Reclass. PT 41 Mar. 24, 1941. Transferred to the U.S. Army Apr. 13, 1942. Destroyed Apr. 15, 1942, en route to Lake Lanao, Mindanao, to prevent capture.
PT 42	Elco-A	July 25, 1941	Ex PTC 22. Reclass. PT 42 Mar. 24, 1941. Sold.
PT 43	Elco-A	July 26, 1941	Ex PTC 23. Reclass. PT 43 Mar. 24, 1941. Damaged by Jap. naval gunfire Jan. 10, 1943. Beached and abandoned at Long. 09° 15.0' South, Lat. 159° 42.0' East.
PT 44	Elco-A	July 30, 1941	Ex PTC 24. Reclass. PT 44 Mar. 24, 1941. Sunk by Jap naval gunfire on Dec. 12, 1942 at Long. 09° 10.0' South, Lat. 159° 45.0' East.
PT 45	Elco-A	Sept. 3, 1941	Reclass. as small boat Apr. 15, 1944. Disposition unknown.
PT 46	Elco-A	Sept. 6, 1941	Reclass. as small boat "C 74095" Apr. 29, 1944. Disposition unknown.
PT 47	Elco-A	Sept. 9, 1941	Sold 1947.
PT 48	Elco-A	Sept. 15, 1941	Reclass. as small boat Oct. 20, 1944. Sold for commercial use. Disposition unknown.
PT 49	Elco-A	Jan. 20, 1942	Reclass. BPT 1 July 3, 1941. Lend-lease to UK Feb. 4, 1942, as MTB 307. Returned Oct. 3, 1945. Sold in Feb. 1947 to the Italian Navy. Renamed GIS-019.
PT 50	Elco-A	Jan. 22, 1942	Reclass. BPT 2 July 3, 1941. Lend-lease to UK Feb. 4, 1942, as MTB 308. Sunk Sept. 14, 1942, at Tobruk, Libya, by Italian aircraft.

Hull Number	Design/ Builder	Completed	Comments
PT 51	Elco-A	Feb. 9, 1942	Reclass. BPT 3 July 3, 1941. Lend-lease to UK Feb. 11, 1942, as MTB 309. Returned Oct. 10, 1945. Destroyed Oct. 26, 1945.
PT 52	Elco-A	Feb. 10, 1942	Reclass. BPT 4 July 3, 1941. Lend-lease to UK Feb. 11, 1942, as MTB 310. Sunk Sept. 14, 1942, by Italian aircraft.
PT 53	Elco-A	Feb. 23, 1942	Reclass. BPT 5 July 3, 1941. Lend-lease to UK Feb. 23, 1942, as MTB 311. Sunk May 2, 1943, by a mine.
PT 54	Elco-A	Feb. 23, 1942	Reclass. BPT 6 July 3, 1941. Lend-lease to UK Feb. 23, 1942, as MTB 312. Sunk Sept. 14, 1942, by German aircraft.
PT 55	Elco-A	Feb. 28, 1942	Reclass. BPT 7 July 3, 1941. Lend-lease to UK Feb. 23, 1942, as MTB 313. Returned March 16, 1946. Sold Jan. 24, 1947.
PT 56	Elco-A	Feb. 28, 1942	Reclass. BPT 8 July 3, 1941. Lend-lease to UK Feb. 28, 1942, as MTB 314. Badly damaged by German aircraft Sept. 14, 1942. Beached to avoid sinking. Salvaged by German forces and commissioned into the German Navy as RA-10. Sunk Sept. 30, 1943, by British aircraft.
PT 57	Elco-A	March 7, 1942	Reclass. BPT 9 July 3, 1941. Lend-lease to UK Feb. 28, 1942, as MTB 315. Returned Nov. 2, 1945. Sold in Feb. 1947 to the Italian Navy. Renamed *GIS-0020*.
PT 58	Elco-A	March 10, 1942	Reclass. BPT 10 July 3, 1941. Lend-lease to UK Feb. 23, 1942, as MTB 316. Sunk July 17, 1943, by gunfire from the Italian cruiser *Scipione Africano*.
PT 59	Elco-A	March 5, 1942	Ex PTC 27. Reclass. BPT 11 June. 19, 1941. Reclass. PT 59 Dec. 12, 1941. Reclass. as small boat "C 102584" Oct. 20, 1944. Sold for use as a commercial vessel. Caught fire and burned in 1966.
PT 60	Elco-A	Feb. 25, 1942	Ex PTC 28. Reclass. BPT 12 June 19, 1941. Reclass. PT 60 Dec. 12, 1941. Converted to a Motor Gunboat in Oct. 1943. Scrapped.
PT 61	Elco-A	Feb. 19, 1942	Ex PTC 29. Reclass. BPT 13 June 19, 1941. Reclass. PT 61 Dec. 12, 1941. Converted to a Motor Gunboat in Oct. 1943. Reclass. as small boat "C 683711" Feb. 6, 1944.
PT 62	Elco-A	Feb. 10, 1942	Ex PTC 30. Reclass. BPT 14 June 19, 1941. Reclass. PT 62 Dec. 12, 1941. Sold.
PT 63	Elco-A	Feb. 7, 1942	Ex PTC 31. Reclass. BPT 15 June 19, 1941. Reclass. PT 63 Dec. 12, 1941. Destroyed by accidental fire June 18, 1944, while moored next to PT 107, after a defective fuel valve on PT 107 caused fuel to leak into the water. The leaking gasoline was ignited by the exhaust blast when PT 107 started her engines. Both boats sunk. Posit.: Long. 01° 45.0' South, Lat. 150° 01.0' East.
PT 64	Elco-A	Jan. 28, 1942	Ex PTC 32. Reclass. BPT 16 June 19, 1941. Reclass. PT 64 Dec. 12, 1941. "Presumed sunk or scrapped by Seventh Fleet."
PT 65	Elco-A	Jan. 24, 1942	Ex PTC 33. Reclass. BPT 17 June 19, 1941. Reclass. PT 65 Dec. 12, 1941. "Presumed scrapped or sunk by Seventh Fleet."
PT 66	Elco-A	Jan. 22, 1942	Ex PTC 34. Reclass. BPT 18 June 19, 1941. Reclass. PT 66 Dec. 12, 1941. Reclass. small boat Feb. 20, 1945.

Hull Number	Design/ Builder	Completed	Comments
PT 67	Elco-A	Jan. 17, 1942	Ex PTC 35. Reclass. BPT 19 June 19, 1941. Reclass. PT 67 Dec. 12, 1941. Destroyed Mar. 17, 1943, by accidental fire along with PT 119. Posit. Long. 09° 02.0′ South, Lat. 149° 20.0′ East.
PT 68	Elco-A	Jan. 13, 1942	Ex PTC 36. Reclass. BPT 20 June 19, 1941. Reclass. PT 68 Dec. 12, 1941. Badly damaged by grounding Sept. 30, 1943. Destroyed by gunfire from PT 191 to prevent capture. Posit. Long. 05° 56.0′ South, Lat. 147° 8.0′ East.

(PT 59–68 were scheduled to be transferred to the UK, as obvious by the BPT classification, and become MTB 317–326. They were retained for U.S. service.)

Hull Number	Design/ Builder	Completed	Comments
PT 69	Huckins	June 30, 1941	Reclass. YP 106 Sept. 24, 1941. Sold Jan. 24, 1947 for commercial service. Last reported as still in existence in 1951.
PT 70	Higgins	June 30, 1941	Reclass. YP 107 Sept. 24, 1941. Sold Sept. 19, 1946.
PT 71	Higgins	July 20, 1942	Destroyed on purpose Oct. 24, 1945, by burning at Brooklyn Navy Yard Annex, Bayonne, N. J.
PT 72	Higgins	July 23, 1942	See comments under PT 71.
PT 73	Higgins	Aug. 12, 1942	Ran aground Jan. 14, 1945. The boat was set afire to prevent capture. Posit. Long. 13° 50.0′ North, Lat. 120° 10.0′ East.
PT 74	Higgins	Aug. 26, 1942	Destroyed on purpose by burning Nov. 23, 1945.
PT 75	Higgins	Aug. 28, 1942	See comments under PT 74.
PT 76	Higgins	Aug. 31, 1942	See comments under PT 74.
PT 77	Higgins	Sept. 3, 1942	Ran aground Feb. 1, 1945. Destroyed to prevent capture. Posit. Long. 13° 55.0′ North., Lat. 120° 36.0′ East.
PT 78	Higgins	Sept. 5, 1942	See comments under PT 74.
PT 79	Higgins	Sept. 8, 1942	Destroyed by naval gunfire Feb. 1, 1945, while maneuvering to prevent running aground. Posit. Long. 13° 55.0′ North., Lat. 120° 36.0′ East.
PT 80	Higgins	Sept. 21, 1942	See comments under PT 74.
PT 81	Higgins	Jan. 11, 1943	See comments under PT 74.
PT 82	Higgins	Nov. 28, 1942	See comments under PT 74.
PT 83	Higgins	Dec. 9, 1942	See comments under PT 74.
PT 84	Higgins	Dec. 3, 1942	See comments under PT 74.
PT 85	Higgins	Dec. 7, 1942	Lend-lease to USSR Feb. 15, 1943. Sunk June 22, 1945, in the Pacific.
PT 86	Higgins	Dec. 9, 1942	Lend-lease to USSR Feb. 15, 1943. Fate unknown.
PT 87	Higgins	Dec. 13, 1942	Lend-lease to USSR Feb. 15, 1943. Sunk June 22, 1945, in the Pacific.
PT 88	Higgins	Dec. 19, 1942	Lend-lease to UK in Apr. 1943 as MTB 419. Returned Oct. 19, 1945. Sold in Feb. 1947.
PT 89	Higgins	Dec. 15, 1942	Lend-lease to USSR 15 Feb. 1943. Fate unknown.
PT 90	Higgins	Dec. 18, 1942	Lend-lease to UK in Apr. 1943 as MTB 420. Returned Oct. 23, 1945. Sold in Feb. 1947.
PT 91	Higgins	Dec. 17, 1942	Lend-lease to UK in Apr. 1943 as MTB 421. Returned Sept. 8, 1945. Destroyed on purpose May 15, 1946.
PT 92	Higgins	Dec. 29, 1942	Lend-lease to UK in Apr. 1943 as MTB 422. Returned Oct. 16, 1945. Sold in Feb. 1947.
PT 93	Higgins	Dec. 30, 1942	Lend-lease to UK in Apr. 1943 as CT 16. Returned May 10, 1946. Sold Sept. 3, 1946.

Hull Number	Design/ Builder	Completed	Comments
PT 94	Higgins	Dec. 29, 1942	Lend-lease to UK in Apr. 1943 as MTB 423. Returned Oct. 19, 1945. Sold Feb. 19, 1947.
PT 95	Huckins	July 23, 1942	Destroyed on purpose by burning Sept. 26, 1945.
PT 96	Huckins	Aug. 22, 1942	Destroyed on purpose Sept. 13, 1945.
PT 97	Huckins	Aug. 29, 1942	See comments under PT 96.
PT 98	Huckins	Sept. 19, 1942	Sold Oct. 14, 1946.
PT 99	Huckins	Sept. 29, 1942	Sold Oct. 14, 1946. Sunk by Hurricane Gloria in 1985.
PT 100	Huckins	Nov. 14, 1942	Sold Oct. 9, 1946, for commercial service. Last known to exist in 1967.
PT 101	Huckins	Nov. 14, 1942	Sold Oct. 10, 1946.
PT 102	Huckins	Nov. 30, 1942	Sold Oct. 21, 1946.
PT 103	Elco-A	June 12, 1942	Destroyed on purpose by burning Nov. 1, 1945.
PT 104	Elco-A	June 19, 1942	See comments under PT 103.
PT 105	Elco-A	June 26, 1942	See comments under PT 103.
PT 106	Elco-A	June 30, 1942	Destroyed on purpose by burning Nov. 6, 1945.
PT 107	Elco-A	July 3, 1942	See comments under PT 63.
PT 108	Elco-A	July 7, 1942	Destroyed on purpose by burning Nov. 11, 1945.
PT 109	Elco-A	July 10, 1942	Rammed and sunk Aug. 2, 1943, by the Japanese destroyer *Amagiri*. Posit. Long. 08° 03.0' South, Lat. 116° 18.0' East.
PT 110	Elco-A	July 14, 1942	Sunk on Jan. 26, 1944, in collision with PT 114 and by explosion of a depth charge accidentally dropped by PT 110 during the collision. Posit. Long. 06° 17.0' South, Lat. 150° 09.0' East.
PT 111	Elco-A	July 16, 1942	Sunk on Feb. 1, 1942, by naval gunfire from a Japanese destroyer.
PT 112	Elco-A	July 18, 1942	Exploded and sunk Jan. 11, 1943, after being hit by naval gunfire from a Japanese destroyer. Posit.: Long. 09° 15.0' South, Lat. 159° 42.0' East.
PT 113	Elco-A	July 23, 1942	Ran aground Aug. 8, 1943. Stripped of all usable parts and abandoned. Posit.: Long. 09° 12.0' South, Lat. 146° 29.0' East.
PT 114	Elco-A	July 24, 1942	Destroyed on purpose by burning Oct. 28, 1945.
PT 115	Elco-A	July 29, 1942	Destroyed on purpose by burning Nov. 9, 1945.
PT 116	Elco-A	July 30, 1942	Destroyed on purpose by burning Nov. 11, 1945.
PT 117	Elco-A	Aug. 4, 1942	Badly damaged by Japanese dive bomber Aug. 1, 1943. Beached to prevent sinking and abandoned. Posit.: Long. 08° 24.0' South, Lat. 157° 19.0' East.
PT 118	Elco-A	Aug. 6, 1942	Badly damaged by grounding Sept. 7, 1943, along with PT 172. Beached to prevent sinking and abandoned. Destroyed by other PT boats to prevent capture. Posit.: Long. 07° 34.0' South, Lat. 165° 35.0' East.
PT 119	Elco-A	Aug. 8, 1942	See comments under PT 67.
PT 120	Elco-A	Aug. 12, 1942	Destroyed on purpose Oct. 26, 1945.
PT 121	Elco-A	Aug. 27, 1942	Accidentally bombed and sunk on Mar. 27, 1944, by an Australian aircraft. Posit.: Long. 05° 17.0' South, Lat. 151° 01.0' East.
PT 122	Elco-A	Aug. 15, 1942	Destroyed on purpose Oct. 28, 1945.
PT 123	Elco-A	Aug. 18, 1942	Sunk on Feb. 1, 1943, by Japanese aircraft.
PT 124	Elco-A	Aug. 20, 1942	Destroyed on purpose by burning Nov. 11, 1945.
PT 125	Elco-A	Aug. 22, 1942	See comments under PT 124.
PT 126	Elco-A	Aug. 27, 1942	Destroyed on purpose Nov. 24, 1945.
PT 127	Elco-A	Aug. 9, 1942	Destroyed on purpose by burning Oct. 26, 1945.
PT 128	Elco-A	Sept. 1, 1942	Destroyed on purpose by burning Nov. 10, 1945.
PT 129	Elco-A	Sept. 4, 1942	Destroyed on purpose by burning Oct. 28, 1945.

Hull Number	Design/ Builder	Completed	Comments
PT 130	Elco-A	Sept. 7, 1942	See comments under PT 129.
PT 131	Elco-A	Sept. 9, 1942	See comments under PT 128.
PT 132	Elco-A	Sept. 11, 1942	See comments under PT 128.
PT 133	Elco-A	Sept. 16, 1942	Exploded and sunk July 15, 1943, after being hit by gunfire from Japanese coastal defense guns. Posit.: Long. 03° 28.0' South, Lat. 143° 34.0' East.
PT 134	Elco-A	Sept. 17, 1942	Destroyed on purpose by burning Nov. 9, 1945.
PT 135	Elco-A	Sept. 21, 1942	Damaged by grounding Apr. 12, 1944. Abandoned and destroyed by gunfire to prevent capture. Posit.: Long. 05° 21.0' South, Lat. 152° 09.5' East.
PT 136	Elco-A	Sept. 23, 1942	Damaged by grounding Sept. 17, 1943. Abandoned and destroyed by gunfire to prevent capture. Posit.: Long. 05° 55.0' South, Lat. 148° 01.0' East.
PT 137	Elco-A	Sept. 25, 1942	Destroyed on purpose by burning Oct. 24, 1945.
PT 138	Elco-A	Sept. 29, 1942	See comments under PT 137.
PT 139	Elco-A	Oct. 13, 1942	Sold Oct. 9, 1946, for commercial service. Scrapped in 1977.
PT 140	Elco-A	Oct. 3, 1942	Sold Oct. 9, 1946 for commercial service. Last reported as still in existence in 1981.
PT 141	Elco-A	Oct. 6, 1942	See comments under PT 139.
PT 142	Elco-A	Oct. 9, 1942	Destroyed on purpose by burning Oct. 28, 1945.
PT 143	Elco-A	Oct. 13, 1942	See comments under PT 142.
PT 144	Elco-A	Oct. 5, 1942	See comments under PT 142.
PT 145	Elco-A	Oct. 17, 1942	Ran aground Jan. 4, 1944. Destroyed by 20-mm gunfire which caused her to burn and explode. Posit.: Long. 05° 34.0' South, Lat. 146° 10.0' East.
PT 146	Elco-A	Oct. 20, 1942	Destroyed on purpose by burning Oct. 26, 1945.
PT 147	Elco-A	Oct. 23, 1942	Ran aground Nov. 18, 1943. Abandoned and destroyed by scuttling charges. Posit.: Long. 05° 55.0' South, Lat. 147° 20.0' East.
PT 148	Elco-A	Oct. 27, 1942	Destroyed on purpose by burning Nov. 1, 1945.
PT 149	Elco-A	Oct. 29, 1942	Destroyed on purpose by burning Oct. 28, 1945.
PT 150	Elco-A	Nov. 2, 1942	See comments under PT 149.
PT 151	Elco-A	Nov. 4, 1942	See comments under PT 149.
PT 152	Elco-A	Nov. 6, 1942	See comments under PT 149.
PT 153	Elco-A	Nov. 10, 1942	Ran aground July 2, 1943. Pulled off and towed to Tulagi, but found to be beyond economical repair. Scrapped.
PT 154	Elco-A	Nov. 13, 1942	Destroyed on purpose by burning Nov. 24, 1945.
PT 155	Elco-A	Nov. 20, 1942	See comments under PT 154.
PT 156	Elco-A	Nov. 18, 1942	See comments under PT 154.
PT 157	Elco-A	Nov. 20, 1942	Destroyed on purpose by burning Nov. 27, 1945.
PT 158	Elco-A	Nov. 23, 1942	Ran aground July 2, 1943. Abandoned and destroyed. Posit.: Long. 08° 20.0' South, Lat. 157° 35.0' East.
PT 159	Elco-A	Nov. 24, 1942	See comments under PT 154.
PT 160	Elco-A	Dec. 7, 1942	See comments under PT 157.
PT 161	Elco-A	Nov. 28, 1942	See comments under PT 154.
PT 162	Elco-A	Dec. 2, 1942	See comments under PT 154.
PT 163	Elco-A	Dec. 4, 1942	Destroyed on purpose Nov. 11, 1945.
PT 164	Elco-A	Dec. 8, 1942	Sunk on Aug. 1, 1943, by Japanese horizontal bomber. Posit.: Long. 08° 25.0' South, Lat. 157° 20.0' East.
PT 165	Elco-A	Dec. 11, 1942	Sunk May 24, 1943, while being transported, along with PTs 167, 171–174 as deck cargo on the SS Stanvac Manila. Posit.: Long. 23° 45.0' South, Lat. 166° 30.0' East.

Hull Number	Design/ Builder	Completed	Comments
PT 166	Elco-A	Dec. 15, 1942	Accidentally strafed and sunk by four U.S. Army B-25 bombers July 20, 1943. Posit.: Long. 08° 15.0' South, Lat. 156° 53.0' East.
PT 167	Elco-A	Dec. 17, 1942	Destroyed on purpose by burning Nov. 11, 1945.
PT 168	Elco-A	Dec. 22, 1942	See comments under PT 167.
PT 169	Elco-A	Dec. 23, 1942	See comments under PT 167.
PT 170	Elco-A	Dec. 28, 1942	See comments under PT 167.
PT 171	Elco-A	Dec. 30, 1942	See comments under PT 167.
PT 172	Elco-A	Jan. 2, 1943	Badly damaged by grounding Sept. 7, 1943. Beached to prevent sinking. Abandoned and destroyed to prevent capture. Posit.: Long. 07° 34.0' South, Lat. 165° 35.0' East.
PT 173	Elco-A	Jan. 28, 1943	See comments under PT 165.
PT 174	Elco-A	Jan. 6, 1943	See comments under PT 167.
PT 175	Elco-A	Jan. 8, 1943	See comments under PT 167.
PT 176	Elco-A	Jan. 12, 1943	See comments under PT 167.
PT 177	Elco-A	Jan. 14, 1943	See comments under PT 167.
PT 178	Elco-A	Jan. 16, 1943	See comments under PT 167.
PT 179	Elco-A	Jan. 19, 1943	See comments under PT 167.
PT 180	Elco-A	Jan. 22, 1943	Sold in May 1946.
PT 181	Elco-A	Jan. 26, 1943	Destroyed on purpose Nov. 11, 1945.
PT 182	Elco-A	Jan. 30, 1943	See comments under PT 167.
PT 183	Elco-A	Feb. 2, 1943	See comments under PT 167.
PT 184	Elco-A	Feb. 4, 1943	See comments under PT 167.
PT 185	Elco-A	Feb. 6, 1943	See comments under PT 167.
PT 186	Elco-A	Feb. 9, 1943	See comments under PT 167.
PT 187	Elco-A	Feb. 12, 1943	Sold in May 1946.
PT 188	Elco-A	Feb. 17, 1943	See comments under PT 149.
PT 189	Elco-A	Feb. 19, 1943	See comments under PT 149.
PT 190	Elco-A	Feb. 19, 1943	Sold in May 1946.
PT 191	Elco-A	Feb. 24, 1943	Sold in May 1946. Resold to the Philippine Republic in Aug. 1946.
PT 192	Elco-A	Feb. 25, 1943	Destroyed on purpose by burning Oct. 26, 1945.
PT 193	Elco-A	Feb. 27, 1943	Ran aground June 24, 1944. Abandoned and set afire to prevent capture. Posit.: Long. 00° 55.0' South, Lat. 134° 52.0' East.
PT 194	Elco-A	Mar. 3, 1943	See comments under PT 192.
PT 195	Elco-A	Mar. 6, 1943	See comments under PT 190.
PT 196	Elco-A	May 3, 1943	See comments under PT 192.
PT 197	Higgins	Jan. 5, 1943	Lend-lease to USSR Feb. 15, 1943. Lost June 22, 1945.
PT 198	Higgins	July 7, 1943	Lend-lease to UK in Apr. 1943 as CT-17. Returned Aug. 2, 1946. Sold Sept. 3, 1946, to the Republic of the Philippines.
PT 199	Higgins	Jan. 23, 1943	See comments under PT 71.
PT 200	Higgins	Jan. 23, 1943	Sunk Feb. 22, 1944, with unknown object off Long Island, N.y. Posit.: Long. 41° 23.0' Long. North, Lat. 71° 01.0' West.
PT 201	Higgins	Jan. 20, 1943	Leased to UK Oct. 17, 1944, as MGB 181. Returned Aug. 8, 1945, and leased the same date to Yugoslavia as MT-1. Scrapped in 1966.
PT 202	Higgins	Jan. 23, 1943	Sunk Aug. 16, 1944, by a German mine. Posit.: Long. 43° 23.0' North, Lat. 06° 43.0' West.

Hull Number	Design/ Builder	Completed	Comments
PT 203	Higgins	Jan. 23, 1943	Leased to UK Oct. 17, 1944, as MGB 189. Returned Jan. 3, 1947. Sold in Mar. 1947 to Turkey.
PT 204	Higgins	Jan. 23, 1943	Leased to UK Oct. 17, 1944, as MGB 182. Returned Aug. 8, 1945, and leased the same date to Yugoslavia as MT-2. Scrapped in 1966.
PT 205	Higgins	Jan. 25, 1943	Leased to UK Oct. 17, 1944, as MGB 190. Returned Jan. 3, 1947. Sold in Mar. 1947 to Turkey.
PT 206	Higgins	Jan. 30, 1943	Leased to UK Oct. 17, 1944, as MGB 177. Returned Oct. 19, 1945. Sold sometime between Apr. 17, 1946, and Feb. 19, 1947, to Italy.
PT 207	Higgins	Feb. 2, 1943	Leased to UK Oct. 17, 1944, as MGB 183. Returned Aug. 8, 1945, and leased the same date to Yugoslavia as MT-3. Scrapped in 1966.
PT 208	Higgins	Feb. 10, 1943	Leased to UK Oct. 17, 1944, as MGB 184. Returned Aug. 8, 1945, and leased the same date to Yugoslavia as MT-4. Scrapped in 1966.
PT 209	Higgins	Feb. 9, 1943	Leased to UK Oct. 17, 1944, as MGB 185. Returned Aug. 8, 1945, and leased the same date to Yugoslavia as MT-5. Scrapped in 1966.
PT 210	Higgins	Feb. 10, 1943	Leased to UK Oct. 17, 1944, as MGB 191. Returned Oct. 23, 1945. Sold sometime between Apr. 17, 1946, and Feb. 19, 1947, of Italy.
PT 211	Higgins	Feb. 11, 1943	Leased to UK Oct. 17, 1944, as MGB 186. Returned Aug. 8, 1945, and leased the same date to Yugoslavia as MT-6. Scrapped in 1966.
PT 212	Higgins	Feb. 18, 1943	Leased to UK Oct. 17, 1944, as MGB 192. Returned Jan. 3, 1947. Sold in Mar. 1947 to Turkey.
PT 213	Higgins	Feb. 15, 1943	Leased to UK Oct. 17, 1944 as MGB 187. Returned Aug. 8, 1945, and leased the same date to Yugoslavia as MT-7. Scrapped in 1966.
PT 214	Higgins	Feb. 18, 1943	Leased to UK Oct. 17, 1944 as MGB 178. Returned Nov. 10, 1945. Sunk Nov. 7, 1945 as target off Malta.
PT 215	Higgins	Feb. 26, 1943	Leased to UK Oct. 17, 1944, as MGB 179. Returned Oct. 23, 1945. Sold sometime between Apr. 17, 1946, and Feb. 19, 1947, to Italy.
PT 216	Higgins	Feb. 26, 1943	Leased to UK Oct. 17, 1944, as MGB 180. Returned Jan. 3, 1947. Sold in March 1947 to Turkey.
PT 217	Higgins	Feb. 28, 1943	Leased to UK Oct. 17, 1944, as MGB 188. Returned Aug. 8, 1945, and leased the same date to Yugoslavia as MT-8. Sunk Nov. 14, 1946.
PT 218	Higgins	Mar. 1, 1943	See comments under PT 202.
PT 219	Higgins	Mar. 4, 1943	Accidentally ran aground Sept. 14, 1943, when her mooring cable parted in a storm. After being pulled off, sunk because of the damage. Salvaged again, she was rated as beyond repair and eventually scrapped.
PT 220	Higgins	Mar. 9, 1943	Destroyed on purpose by burning Nov. 26, 1945.
PT 221	Higgins	Mar. 11, 1943	See comments under PT 220.
PT 222	Higgins	Mar. 15, 1943	See comments under PT 220.
PT 223	Higgins	Mar. 13, 1943	See comments under PT 220.
PT 224	Higgins	Mar. 15, 1943	Sold in May 1946.
PT 225	Higgins	Mar. 20, 1943	Destroyed on purpose by burning Nov. 19, 1945.
PT 226	Higgins	Mar. 20, 1943	Sold in May 1946.
PT 227	Higgins	Mar. 25, 1943	Destroyed on purpose by burning Nov. 19, 1945.

Hull Number	Design/ Builder	Completed	Comments
PT 228	Higgins	Mar. 29, 1943	Sold in May 1946.
PT 229	Higgins	Mar. 25, 1943	Sold in May 1946.
PT 230	Higgins	Mar. 29, 1943	Destroyed on purpose by burning Nov. 19, 1945.
PT 231	Higgins	Mar. 31, 1943	Sold in May 1946.
PT 232	Higgins	Mar. 31, 1943	Sold in May 1946.
PT 233	Higgins	Apr. 7, 1943	Destroyed on purpose by burning Nov. 19, 1945.
PT 234	Higgins	Apr. 14, 1943	Sold in May 1946.
PT 235	Higgins	Apr. 17, 1943	Destroyed on purpose by burning Nov. 19, 1945.
PT 236	Higgins	Apr. 19, 1943	Sold in May 1946.
PT 237	Higgins	Apr. 22, 1943	Sold in May 1946.
PT 238	Higgins	Apr. 22, 1943	Sold in May 1946.
PT 239	Higgins	Apr. 30, 1943	Burned and sunk at the dock on Dec. 14, 1943, due to accidental fire. Posit.: Long. 07° 42.0′ South, Lat. 156° 47.0′ East.
PT 240	Higgins	Apr. 30, 1943	Sold in May 1946.
PT 241	Higgins	May 12, 1943	Destroyed on purpose by burning Nov. 19, 1945.
PT 242	Higgins	May 14, 1943	Destroyed on purpose by burning Nov. 19, 1945.
PT 243	Higgins	May 14, 1943	Destroyed on purpose by burning Nov. 26, 1945.
PT 244	Higgins	May 24, 1943	Destroyed on purpose by burning Nov. 26, 1945.
PT 245	Higgins	May 19, 1943	Sold in May 1946.
PT 246	Higgins	May 24, 1943	Destroyed on purpose by burning Nov. 26, 1945.
PT 247	Higgins	May 25, 1943	Sunk May 5, 1944, by a hit in the engine room from a large Japanese Coastal Defense gun. Posit.: Long. 06° 38.0′ South, Lat. 156° 01.0′ East.
PT 248	Higgins	May 26, 1943	Destroyed on purpose by burning Nov. 24, 1945.
PT 249	Higgins	May 28, 1943	Sold in May 1946.
PT 250	Higgins	May 31, 1943	Sold in May 1946.
PT 251	Higgins	May 31, 1943	Sunk Feb. 26, 1944, by a direct hit from a coastal defense gun after running hard aground. Posit.: Long. 06° 30.0′ South, Lat. 155° 10.0′ East.
PT 252	Higgins	June 15, 1943	Destroyed on purpose by burning Nov. 24, 1945.
PT 253	Higgins	June 14, 1943	Sold in May 1946.
PT 254	Higgins	June 16, 1943	Sold in May 1946.
PT 255	Huckins	Feb. 25, 1943	Sold Sept. 1, 1948.
PT 256	Huckins	Feb. 26, 1943	Sold Sept. 1, 1948.
PT 257	Huckins	Mar 27, 1943	Sold Apr. 11, 1947, for commercial service. Last reported as still in existence in 1953.
PT 258	Huckins	Mar. 29, 1943	Sold Apr. 11, 1947.
PT 259	Huckins	May 25, 1943	Sold Mar. 25, 1947, for commercial service. Last reported as still in existence in 1951.
PT 260	Huckins	May 26, 1943	See comments under PT 260.
PT 261	Huckins	June 26, 1943	Sold Apr. 11, 1947, for scrapping.
PT 262	Huckins	July 7, 1943	Sold Mar. 25, 1947, for scrapping.
PT 263	Huckins	July 31, 1943	Sold Apr. 11, 1947, for scrapping.
PT 264	Huckins	Sept. 7, 1943	Sold July 7, 1947, for scrapping.
PT 265	Higgins	Aug. 24, 1943	Lend-lease to USSR Nov. 9, 1943. Declared "unfit" by the Soviet Navy in 1954. Reported destroyed on purpose by the USSR with demolition charges after thewar, but not verified. Stricken from the U.S. Naval Vessel Register Jan. 1, 1983, as a result of the Oct. 18, 1972, treaty between the USSR and the United States, which settled "all rights, claims, benefits and obligations" of the two governments that arose during the World War II period.

Hull Number	Design/ Builder	Completed	Comments
PT 266	Higgins	Aug. 25, 1943	Lend-lease to USSR Nov. 9, 1943. Sunk in the war.
PT 267	Higgins	Aug. 26, 1943	Lend-lease to USSR Nov. 9, 1943. See comments under PT 265.
PT 268	Higgins	Aug. 27, 1943	Lend-lease to USSR Nov. 9, 1943. See comments under PT 265.
PT 269	Higgins	Aug. 28, 1943	Lend-lease to USSR Nov. 9, 1943. See comments under PT 265.
PT 270	Higgins	Aug. 30, 1943	Lend-lease to USSR Nov. 9, 1943. See comments under PT 265.
PT 271	Higgins	Aug. 31, 1943	Lend-lease to USSR Nov. 17, 1943. See comments under PT 265.
PT 272	Higgins	Sept. 1, 1943	Lend-lease to USSR Nov. 17, 1943. Sunk in the war.
PT 273	Higgins	Sept. 3, 1943	Lend-lease to USSR Nov. 17, 1943. See comments under PT 265.
PT 274	Higgins	Sept. 13, 1943	Lend-lease to USSR Nov. 17, 1943. See comments under PT 265.
PT 275	Higgins	Sept. 13, 1943	Lend-lease to USSR Nov. 17, 1943. Sunk in the war.
PT 276	Higgins	Sept. 20, 1943	Lend-lease to USSR Nov. 17, 1943. See comments under PT 265.
PT 277	Higgins	July 7, 1943	Destroyed on purpose by burning Nov. 26, 1945.
PT 278	Higgins	July 9, 1943	Sold in Dec. 1946.
PT 279	Higgins	June 28, 1943	Sunk Feb. 11, 1944, in a collision with PT 282. Posit.: Long. 05° 30.0′ South, Lat. 154° 15.0′ East.
PT 280	Higgins	June 28, 1943	Destroyed on purpose by burning Nov. 26, 1945.
PT 281	Higgins	July 8, 1943	Destroyed on purpose by burning on Nov. 26, 1945.
PT 282	Higgins	July 10, 1943	See comments under PT 280.
PT 283	Higgins	July 12, 1943	Sunk March 17, 1944, by hits from Japanese machine guns and a hit from a 5″ shell fired by the *USS Guest*. Posit.: Long. 06° 27.0′ South, Lat. 155° 08.0′ East.
PT 284	Higgins	July 21, 1943	Destroyed on purpose by burning Nov. 26, 1945.
PT 285	Higgins	July 16, 1943	See comments under PT 284.
PT 286	Higgins	Aug. 4, 1943	See comments under PT 284.
PT 287	Higgins	July 22, 1943	See comments under PT 284.
PT 288	Higgins	July 23, 1943	See comments under PT 284.
PT 289	Higgins	Sept. 20, 1943	Lend-lease to USSR Dec. 3, 1943. See comments under PT 265.
PT 290	Higgins	Sept. 22, 1943	Lend-lease to USSR Dec. 3, 1943. See comments under PT 265.
PT 291	Higgins	Sept. 25, 1943	Lend-lease to USSR Dec. 3, 1943. Sunk in the war.
PT 292	Higgins	Sept. 24, 1943	Lend-lease to USSR Dec. 3, 1943. See comments under PT 265.
PT 293	Higgins	Sept. 25, 1943	Lend-lease to USSR Dec. 3, 1943. See comments under PT 265.
PT 294	Higgins	Sept. 28, 1943	Lend-lease to USSR Dec. 3, 1943. See comments under PT 265.
PT 295	Higgins	Oct. 15, 1943	Sold Aug. 27, 1948.
PT 296	Higgins	Oct. 18, 1943	Sold and removed from U.S. naval custody July 8, 1948. Used for commercial service. Hulk sunk in a storm off Staten Island, NY, in 1990.
PT 297	Higgins	Oct. 20, 1943	Destroyed on purpose by burning Nov. 26, 1945.
PT 298	Higgins	Oct. 26, 1943	Sold in May 1946.
PT 299	Higgins	Oct. 26, 1943	Sold in May 1946.
PT 300	Higgins	Oct. 29, 1943	Sunk Dec. 18, 1944, by a kamikaze. Posit.: Long. 12° 19.0′ South, Lat. 121° 05.0′ East.
PT 301	Higgins	Nov. 4, 1943	Irreparably damaged Nov. 7, 1944, by accidental engine-room explosion. Scrapped at San Pedro, Calif.
PT 302	Higgins	Nov. 9, 1943	Sold Mar. 19, 1948.
PT 303	Higgins	Nov. 29, 1943	Sold July 20, 1948, for commercial service. Last reported as still in existence in 1989.
PT 304	Higgins	Nov. 23, 1943	Sold July 19, 1948, for commercial service. Last reported as still in existence in 1963.

Hull Number	Design/ Builder	Completed	Comments
PT 305	Higgins	Dec. 8, 1943	Sold June 18, 1948, for commercial service. Cut down to 65 ft. length. Still exists in an operating condition, being owned by Mr. David Crow, Tilgham Island, Md.
PT 306	Higgins	Dec. 3, 1943	Sold Apr. 1, 1948, for commercial service. Last reported as still in existence in 1963.
PT 307	Higgins	Dec. 2, 1943	Sold Mar. 19, 1948, for commercial service. Ran aground in 1951 and stranded.
PT 308	Higgins	Jan. 24, 1944	Sold July 19, 1948, for commercial service. Sunk in the early 1990s in a canal at Dagsboro, Dela. Parts salvaged to aid in restoring PT 309.
PT 309	Higgins	Jan. 26, 1944	Sold June 18, 1948, for commercial service. In 1994–95 the boat was purchased by the Admiral Nimitz Museum and Historical Center, Fredericksburg, Texas for restoration to her original configuration. From 1998 she has been on display.
PT 310	Higgins	Jan. 27, 1944	Sold Mar. 12, 1948.
PT 311	Higgins	Jan. 25, 1944	Sunk Nov. 18, 1944, by a German mine. Posit.: Long. 43° 41.0′ South, Lat. 09° 37.0′ East.
PT 312	Higgins	Jan. 29, 1944	Sold June 21, 1948, for commercial service. Last reported as still in existence in 1955.
PT 313	Higgins	Jan. 31, 1944	Sold July 19, 1948.
PT 314	Elco-A	Mar. 11, 1943	Sold Jan. 21, 1948. Scrapped in 1996 in a Cayaha, N.Y., boatyard.
PT 315	Elco-A	Mar. 15, 1943	Sold May 21, 1948.
PT 316	Elco-A	Mar. 17, 1943	Sold Dec. 29, 1947, for commercial service. Last reported as still in existence in 1975.
PT 317	Elco-A	Mar. 19, 1943	Sold Jan. 21, 1948.
PT 318	Elco-A	Mar. 23, 1943	Sold in May 1946.
PT 319	Elco-A	Mar. 26, 1943	See comments under PT 318.
PT 320	Elco-A	Mar. 27, 1943	Sunk on Nov. 5, 1944, by a Japanese aircraft. Posit.: Long. 11° 11.0′ North, Lat. 125° 05.0′ East.
PT 321	Elco-A	Mar. 30, 1943	Ran aground Nov. 10, 1944. Posit.: Long. 11° 25.0′ North, Lat. 124° 19.0′ East.
PT 322	Elco-A	Apr. 2, 1943	Ran aground Nov. 23, 1943. Posit.: Long. 06° 09.0′ South, Lat. 147° 36.0′ East.
PT 323	Elco-A	Apr. 6, 1943	Irreparably damaged Dec. 10, 1944, after being hit by a kamikaze. Beached and abandoned. Posit.: Long. 10° 33.0′ North, Lat. 125° 14.0′ East.
PT 324	Elco-A	Apr. 8, 1943	Destroyed on purpose by burning Nov. 10, 1945.
PT 325	Elco-A	Apr. 10, 1943	See comments under PT 324.
PT 326	Elco-A	Apr. 13, 1943	See comments under PT 318.
PT 327	Elco-A	May 15, 1943	See comments under PT 324.
PT 328	Elco-A	Apr. 17, 1943	See comments under PT 318.
PT 329	Elco-A	Apr. 21, 1943	See comments under PT 324.
PT 330	Elco-A	Apr. 23, 1943	See comments under PT 324.
PT 331	Elco-A	Apr. 27, 1943	See comments under PT 324.
PT 332	Elco-A	Apr. 29, 1943	See comments under PT 318.
PT 333	Elco-A	May 1, 1943	See comments under PT 318.
PT 334	Elco-A	May 5, 1943	See comments under PT 318.
PT 335	Elco-A	May 7, 1943	See comments under PT 318.
PT 336	Elco-A	May 12, 1943	Destroyed on purpose by burning Nov. 6, 1945.
PT 337	Elco-A	May 14, 1943	Sunk Mar. 7, 1944, by a Jap. coastal defense gun. Posit.: Long. 04° 09.0′ South, Lat. 144° 50.0′ East.

Hull Number	Design/ Builder	Completed	Comments
PT 338	Elco-A	May 18, 1943	Irreparably damaged Jan. 28, 1945, by running aground. Destroyed Jan. 31, 1945. Posit.: Long. 12° 06.45' North, Lat. 121° 23.15' East.
PT 339	Elco-A	May 22, 1943	Irreparably damaged May 27, 1944, by running aground. Posit.: Long. 042° 01.0' South, Lat. 144° 44.0' East.
PT 340	Elco-A	May 25, 1943	See comments under PT 318.
PT 341	Elco-A	May 28, 1943	See comments under PT 318.
PT 342	Elco-A	May 31, 1943	See comments under PT 318.
PT 343	Elco-A	June 1, 1943	See comments under PT 318.
PT 344	Elco-A	June 7, 1943	See comments under PT 318.
PT 345	Elco-A	June 8, 1943	Destroyed on purpose by burning Nov. 9, 1945.
PT 346	Elco-A	June 10, 1943	Sunk accidentally April 29, 1944, by U.S. aircraft. Posit.: Long. 04° 13.0' South, Lat. 151° 27.0' East.
PT 347	Elco-A	June 15, 1943	Ran aground Apr. 29, 1944. While salvage was being attempted, attacked by U.S. aircraft and sunk. Posit.: Long. 04° 13.0' South, Lat. 151° 27.0' East.
PT 348	Elco-A	June 17, 1943	See comments under PT 318.
PT 349	Elco-A	June 18, 1943	See comments under PT 318.
PT 350	Elco-A	June 22, 1943	See comments under PT 345.
PT 351	Elco-A	June 25, 1943	See comments under PT 345.
PT 352	Elco-A	June 20, 1943	See comments under PT 345.
PT 353	Elco-A	July 2, 1943	Accidentally sunk Mar. 27, 1944, by Australian aircraft. Posit.: Long. 05° 17.0' South, Lat. 151° 01.0' East.
PT 354	Elco-A	July 6, 1943	See comments under PT 318.
PT 355	Elco-A	July 8, 1943	See comments under PT 318.
PT 356	Elco-A	July 10, 1943	See comments under PT 318.
PT 358	Elco-A	July 23, 1943	See comments under PT 318.
PT 359	Elco-A	June 16, 1943	See comments under PT 318.
PT 360	Elco-A	July 20, 1943	See comments under PT 318.
PT 361	Elco-A	July 27, 1943	See comments under PT 318.
PT 362	Elco-B	May 18, 1943	Destroyed on purpose by burning Nov. 1, 1945.
PT 363	Elco-B	June 5, 1943	Sunk Nov. 25, 1944, by Jap. coastal defense guns and small arms fire. Posit.: Long. 00° 55.0' North, Lat. 127° 50.0' East.
PT 364	Elco-B	June 8, 1943	See comments under PT 362.
PT 365	Elco-B	June 12, 1943	See comments under PT 362.
PT 366	Elco-B	June 8, 1943	See comments under PT 318.
PT 367	Elco-B	June 23, 1943	See comments under PT 362.
PT 368	Scott-Paine	Apr. 19, 1943	Orig. built for Netherlands as TM-32. Reverse lend-lease to U.S. Navy as PT 368 May 3, 1943. Ran aground Oct. 11, 1944. Posit.: Long. 01° 59.0' North, Lat. 127° 57.0' East.
PT 369	Scott-Paine	Mar. 27, 1943	Orig. built for Netherlands as TM-35. Reverse lend-lease to U.S. Navy as PT 369 May 3, 1943. Destroyed on purpose by burning Nov. 1, 1945.
PT 370	Scott-Paine	Apr. 22, 1943	Orig. built for Netherlands as TM-36. Reverse lend-lease to U.S. Navy as PT 370 July 10, 1943. See comments under PT 369 for disposition.
PT 371	Scott-Paine	Apr. 10, 1943	Orig. built for Netherlands as TM-37. Reverse lend-lease to U.S. Navy as PT 371 July 10, 1943. Ran aground Sept. 19, 1944. Destroyed to prevent capture. Posit.: Long. 02° 05.0' North, Lat. 127° 51.0' East.
PT 372	Elco-A	Aug. 3, 1943	See comments under PT 318.
PT 373	Elco-A	Aug. 5, 1943	See comments under PT 318.

Hull Number	Design/ Builder	Completed	Comments
PT 374	Elco-A	Aug. 6, 1943	See comments under PT 318.
PT 375	Elco-A	Aug. 10, 1943	See comments under PT 318.
PT 376	Elco-A	Aug. 12, 1943	See comments under PT 318.
PT 377	Elco-A	Aug. 14, 1943	See comments under PT 318.
PT 378	Elco-A	Aug. 17, 1943	See comments under PT 318.
PT 379	Elco-A	Aug. 20, 1943	See comments under PT 318.
PT 380	Elco-A	Aug. 24, 1943	See comments under PT 318.
PT 381	Elco-A	Aug. 26, 1943	See comments under PT 318.
PT 382	Elco-A	Aug. 28, 1943	See comments under PT 318.
PT 383	Elco-A	Aug. 28, 1943	See comments under PT 318.
PT 384	Vosper-A	May 6, 1943	Lend-lease to UK May 6, 1944, as MTB 396. Returned Sept. 10, 1945. Destroyed on purpose by burning Oct. 26, 1945.
PT 385	Vosper-A	May 13, 1944	Lend-lease to UK May 13, 1944, as MTB 397. Returned Mar. 16, 1946. Sold Jan. 24, 1947, to Egypt.
PT 386	Vosper-A	May 25, 1944	Lend-lease to UK May 25, 1944, as MTB 398. Returned Oct. 16, 1945. Sold Jan. 24, 1947, to Italy. Trans. to the Italian Navy as GIS-0012 in 1951. Scrapped 1959.
PT 387	Vosper-A	June 1, 1943	Lend-lease to UK June 1, 1944, as MTB 399. Returned Mar. 16, 1946. Sold Jan. 24, 1947, to Egypt.
PT 388	Vosper-A	June 13, 1943	Lend-lease to UK June 13, 1944, as MTB 400. Returned Mar. 16, 1946. Sold Feb. 19, 1947, to Italy. Trans. to the Italian Navy as GIS-001 Mar. 24, 1948. Scrapped in 1959.
PT 389	Vosper-A	July 8, 1944	Lend-lease to UK July 8, 1944, as MTB 401. Returned Oct. 23, 1945. Sold Feb. 19, 1947, to Italy. Trans. to the Italian Navy as GIS-002 Apr. 1, 1948. Scrapped 1960.
PT 390	Vosper-A	June 29, 1944	Lend-lease to UK June 29, 1944, as MTB 402. Returned Oct. 16, 1945. Sold Feb. 19, 1947, to Italy. Trans. to the Italian Navy as GIS-004 Feb. 1, 1948. Scrapped in 1959.
PT 391	Vosper-A	July 11, 1943	Lend-lease to UK July 11, 1944, as MTB 403. Returned Oct. 18, 1945. Sold Jan. 24, 1947, to Italy. Trans. to the Italian Navy as GIS-003 Feb. 1, 1948. Scrapped in 1960.
PT 392	Vosper-A	July 22, 1944	Lend-lease to UK July 22, 1944, as MTB 404. Returned Nov. 7, 1945. Sold Feb. 19, 1947, to Italy. Trans. to the Italian Navy as GIS-013 Apr. 4, 1948. Scrapped in 1960.
PT 393	Vosper-A	Aug. 11, 1944	Lend-lease to UK Aug. 11, 1944, as MTB 405. Returned Nov. 10, 1945. Sold Feb. 18, 1947 to Italy. Trans. to the Italian Navy as GIS-005 Apr. 4, 1948. Scrapped in 1962.
PT 394	Vosper-A	Aug. 2, 1944	Lend-lease to UK Aug. 2, 1944, as MTB 406. Returned Nov. 7, 1945. Sold Feb. 19, 1947, to Italy. Trans. to the Italian Navy as GIS-006 Apr. 4, 1948. Scrapped in 1962.
PT 395	Vosper-A	Aug. 30, 1944	Lend-lease to UK Aug. 30, 1944, as MTB 407. Returned Nov. 10, 1945. Trans. to U.S. Army Apr. 1, 1946. Returned. Sold Feb. 19, 1947.
PT 396	Vosper-A	Sept. 9, 1944	Lend-lease to UK Sept. 9, 1944, as MTB 408. Returned Nov. 10, 1945. Sold Feb. 19, 1947, to Italy. Trans. to the Italian Navy as GIS-0011 Apr. 4, 1948. Scrapped in 1959.
PT 397	Vosper-A	Oct. 11, 1944	Lend-leased to UK Oct. 11, 1944, as MTB 409. Returned Nov. 7, 1945. Sold Feb. 19, 1947, to Italy. Trans. to the Italian Navy as GIS-008 Apr. 4, 1948. Scrapped in 1959.
PT 398	Vosper-A	Oct. 6, 1944	Lend-lease to UK Oct. 6, 1944, as MTB 410. Returned Nov. 7, 1945. Sold Feb. 19, 1947 to Italy. Trans. to the Italian Navy as GIS-007 Apr. 4, 1948. Scrapped in 1959.

Hull Number	Design/ Builder	Completed	Comments
PT 399	Vosper-A	Oct. 30, 1944	Lend-lease to UK Oct. 30, 1944, as MTB-411. Returned Nov. 10, 1945. Sold Feb. 19, 1947, to Italy. Trans. to the Italian Navy as GIS-028 July 21, 1948. Scrapped in 1959.
PT 400	Vosper-B	Jan. 17, 1944	Lend-lease to USSR Jan. 24, 1944. Returned June 16, 1954. Sold Aug. 11, 1954 for scrapping.
PT 401	Vosper-B	Jan. 17, 1944	Lend-lease to USSR Jan. 24, 1944. Returned May 27, 1944. Sold Aug. 11, 1954, for scrapping.
PT 402	Vosper-B	Jan. 20, 1944	Lend-lease to USSR Feb. 22, 1944, as TKA-231. Returned May 27, 1944. Sold Aug. 11, 1954, for scrapping.
PT 403	Vosper-B	Jan. 20, 1944	Lend-lease to USSR Feb. 22, 1944, as TKA-232. Returned May 27, 1944. Sold Aug. 11, 1954, for scrapping.
PT 404	Vosper-B	Jan. 24, 1944	Lend-lease to USSR Feb. 22, 1944, as TKA-233. Returned May 27, 1944. Sold Aug. 11, 1954, for scrapping.
PT 405	Vosper-B	Jan. 24, 1944	Lend-leased USSR Feb. 22, 1944, as TKA-234. Returned May 27, 1944. Sold Aug. 11, 1954 for scrapping.
PT 406	Vosper-B	Jan. 31, 1944	Lend-lease to USSR Feb. 24, 1944, as TKA-243. Returned July 2, 1955. Fate unknown.
PT 407	Vosper-B	Jan. 31, 1944	Lend-lease to USSR Feb. 24, 1944, as TKA-244. Returned July 2, 1955. Fate unknown.
PT 408	Vosper-B	Feb. 4, 1944	Lend-lease to USSR Feb. 24, 1944, as TKA-235. Returned May 27, 1944. Sold Aug. 11, 1954 for scrapping.
PT 409	Vosper-B	Feb. 9, 1944	Lend-lease to USSR Feb. 24, 1944, as TKA-447. Returned May 27, 1944. Sold Aug. 11, 1954, for scrapping.
PT 410	Vosper-B	Feb. 23, 1944	Lend-lease to USSR Mar. 2, 1944, as TKA-237. Returned July 9, 1955. Fate unknown.
PT 411	Vosper-B	Feb. 23, 1944	Lend-lease to USSR Mar. 2, 1944, as TKA-238. Destroyed June 29, 1956, in Pechenga Gulf, Barents Sea, USSR under U.S. supervision.
PT 412	Vosper-B	Feb. 29, 1944	Lend-lease to USSR Mar. 5, 1944, as TKA-239. Sunk July 15, 1944, by German Subchaser *UJ-1211* off North Cape, Norway.
PT 413	Vosper-B	Feb. 29, 1944	Lend-lease to USSR Mar. 5, 1944, as TKA-240. Returned on July 5,1955. Fate unknown.
PT 414	Vosper-B	Mar. 9, 1944	Lend-lease to USSR June 8, 1944, as TKA-246. Reported destroyed on purpose by the USSR with demolition charges after the war, but not verified. Stricken from the U.S. Naval Vessel Register Jan. 1, 1983, as a result of the Oct. 18, 1972, treaty between the USSR and the United States which settled "all rights, claims, benefits and obligations of the two governments that arose during the World War II period."
PT 415	Vosper-B	Mar. 9, 1944	Lend-lease to USSR June 8, 1944, as TKA-247. Destroyed on purpose by the USSR with demolition charges after the war.
PT 416	Vosper-B	Mar. 14, 1944	Lend-lease to USSR June 8, 1944, as TKA-248. See comments under PT 414 for disposition.
PT 417	Vosper-B	Mar. 18, 1944	Lend-lease to USSR Aug. 11, 1944. See comments under PT 415 for disposition.
PT 418	Vosper-B	Mar. 23, 1944	Lend-lease to USSR Aug. 9, 1944. See comments under PT 415 for disposition.
PT 419	Vosper-B	Mar. 23, 1944	Lend-lease to USSR Aug. 11, 1944. See comments under PT 415 for disposition.

Hull Number	Design/Builder	Completed	Comments
PT 420	Vosper-B	Apr. 5, 1944	Lend-lease to USSR July 12, 1944. See comments under PT 414 for disposition.
PT 421	Vosper-B	Apr. 13, 1944	Lend-lease to USSR Aug. 9, 1944. See comments under PT 414 for disposition.
PT 422	Vosper-B	Apr. 13, 1944	Lend-lease to USSR July 12, 1944. See comments under PT 414 for disposition.
PT 423	Vosper-B	Apr. 21, 1944	Lend-lease to USSR Aug. 9, 1944. See comments under PT 415 for disposition.
PT 424	Vosper-B	May 5, 1944	Lend-lease to USSR July 12, 1944. Returned July 5, 1955. Fate unknown.
PT 425	Vosper-B	May 9, 1944	Lend-lease to USSR July 12, 1944. Returned July 5, 1955. Fate unknown.
PT 426	Vosper-B	May 16, 1944	Lend-lease to USSR July 12, 1944. Returned July 6, 1955. Fate unknown.
PT 427	Vosper-B	May 19, 1944	Lend-lease to USSR July 12, 1944. Returned July 6, 1955. Fate unknown.
PT 428	Vosper-B	May 25, 1944	Lend-lease to USSR Oct. 5, 1944. See comments under PT 414 for disposition.
PT 429	Vosper-B	May 31, 1944	Lend-lease to USSR Oct. 5, 1944. See comments under PT 415 for disposition.
PT 430	Vosper-C	Feb. 14, 1944	Lend-lease to USSR Feb. 25, 1944, as TKA-241. Returned July 14, 1955. Fate unknown.
PT 431	Vosper-C	Feb. 6, 1944,	Lend-lease to USSR Mar. 4, 1944, as TKA-242. Returned July 14, 1955. Fate unknown.
PT 432	Vosper-C	Feb. 29, 1944	Lend-lease to USSR Mar. 5, 1944, as TKA-243. Returned July 14, 1955. Fate unknown.
PT 433	Vosper-C	Mar. 17, 1944	Lend-lease to USSR June 8, 1944, as TKA-249. See comments under PT 415 for disposition.
PT 434	Vosper-C	Mar. 17, 1944	Lend-lease to USSR June 8, 1944, as TKA-240. Sunk during the war.
PT 435	Vosper-C	Mar. 17, 1944	Lend-lease to USSR June 8, 1944, as TKA-251. See comments under PT 414 for disposition.
PT 436	Vosper-C	Mar. 30, 1944	Lend-lease to USSR Sept. 18, 1944. See comments under PT 414 for disposition.
PT 437	Vosper-C	Mar. 30, 1944	Lend-lease to USSR Sept. 18, 1944. See comments under PT 414 for disposition.
PT 438	Vosper-C	Apr. 6, 1944	Lend-lease to USSR Oct. 5, 1944. Sunk during the war.
PT 439	Vosper-C	Apr. 27, 1944	Lend-lease to USSR Oct. 5, 1944. Returned July 6, 1955. Fate unknown.
PT 440	Vosper-C	Apr. 13, 1944	Lend-lease to USSR Aug. 9, 1944. See comments under PT 414 for disposition.
PT 441	Vosper-C	Apr. 20, 1944	Lend-lease to USSR Oct. 5, 1944. Sunk during the war.
PT 442	Vosper-C	Apr. 27, 1944	Lend-lease to USSR Oct. 5, 1944. Returned July 6, 1955. Fate unknown.
PT 443	Vosper-C	May 4, 1944	Lend-lease to USSR Sept. 18, 1944. Returned July 6, 1955. Fate unknown.
PT 444	Vosper-C	May 4, 1944	Lend-lease to USSR Sept. 18, 1944. See comments under PT 415 for disposition.
PT 445	Vosper-C	May 19, 1944	Lend-lease to USSR July 17, 1944. See comments under PT 415 for disposition.
PT 446	Vosper-C	May 25, 1944	Lend-lease to USSR Oct. 5, 1944. Returned July 6, 1955. Fate unknown.

Hull Number	Design/ Builder	Completed	Comments
PT 447	Vosper-C	May 18, 1944	Lend-lease to USSR July 17, 1944. See comments under PT 415 for disposition.
PT 448	Vosper-C	June 7, 1944	Lend-lease to USSR July 9, 1944, as pendant no. "246." Returned July 14, 1945. Fate unknown.
PT 449	Vosper-C	May 25, 1944	Lend-lease to USSR Oct. 5, 1944. See comments under PT 415 for disposition.
PT 450	Higgins	Feb. 3, 1944	Sold June 25, 1948, for commercial service. Burned and sunk in 1955.
PT 451	Higgins	Jan. 31, 1944	Sold March 31, 1948, for commercial service. Last reported that abandoned hull still exists as of 1996.
PT 452	Higgins	Feb. 5, 1944	Sold July 19, 1948.
PT 453	Higgins	Mar. 14, 1944	Sold in May 1946.
PT 454	Higgins	Feb. 8, 1944	Sold in May 1946.
PT 455	Higgins	Feb. 15, 1944	Sold in May 1946.
PT 456	Higgins	Mar. 9, 1944	Sold June 21, 1948.
PT 457	Higgins	Mar. 15, 1944	Sold July 20, 1948, for commercial service. Cut down to 62' 9" length. Last reported as still in existence, owned by Mr. Joe Stanislayczwk, Highlands, N.J.
PT 458	Higgins	Mar. 18, 1944	Sold June 21, 1948, for commercial service. Last reported as still in existence in 1961.
PT 459	Higgins	Mar. 24, 1944	Sold June 18, 1948, for commercial service. Cut down to 65' length. Last reported as still in existence, operating out of Fire Island, N.Y., as a charter and ferry boat.
PT 460	Higgins	Mar. 7, 1944	Sold June 21, 1948.
PT 461	Higgins	Mar. 28, 1944	Sold June 21, 1948, for commercial service. Burned and sunk in 1959.
PT 462	Higgins	Mar. 29, 1944	Sold in May 1946.
PT 463	Higgins	Apr. 1, 1944	Sold in May 1946.
PT 464	Higgins	Apr. 5, 1944	Sold in May 1946.
PT 465	Higgins	Apr. 13, 1944	Sold in May 1946.
PT 466	Higgins	Apr. 17, 1944	Sold in May 1946.
PT 467	Higgins	Apr. 20, 1944	Sold in May 1946.
PT 468	Higgins	Apr. 24, 1944	Sold in May 1946.
PT 469	Higgins	Apr. 28, 1944	Sold in May 1946.
PT 470	Higgins	Apr. 29, 1944	Sold in May 1946.
PT 471	Higgins	May 5, 1944	Sold in May 1946.
PT 472	Higgins	May 11, 1944	Sold in May 1946.
PT 473	Higgins	May 16, 1944	Sold in May 1946.
PT 474	Higgins	June 9, 1944	Destroyed on purpose Nov. 2, 1945.
PT 475	Higgins	June 15, 1944	Sold in May 1946.
PT 476	Higgins	June 16, 1944	Sold in May 1946.
PT 477	Higgins	July 1, 1944	Destroyed on purpose Nov. 2, 1945.
PT 478	Higgins	June 28, 1944	Sold in May 1946.
PT 479	Higgins	July 11, 1944	Sold in May 1946.
PT 480	Higgins	July 15, 1944	Sold in May 1946.
PT 481	Higgins	July 22, 1944	Sold in May 1946.
PT 482	Higgins	Aug. 3, 1944	Sold in May 1946.
PT 483	Higgins	Aug. 12, 1944	Sold in May 1946.
PT 484	Higgins	Aug. 30, 1944	Sold in May 1946.
PT 485	Higgins	Aug. 29, 1944	Sold in May 1946.

Hull Number	Design/ Builder	Completed	Comments
PT 486	Elco-A	Nov. 25, 1943	Stricken from the Navy List Feb. 7, 1946. Reinstated on the Navy List Aug. 15, 1946. Reclass. as small boat "C 105335" Aug. 27, 1946. Sold for commercial service. Last reported to still be in existence, owned by Mr. Charles Schumann, Wildwood, N.J., operated as a daily summer sightseeing boat.
PT 487	Elco-A	Jan. 10, 1944	Stricken from the Navy List Feb. 25, 1946. Reinstated Aug. 15, 1946. Reclass. as small boat "C 105336" Aug. 27, 1946. Fate unknown.
PT 488	Elco-A	Nov. 23, 1943	Sold in May 1946.
PT 489	Elco-A	Nov. 26, 1943	See comments under PT 488 for disposition.
PT 490	Elco-A	Nov. 29, 1943	See comments under PT 488 for disposition.
PT 491	Elco-A	Nov. 30, 1943	See comments under PT 488 for disposition.
PT 492	Elco-A	Dec. 3, 1943	See comments under PT 488 for disposition.
PT 493	Elco-A	Dec. 6, 1943	Sunk Oct. 25, 1944, by coastal guns. Beached and abandoned. Posit.: Long. 10° 15.0′ North, Lat. 125° 23.0′ East.
PT 494	Elco-A	Dec. 9, 1943	See comments under PT 488 for disposition.
PT 495	Elco-A	Dec. 13, 1943	See comments under PT 488 for disposition.
PT 496	Elco-A	Dec. 14, 1943	See comments under PT 488 for disposition.
PT 497	Elco-A	Dec. 18, 1943	See comments under PT 488 for disposition.
PT 498	Elco-A	Dec. 21, 1943	Lend-lease to USSR Mar. 4, 1945. See comments under PT 415 for disposition.
PT 499	Elco-A	Dec. 23, 1943	Lend-lease to USSR Dec. 30, 1944. Fate unknown.
PT 500	Elco-A	Dec. 27, 1943	Lend-lease to USSR Dec. 30, 1944. See comments under PT 411 for disposition.
PT 501	Elco-A	Dec. 29, 1943	Lend-lease to USSR Jan. 31, 1945. See comments under PT 415 for disposition.
PT 502	Elco-A	Dec. 31, 1943	Lend-lease to USSR Jan. 31, 1945. See comments under PT 414 for disposition.
PT 503	Elco-A	Jan. 5, 1944	Lend-lease to USSR Dec. 30, 1944. See comments under PT 415 for disposition.
PT 504	Elco-A	Jan. 11, 1944	Lend-lease to USSR Dec. 30, 1944. See comments under PT 415 for disposition.
PT 505	Elco-A	Jan. 13, 1944	Stricken from the Navy List Feb. 25, 1946. Reinstated on the Navy List Aug. 15, 1946. Reclass. as small boat Aug. 27, 1946. Sold Sept. 25, 1947, for commercial service. Last reported still in existence in 1955.
PT 506	Elco-A	Jan. 15, 1944	Lend-lease to USSR Jan. 31, 1945. See comments under PT 414 for disposition.
PT 507	Elco-A	Jan. 18, 1944	Lend-lease to USSR Mar. 4, 1945. See comments under PT 414 for disposition.
PT 508	Elco-A	Jan. 21, 1944	Lend-lease to USSR Jan. 31, 1945. See comments under PT 414 for disposition.
PT 509	Elco-A	Jan. 25, 1944	Sunk Aug. 9, 1944, by naval gunfire from a German minesweeper. Posit.: Long. 49° 11.0′ North, Lat. 02° 15.0′ West.
PT 510	Elco-A	Feb. 4, 1944	Lend-lease to USSR Dec. 30, 1944. See comments under PT 415 for disposition.
PT 511	Elco-A	Feb. 7, 1944	Lend-lease to USSR Dec. 30, 1944. See comments under PT 415 for disposition.
PT 512	Elco-A	Feb. 9, 1944	Lend-lease to USSR Dec. 30, 1944. See comments under PT 415 for disposition.

Hull Number	Design/ Builder	Completed	Comments
PT 513	Elco-A	Feb. 12, 1944	Lend-lease to USSR Dec. 30, 1944. See comments under PT 415 for disposition.
PT 514	Elco-A	Feb. 14, 1944	Lend-lease to USSR Mar. 4, 1945. See comments under PT 414 for disposition.
PT 515	Elco-A	Feb. 17, 1944	Lend-lease to USSR Mar. 4, 1945. See comments under PT 415 for disposition.
PT 516	Elco-A	Feb. 24, 1944	Lend-lease to USSR Apr. 7, 1945. See comments under PT 411 for disposition.
PT 517	Elco-A	Feb. 25, 1944	Lend-lease to USSR Apr. 7, 1945. Returned July 2, 1955. Fate unknown.
PT 518	Elco-A	Feb. 29, 1944	Lend-lease to USSR Apr. 7, 1945. See comments under PT 411 for disposition.
PT 519	Elco-A	Mar. 1, 1944	Lend-lease to USSR Apr. 7, 1945. See comments under PT 411 for disposition.
PT 520	Elco-A	Mar. 7, 1944	Lend-lease to USSR Apr. 7, 1945. See comments under PT 411 for disposition.
PT 521	Elco-A	Mar. 11, 1944	Lend-lease to USSR Apr. 7, 1945. See comments under PT 411 for disposition.
PT 522	Elco-A	Mar. 17, 1944	See comments under PT 488 for disposition.
PT 523	Elco-A	Feb. 8, 1944	See comments under PT 488 for disposition.
PT 524	Elco-A	Mar. 24, 1944	See comments under PT 488 for disposition.
PT 525	Elco-A	Mar. 30, 1944	See comments under PT 488 for disposition.
PT 526	Elco-A	Apr. 5, 1944	See comments under PT 488 for disposition.
PT 527	Elco-A	Apr. 11, 1944	See comments under PT 488 for disposition.
PT 528	Elco-A	Apr. 17, 1944	See comments under PT 488 for disposition.
PT 529	Elco-A	Apr. 22, 1944	See comments under PT 488 for disposition.
PT 530	Elco-A	Apr. 27, 1944	See comments under PT 488 for disposition.
PT 531	Elco-A	May 4, 1944	See comments under PT 488 for disposition.
PT 532	Elco-A	May 11, 1944	See comments under PT 488 for disposition.
PT 533	Elco-A	May 17, 1944	Sold in May 1946.
PT 534	Elco-A	May 24, 1944	See comments under PT 533 for disposition.
PT 535	Elco-A	May 29, 1944	See comments under PT 533 for disposition.
PT 536	Elco-A	June 3, 1944	See comments under PT 533 for disposition.
PT 537	Elco-A	June 9, 1944	See comments under PT 533 for disposition.
PT 538	Elco-A	June 15, 1944	See comments under PT 533 for disposition.
PT 539	Elco-A	June 21, 1944	See comments under PT 533 for disposition.
PT 540	Elco-A	June 28, 1944	See comments under PT 533 for disposition.
PT 541	Elco-A	July 5, 1944	See comments under PT 533 for disposition.
PT 542	Elco-A	July 10, 1944	See comments under PT 533 for disposition.
PT 543	Elco-A	July 15, 1944	See comments under PT 533 for disposition.
PT 544	Elco-A	July 21, 1944	See comments under PT 533 for disposition.
PT 545	Elco-A	Sept. 8, 1944	Sold Aug. 23, 1946.
PT 546	Elco-A	Sept. 3, 1943	Ex RPT 13. Reclass. PT 546 May 10, 1943. See comments under PT 488 for disposition.
PT 547	Elco-A	Oct. 4, 1943	Ex RPT 14. Reclass. PT 547 May 10, 1943. See comments under PT 488 for disposition.
PT 548	Elco-A	Sept. 7, 1943	Ex RPT 15. Reclass. PT 548 May 10, 1943. See comments under PT 488 for disposition.
PT 549	Elco-A	Sept. 10, 1943	Ex RPT 16. Reclass. PT 549 May 10, 1943. See comments under PT 488 for disposition.
PT 550	Elco-A	Sept. 14, 1943	Ex RPT 17. Reclass. PT 550 May 10, 1943. See comments under PT 488 for disposition.

Hull Number	Design/ Builder	Completed	Comments
PT 551	Elco-A	Sept. 16, 1943	Ex RPT 18. Reclass. PT 551 May 10, 1943. See comments under PT 488 for disposition.
PT 552	Elco-A	Oct. 16, 1943	Ex RPT 19. Reclass. PT 552 May 10, 1943. See comments under PT 414 for disposition.
PT 553	Elco-A	Oct. 18, 1943	Ex RPT 20. Reclass. PT 553 May 10, 1943. Lend-lease to USSR Apr. 12, 1945. See comments under PT 411 for disposition.
PT 554	Elco-A	Oct. 21, 1943	Ex RPT 21. Reclass. PT 554 May 10, 1943. Lend-lease to USSR May 8, 1945. See comments under PT 411 for disposition.
PT 555	Elco-A	Oct. 26, 1943	Ex RPT 22. Reclass. PT 555 May 10, 1943. Irreparably damaged after hitting a German mine Sept. 16, 1944. Posit.: Long. 43° 19.0' North, Lat. 05° 30.0' East. Written off as constructive total loss and scrapped.
PT 556	Elco-A	Oct. 28, 1943	Ex RPT 23. Reclass. PT 556 May 10, 1943. Lend-lease to USSR Apr. 12, 1945. See comments under PT 411 for disposition.
PT 557	Elco-A	Oct. 30, 1943	Ex RPT 24. Reclass. PT 557 May 10, 1943. Reclass. as small boat "C 105338" Aug. 27, 1946. Sold 1946–47 for commercial service. Last reported still in existence in 1981.
PT 558	Elco-A	Nov. 2, 1943	Ex RPT 25. Reclass. PT 558 May 10, 1943. Sold Mar. 12, 1948, for commercial service. Sunk in collision in 1970.
PT 559	Elco-A	Nov. 4, 1943	Ex RPT 26. Reclass. PT 559 May 10, 1943. Reclass. as small boat "C 105339" Aug. 27, 1946. Sold.
PT 560	Elco-A	Nov. 6, 1943	Ex RPT 27. Reclass. PT 560 May 10, 1943. Lend-lease to USSR May 8, 1945, as TKA-584(?). See comments under PT 411 for disposition.
PT 561	Elco-A	Nov. 9, 1943	Ex RPT 28. Reclass. PT 561 May 10, 1943. Lend-lease to USSR Apr. 12, 1945, as TKA-581(?). See comments under PT 411 for disposition.
PT 562	Elco-A	Nov. 11, 1943	Ex RPT 29. Reclass. PT 562 May 10, 1943. Lend-lease to USSR Apr. 7, 1945, as TKA-585(?). See comments under PT 411 for disposition.
PT 563	Elco-A	Nov. 22, 1943	Ex RPT 30. Reclass. PT 563 May 10, 1943. Lend-lease to USSR Apr. 12, 1945, as TKA-582(?). See comments under PT 411 for disposition.
PT 564	Higgins	June 30, 1943	Built as private speculation. Acquired by the Navy Sept. 2, 1943. Extremely successful design, but never put into production because it could not carry the armament necessary when PTs were used as "Gunboats" on some missions. Sold July 2, 1948. Removed from Naval Custody the same date.
PT 565	Elco-A	Dec. 8, 1944	See comments under PT 488 for disposition.
PT 566	Elco-A	Dec. 13, 1944	See comments under PT 488 for disposition.
PT 567	Elco-A	Dec. 15, 1944	See comments under PT 488 for disposition.
PT 568	Elco-A	Dec. 19, 1944	See comments under PT 488 for disposition.
PT 569	Elco-A	Dec. 23, 1944	See comments under PT 488 for disposition.
PT 570	Elco-A	Dec. 29, 1944	See comments under PT 488 for disposition.
PT 571	Elco-A	Jan. 13, 1945	See comments under PT 488 for disposition.
PT 572	Elco-A	Jan. 19, 1945	See comments under PT 488 for disposition.
PT 573	Elco-A	Jan. 23, 1945	See comments under PT 488 for disposition.
PT 574	Elco-A	Feb. 7, 1945	See comments under PT 488 for disposition.
PT 575	Elco-A	Feb. 7, 1945	Sold in May 1946.

Hull Number	Design/ Builder	Completed	Comments
PT 576	Elco-A	Feb. 12, 1945	See comments under PT 575 for disposition.
PT 577	Elco-A	Feb. 20, 1945	See comments under PT 575 for disposition.
PT 578	Elco-A	Feb. 24, 1945	See comments under PT 575 for disposition.
PT 579	Elco-A	Mar. 1, 1945	See comments under PT 575 for disposition.
PT 580	Elco-A	Mar. 3, 1945	See comments under PT 575 for disposition.
PT 581	Elco-A	Mar. 8, 1945	See comments under PT 575 for disposition.
PT 582	Elco-A	Mar. 13, 1945	See comments under PT 575 for disposition.
PT 583	Elco-A	Mar. 19, 1945	See comments under PT 575 for disposition.
PT 584	Elco-A	Mar. 22, 1945	See comments under PT 575 for disposition.
PT 585	Elco-A	Mar. 27, 1945	See comments under PT 575 for disposition.
PT 586	Elco-A	Mar. 30, 1945	See comments under PT 575 for disposition.
PT 587	Elco-A	Apr. 4, 1945	See comments under PT 575 for disposition.
PT 588	Elco-A	Apr. 10, 1945	See comments under PT 575 for disposition
PT 589	Elco-A	Apr. 13, 1945	See comments under PT 575 for disposition.
PT 590	Elco-A	Apr. 16, 1945	See comments under PT 575 for disposition.
PT 591	Elco-A	Apr. 19, 1945	See comments under PT 575 for disposition.
PT 592	Elco-A	Apr. 21, 1945	See comments under PT 575 for disposition.
PT 593	Elco-A	Apr. 25, 1945	See comments under PT 575 for disposition.
PT 594	Elco-A	Apr. 28, 1945	See comments under PT 575 for disposition.
PT 595	Elco-A	May 5, 1945	See comments under PT 575 for disposition.
PT 596	Elco-A	May 10, 1945	See comments under PT 575 for disposition.
PT 597	Elco-A	May 16, 1945	See comments under PT 575 for disposition.
PT 598	Elco-A	May 21, 1945	See comments under PT 575 for disposition.
PT 599	Elco-A	May 25, 1945	See comments under PT 575 for disposition
PT 600	Elco-A	May 30, 1945	Sold in May 1946.
PT 601	Elco-A	June 5, 1945	Reclass. as "floating equipment" Dec. 3, 1948, and renumbered "RCT-1." Reclass. as small boat "C 6083" July 14, 1952. Sold. Converted for commercial service. Abandoned in 1975.
PT 602	Elco-A	June 8, 1945	Reclass. as "floating equipment" Dec. 3, 1948, and renumbered "RCT-2." Trans. to Norway May 2, 1951 as Snogg (P-954). Renamed Knurr shortly after. Returned Dec. 1, 1961. Scrapped 1962 in country.
PT 603	Elco-A	June 28, 1945	Reclass. as "floating equipment" Dec. 3, 1948, and renumbered "RCT-3". Trans. to Norway June 16, 1951, as Sel (P-950). Returned Dec. 1, 1961. Scrapped in 1962 in country.
PT 604	Elco-A	June 13, 1945	Reclass. as "floating equipment" Dec. 3, 1948, and renumbered "RCT-4." Trans. to Norway May 2, 1951, as Sild (P-951). Returned Dec. 1, 1961. Scrapped in 1962 in country.
PT 605	Elco-A	June 18, 1945	Reclass. as "floating equipment" Dec. 3, 1948, and renumbered "RCT-5." Trans. to Norway May 2, 1951, as Skrei (P-952). Returned 1962. Scrapped 1962 in country.
PT 606	Elco-A	June 23, 1945	Reclass. as "floating equipment" Dec. 3, 1948, and renumbered "RCT-6." Trans. to Norway May 2, 1951, as Snarren (P-953). Renamed Lyr. Returned in 1962. Scrapped 1962 in country.
PT 607	Elco-A	July 4, 1945	Sold May 14, 1947.
PT 608	Elco-A	July 14, 1945	Reclass. as "floating equipment" Dec. 3, 1948, and renumbered "RCT-8." Trans. to Norway Mar. 16, 1951, as Springer (P-955). Returned in 1966. Scrapped in country.

Hull Number	Design/ Builder	Completed	Comments
PT 609	Elco-A	July 9, 1945	Reclass. as "floating equipment" Dec. 3, 1948, and renumbered "RCT-9." Trans. to Norway Mar. 16, 1951, as *Hai* (P-956). Returned in 1966. Scrapped in country.
PT 610	Elco-A	July 19, 1945	Reclass. as "floating equipment" Dec. 3, 1948, and renumbered "RCT-10." Trans. to Norway June 16, 1951, as *Hauk* (P-957). Renamed *Laks* in the late 1950s. Returned in 1966. Scrapped in country.
PT 611	Elco-A	July 25, 1945	Reclass. as "floating equipment" Dec. 3, 1948, and renumbered "RCT-11." Trans. to Norway Mar. 16, 1951, as *Hval* (P-958). Returned in 1966. Scrapped in country.
PT 612	Elco-A	July 31, 1945	Reclass. as "floating equipment" Dec. 3, 1948, and renumbered "RCT-12." Trans. to Norway Mar. 16, 1951, as *Delfin* (P-959). Returned Dec. 1, 1961. Scrapped in 1962 in country.
PT 613	Elco-A	Aug. 10, 1945	Trans. to South Korea Jan. 24, 1952, as *Olpaemi* (PT 26). Destroyed on Sept. 18, 1952, by explosion and resulting fire at Chinhae Naval Shipyard, Chinhae, South Korea. Remains broken up.
PT 614	Elco-A	Aug. 14, 1945	Reclass. as small boat "C 105340" on Aug. 26, 1946. Fate unknown.
PT 615	Elco-A	Sept. 5, 1945	Reclass. as small boat "C 105341" Aug. 26, 1946. Sold in 1946–47 and converted for commercial service. Still in existence operating out of Philadelphia, Penn.
PT 616	Elco-A	Sept. 11, 1945	Trans. South Korea Jan. 24, 1952, as *Kal mae ki* (PT 23). Returned in 1968. Scrapped in country.
PT 617	Elco-A	Sept. 21, 1945	Sold in Sept. 1947 for commercial service. Acquired by PT Boats Inc., Germantown, TN, in 1979 and restored. Now on display at Battleship Cove, Fall River, Mass.
PT 618	Elco-A	Sept. 24, 1945	Reclass. as small boat "C 105342" Aug. 26, 1946. Fate unknown.
PT 619	Elco-A	Oct. 1, 1945	Trans. South Korea Jan. 24, 1952, as *Kiroki* (PT 25). Sold to South Korea in 1963 for scrapping. Hulk still in existence in early 1968. Donated to PT Boats Inc., Germantown, Tenn., in 1968. Shipped back to the United States. Found to be beyond restoration and repair. Cannibalized to assist in the restoration of PT 617. Remains destroyed by burning.
PT 620	Elco-A	Oct. 5, 1945	Trans. South Korea Jan. 24, 1952, as *Jebi* (PT 27). Returned in 1963. Scrapped in 1964 in country.
PT 621	Elco-A	Oct. 12, 1945	Sold July 15, 1947, for commercial service. Last reported as still in existence in 1953.
PT 622	Elco-A	Oct. 24, 1945	Sold Mar. 24, 1947.
PT 623	Elco-A	-----	Keel laid Apr. 30, 1945. Construction canceled Sept. 12, 1945. Completed for commercial service.
PT 624	Elco-A	-----	Keel laid May 4, 1945. Construction canceled Sept. 12, 1945. Completed for commercial service. Last reported as still in existence in 1963.
PT 625	Higgins	Dec. 7, 1944	Lend-leased USSR May 22, 1945. See comments under PT 415 for disposition.
PT 626	Higgins	Dec. 18, 1944	Lend-leased USSR Navy May 22, 1945. See comments under PT 414 for disposition.
PT 627	Higgins	Jan. 7, 1945	Lend-lease to USSR May 22, 1945. See comments under PT 414 for disposition.

Hull Number	Design/ Builder	Completed	Comments
PT 628	Higgins	Jan. 16, 1945	Lend-lease to USSR May 22, 1945. See comments under PT 414 for disposition.
PT 629	Higgins	Jan. 29, 1945	Lend-lease to USSR June 8, 1945. See comments under PT 414 for disposition.
PT 630	Higgins	Feb. 8, 1945	Lend-lease to USSR June 8, 1945. See comments under PT 414 for disposition.
PT 631	Higgins	Feb. 18, 1945	Lend-lease to USSR June 8, 1945. See comments under PT 415 for disposition.
PT 632	Higgins	Mar. 15, 1945	Lend-lease to USSR June 8, 1945. See comments under PT 414 for disposition.
PT 633	Higgins	Mar. 14, 1945	Lend-lease to USSR June 8, 1945. See comments under PT 414 for disposition.
PT 634	Higgins	Mar. 21, 1945	Lend-lease to USSR June 8, 1945. See comments under PT 414 for disposition.
PT 635	Higgins	Mar. 23, 1945	Lend-lease to USSR June 8, 1945. See comments under PT 414 for disposition.
PT 636	Higgins	Mar. 26, 1945	Lend-lease to USSR June 8, 1945. See comments under PT 414 for disposition.
PT 637	Higgins	Apr. 10, 1945	Lend-lease to USSR June 30, 1945. See comments under PT 414 for disposition.
PT 638	Higgins	Apr. 12, 1945	Lend-lease to USSR June 30, 1945. See comments under PT 414 for disposition.
PT 639	Higgins	Apr. 16, 1945	Lend-lease to USSR June 30, 1945. See comments under PT 414 for disposition.
PT 640	Higgins	Apr. 18, 1945	Lend-lease to USSR June 30, 1945. See comments under PT 414 for disposition.
PT 641	Higgins	Apr. 23, 1945	Lend-lease to USSR Aug. 3, 1945. See comments under PT 414 for disposition.
PT 642	Higgins	Apr. 28, 1945	Lend-lease to USSR Aug. 3, 1945. See comments under PT 414 for disposition.
PT 643	Higgins	May 2, 1945	Lend-lease to USSR Aug. 3, 1945. See comments under PT 414 for disposition.
PT 644	Higgins	May 11, 1945	Lend-lease to USSR Aug. 3, 1945. See comments under PT 414 for disposition.
PT 645	Higgins	May 13, 1945	Lend-lease to USSR Aug. 23, 1945. See comments under PT 414 for disposition.
PT 646	Higgins	May 17, 1945	Lend-lease to USSR Aug. 23, 1945. See comments under PT 414 for disposition.
PT 647	Higgins	May 22, 1945	Lend-lease to USSR Aug. 23, 1945. See comments under PT 414 for disposition.
PT 648	Higgins	May 26, 1945	Lend-lease to USSR Aug. 23, 1945. See comments under PT 414 for disposition.
PT 649	Higgins	May 30, 1945	Lend-lease to USSR Aug. 30, 1945. See comments under PT 414 for disposition.
PT 650	Higgins	June 15, 1945	Lend-lease to USSR Aug. 30, 1945. See comments under PT 414 for disposition.
PT 651	Higgins	June 20, 1945	Lend-lease to USSR Aug. 30, 1945. See comments under PT 415 for disposition.
PT 652	Higgins	June 26, 1945	Lend-lease to USSR Aug. 30, 1945. See comments under PT 414 for disposition.
PT 653	Higgins	June 29, 1945	Lend-lease to USSR Aug. 30, 1945. See comments under PT 414 for disposition.

Hull Number	Design/ Builder	Completed	Comments
PT 654	Higgins	July 6, 1945	Lend-lease to USSR Aug. 30, 1945. See comments under PT 414 for disposition.
PT 655	Higgins	July 11, 1945	Lend-lease to USSR Aug. 30, 1945. See comments under PT 414 for disposition.
PT 656	Higgins	July 17, 1945	Lend-lease to USSR Aug. 30, 1945. See comments under PT 414 for disposition.
PT 657	Higgins	July 21, 1945	Was to have been Lend-lease to USSR, but trans. canceled due to the end of the war. Sold Nov. 14, 1946, for commercial service. Still exists, operating out of San Diego, CA.
PT 658	Higgins	July 30, 1945	Was to have been Lend-lease to USSR, but trans. canceled due to the end of the war. Reclass. as small boat "C 105343" Aug. 26, 1946. Assigned to the Bureau of Aeronautics as a remote-controlled target. Stationed at the Naval Air Facility, Point Mugu, Calif. Reclass. as "floating equipment" Dec. 3, 1948. Sold June 30, 1958. Acquired in 1993 by Save the PT Boats Inc. in Oregon. Museum/memorial at the Naval Reserve Center, Swan Island, Portland, Ore., having been fully restored.
PT 659	Higgins	Aug. 2, 1945	Was to have been Lend-leased to USSR, but trans. canceled due to the end of the war. Reclass. as small boat "C 105344" Aug. 26, 1946. Assigned to the Bureau of Aeronautics as a remote-controlled target. Stationed at the Naval Air Facility, Point Mugu, Calif. Reclass. as "floating equipment" Dec. 3, 1948. Trans. to Naval Inshore Undersea Warfare Group One Sept. 13, 1968. Trans. back to Point Mugu for use as a remote-controlled target May 27, 1970. Donated to Save the PT Boats, Inc. in Oregon. Museum/memorial at Fort Vancouver National Historical Site, Vancouver, Wash., having been fully restored.
PT 660	Higgins	Aug. 10, 1945	Was to have been Lend-leased to USSR, but trans. canceled due to the end of the war. Reclass. as small boat "C 105345" Aug. 26, 1946. Assigned to the Bureau of Aeronautics as a remote-controlled target. Stationed at the Naval Air Facility, Point Mugu, Calif. Reclass. as "floating equipment" Dec. 3, 1948. Sunk as a target off Port Hueneme, Calif., in the early 1990s.
PT 661	Vosper-B	Oct. 30, 1944	Lend-lease to USSR Nov. 26, 1944. Returned July 2, 1955. Fate unknown.
PT 662	Vosper-B	Nov. 18, 1944	Trans. to USSR in a knocked-down condition (kit form) Dec. 12, 1944, under Lend-lease. Returned July 9, 1955. Fate unknown.
PT 663	Vosper-B	Nov. 18, 1944	Trans. to USSR in a knocked-down condition (kit form) Dec. 12, 1944, under Lend-lease. Returned July 14, 1955. Fate unknown.
PT 664	Vosper-B	Nov. 18, 1944	Trans. to USSR in a knocked-down condition (kit form) Dec. 12, 1944, under Lend-lease. Returned July 14, 1955. Fate unknown.
PT 665	Vosper-B	Nov. 18, 1944	Trans. to USSR in a knocked-down condition (kit form) Dec. 12, 1944, under Lend-lease. Returned July 9, 1955. Fate unknown.

Hull Number	Design/ Builder	Completed	Comments
PT 666	Vosper-B	Nov. 18, 1944	Trans. to USSR in a knocked-down condition (kit form) Dec. 12, 1944, under Lend-lease. Returned July 14, 1955. Fate unknown.
PT 667	Vosper-B	Nov. 18, 1944	Trans. to USSR in a knocked-down condition (kit form) Dec. 12, 1944, under Lend-lease. Returned July 14, 1955. Fate unknown.
PT 668	Vosper-B	Nov. 18, 1944	Trans. to USSR in a knocked-down condition (kit form) Dec. 12, 1944, under Lend-lease. Returned July 20, 1955. Fate unknown.
PT 669	Vosper-B	Nov. 18, 1944	Trans. to USSR in a knocked-down condition (kit form) Dec. 12, 1944, under Lend-lease. Returned July 14, 1955. Fate unknown.
PT 670	Vosper-B	Nov. 18, 1944	Trans. to USSR in a knocked-down condition (kit form) Dec. 12, 1944, under Lend-lease. Returned July 2, 1955. Fate unknown.
PT 671	Vosper-B	Nov. 18, 1944	Trans. to USSR in a knocked-down condition (kit form) Dec. 12, 1944, under Lend-lease. Returned July 2, 1955. Fate unknown.
PT 672	Vosper-B	Nov. 18, 1944	Trans. to USSR in a knocked-down condition (kit form) Dec. 12, 1944, under Lend-lease. Returned July 9, 1955. Fate unknown.
PT 673	Vosper-B	Nov. 18, 1944	Trans. to USSR in a knocked-down condition (kit form) Dec. 12, 1944, under Lend-lease. Returned July 9, 1955. Fate unknown.
PT 674	Vosper-B	Nov. 18, 1944	Trans. to USSR in a knocked-down condition (kit form) Dec. 12, 1944, under Lend-lease. Returned July 14, 1955. Fate unknown.
PT 675	Vosper-B	Nov. 18, 1944	Trans. to USSR in a knocked-down condition (kit form) Dec. 12, 1944, under Lend-lease. Returned July 14, 1955. Fate unknown.
PT 676	Vosper-B	Dec. 6, 1944	Lend-leased USSR Dec. 25, 1944. Returned July 9, 1955. Fate unknown.
PT 677	Vosper-B	Dec. 6, 1944	Lend-leased USSR Dec. 25, 1944. Returned July 9, 1955. Fate unknown.
PT 678	Vosper-B	Dec. 13, 1944	Lend-leased USSR Jan. 8, 1945. Returned July 2, 1955. Fate unknown.
PT 679	Vosper-B	Dec. 13, 1944	Lend-leased USSR Jan. 8, 1945. Returned July 2, 1955. Fate unknown.
PT 680	Vosper-B	Dec. 19, 1944	Lend-leased USSR Mar. 3, 1945. Returned July 9, 1955. Fate unknown.
PT 681	Vosper-B	Dec. 19, 1944	Lend-leased USSR Mar. 3, 1945. Returned July 20, 1955. Fate unknown.
PT 682	Vosper-B	Dec. 27, 1944	Lend-leased USSR Mar. 15, 1945. Returned July 20, 1955. Fate unknown.
PT 683	Vosper-B	Jan. 1, 1945	Lend-leased USSR Mar. 15, 1945. Destroyed June 29, 1956, in Pechenga Gulf, Barents Sea, USSR under U.S. supervision.
PT 684	Vosper-B	Feb. 12, 1945	Lend-leased USSR Apr. 11, 1945. See comments under PT 683 for disposition.
PT 685	Vosper-B	Feb. 14, 1945	Lend-leased USSR Apr. 11, 1945. See comments under PT 683 for disposition.
PT 686	Vosper-B	Feb. 23, 1945	Lend-leased USSR Apr. 11, 1945. See comments under PT 683 for disposition.

Hull Number	Design/ Builder	Completed	Comments
PT 687	Vosper-B	Feb. 23, 1945	Lend-leased USSR May 16, 1945. See comments under PT 683 for disposition.
PT 688	Vosper-B	Mar. 2, 1945	Lend-leased USSR May 16, 1945. See comments under PT 683 for disposition.
PT 689	Vosper-B	Mar. 3, 1945	Lend-leased USSR May 18, 1945. See comments under PT 683 for disposition.
PT 690	Vosper-B	Mar. 7, 1945	Lend-leased USSR May 18, 1945. See comments under PT 683 for disposition.
PT 691	Vosper-B	Mar. 9, 1945	Lend-leased USSR May 19, 1945. See comments under PT 683 for disposition.
PT 692	Vosper-B	Mar. 10, 1945	Lend-leased USSR May 19, 1945. See comments under PT 683 for disposition.
PT 693	Vosper-B	Mar. 21, 1945	Was to have been Lend-leased to USSR. Trans. canceled while en route to USSR. Trans. to the War Shipping Administration Aug. 15, 1946, for disposal. Sold in 1946 for commercial service. Last reported as still in existence in 1981.
PT 694	Vosper-B	Apr. 5, 1945	Was to have been Lend-leased to USSR. Trans. canceled while en route to USSR. Trans. to the War Shipping Administration Aug. 15, 1946, for disposal. Sold in 1946 to Howard Hughes. Served as a tender to his seaplane "Spruce Goose." In late 1950s sold to the studio that made the TV show "McHale's Navy" for use in that show. Became "PT 73." Sold after show was canceled. Sunk in a storm in March 1993 at Santa Barbara, Calif.
PT 695	Vosper-B	Apr. 5, 1945	Was to have been Lend-leased to USSR. Trans. canceled while en route to USSR. Trans. to the War Shipping Administration Aug. 15, 1946, for disposal. Sold in 1946 for commercial service. Still in existence at Rio Vista, Calif.
PT 696	Vosper-B	Apr. 14, 1945	Was to have been Lend-leased to USSR. Trans. canceled while en route to USSR. Trans. to the War Shipping Administration Aug. 15, 1946, for disposal. Sold in 1946 for commercial service. Sunk in the early 1980s after striking a floating telephone pole in San Francisco Bay, Calif.
PT 697	Vosper-B	Apr. 18, 1945	Was to have been Lend-leased to USSR. Canceled. Sold and removed from Navy custody Sept. 11, 1946. Last reported as still in existence in 1952.
PT 698	Vosper-B	Apr. 21, 1945	Was to have been Lend-leased to USSR. Canceled. Sold and removed from Navy custody Sept. 11, 1946.
PT 699	Vosper-B	May 1, 1945	Was to have been Lend-leased to USSR. Canceled. Sold and removed from Navy custody Sept. 19, 1946.
PT 700	Vosper-B	May 3, 1945	Was to have been Lend-leased to USSR. Canceled. Sold and removed from Navy custody Oct. 21, 1946.
PT 701	Vosper-B	May 9, 1945	Was to have been Lend-leased to USSR. Canceled. Sold and removed from Navy custody Sept. 11, 1946. Converted for merchant service. Last reported as still in existence in 1951.
PT 702	Vosper-B	May 14, 1945	Was to have been Lend-leased to USSR. Canceled. Sold and removed from Navy custody Sept. 17, 1946.

Hull Number	Design/ Builder	Completed	Comments
PT 703	Vosper-B	May 22, 1945	Was to have been Lend-leased to USSR. Canceled. Trans. to the War Shipping Administration for disposal June 25, 1946. Converted for merchant service. Foundered in 1954.
PT 704	Vosper-B	May 26, 1945	Was to have been Lend-leased to USSR. Canceled. Trans. to the War Shipping Administration for disposal July 16, 1946. Converted for merchant service. Last reported as still in existence in 1974.
PT 705	Vosper-B	May 30, 1945	Was to have been Lend-leased to USSR. Canceled. Trans. to the War Shipping Administration for disposal July 10, 1946. Converted for merchant service. Postwar records on this boat are confusing as this boat is recorded as operating in the United States and Central America at the same time.
PT 706	Vosper-B	June 8, 1945	Was to have been Lend-leased to USSR. Canceled. Trans. to the War Shipping Administration for disposal June 25, 1946. Converted for merchant service. Last reported as still in existence in 1964.
PT 707	Vosper-B	June 14, 1945	Was to have been Lend-leased to USSR. Canceled. Trans. to the War Shipping Administration for disposal June 25, 1946. Converted for merchant service. Last reported as still in existence in 1948.
PT 708	Vosper-B	June 23, 1945	Was to have been Lend-leased to USSR. Canceled. Trans. to the Maritime Commission for disposal Aug. 12, 1946. Converted for merchant service. Caught fire and burned in 1972.
PT 709	Vosper-B	June 27, 1945	Was to have been Lend-leased to USSR. Canceled. Trans. to the War Shipping Administration for disposal July 17, 1946. Converted for merchant service. Last reported as still in existence in 1956.
PT 710	Vosper-B	July 4, 1945	Was to have been Lend-leased to USSR. Canceled. Trans. to the War Shipping Administration for disposal June 25, 1946. Converted for merchant service. Last reported as still in existence in 1948.
PT 711	Vosper-B	July 11, 1945	Was to have been Lend-leased to USSR. Canceled. Trans. to the War Shipping Administration for disposal July 17, 1946.
PT 712	Vosper-B	July 18, 1945	Was to have been Lend-leased to USSR. Canceled. Trans. to the Maritime Commission for disposal Sept. 13, 1946. Converted for merchant service. Fate unknown.
PT 713	Vosper-B	July 19, 1945	Was to have been Lend-leased to USSR. Canceled. Trans. to the Maritime Commission for disposal Sept. 13, 1946. Converted for merchant service. Last reported as still in existence in 1978 rotting away at Yanks Boat Yard.
PT 714	Vosper-B	July 23, 1945	Was to have been Lend-leased to USSR. Canceled. Trans. to the Maritime Commission for disposal Sept. 11, 1946. Converted for merchant service. Last reported as still in existence in 1964.
PT 715	Vosper-B	July 29, 1945	Was to have been Lend-leased to USSR. Canceled. Trans. to Cuba Aug. 14, 1946, as *R-41*. Sunk Oct. 5, 1948, in a hurricane, but salvaged, repaired, and converted to search and rescue craft. Disposed of in 1976.

Hull Number	Design/ Builder	Completed	Comments
PT 716	Vosper-B	Aug. 2, 1945	Was to have been Lend-leased to USSR. Canceled. Trans. to Cuba July 19, 1946, as *R-42*. Sunk Oct. 5, 1948, in a hurricane, but salvaged, repaired and converted to search and rescue craft. Disposed of in 1976.
PT 717	Vosper-B	Aug. 2, 1945	Was to have been Lend-leased to USSR. Canceled. Sold June 26, 1947.
PT 718	Vosper-B	Aug. 15, 1945	Was to have been Lend-leased to USSR. Canceled. Trans. to the Maritime Commission for disposal June 27, 1947. Sold.
PT 719	Vosper-B	Aug. 24, 1945	Was to have been Lend-leased to USSR. Canceled. Trans. to the Maritime Commission for disposal June 27, 1947. Sold 1947 for commercial service. Caught fire and burned in 1975. Constructive total loss.
PT 720	Vosper-B	Aug. 29, 1945	Was to have been Lend-leased to USSR. Canceled. Trans. to the Maritime Commission for disposal June 18, 1947. Sold.
PT 721	Vosper-B	Sept. 4, 1945	Was to have been Lend-leased to USSR. Canceled. Sold July 21, 1947.
PT 722	Vosper-B	Sept. 6, 1945	Was to have been Lend-leased to USSR. Canceled. Trans. to the Maritime Commission for disposal Aug. 15, 1947. Sold.
PT 723	Vosper-B	Sept. 14, 1945	Was to have been Lend-leased to USSR. Canceled. Trans. To Maritime Commission for disposal Apr. 12, 1947. Sold.
PT 724	Vosper-B	Sept. 21, 1945	Was to have been Lend-leased to USSR. Canceled. Trans. to the Maritime Commission for disposal July 18, 1947. Sold in 1947. Converted for commercial service. Still in existence.
PT 725	Vosper-B	Oct. 1, 1945	Was to have been Lend-leased to USSR. Canceled. Trans. to the Maritime Commission for disposal Aug. 18, 1947. Sold.
PT 726	Vosper-B	Oct. 6, 1945	Was to have been Lend-leased to USSR. Canceled. Trans. to the Maritime Commission for disposal June 20, 1947. Sold Aug. 16, 1947.
PT 727	Vosper-B	Oct. 13, 1945	Was to have been Lend-leased to USSR. Canceled. Trans. to the Maritime Commission for disposition June 20, 1947. Sold.
PT 728	Vosper-B	Oct. 20, 1945	Was to have been Lend-leased to USSR. Canceled. Trans. to the Maritime Commission for disposal Aug. 16, 1947. Sold Aug. 18, 1947. Converted for commercial service. Still in existence under the [text missing] operating out of Key West, FL.
PT 729	Vosper-B	Oct. 27, 1945	Was to have been Lend-leased to USSR. Canceled. Reclass. as small boat "C 104348" Nov. 16, 1945. Trans. to the Maritime Commission for disposal Sept. 12, 1947. Sold.
PT 730	Vosper-B	Oct. 30, 1945	Was to have been Lend-leased to USSR. Canceled. Reclass. as a small boat "C 104347" Nov. 16, 1945. Trans. to the Maritime Commission for disposal Sept. 12, 1947. Sold Dec. 5, 1947.
PT 731	Elco-A	Sept. 19, 1944	Lend-leased USSR Oct. 25, 1944. See comments under PT 411 for disposition.

Hull Number	Design/ Builder	Completed	Comments
PT 732	Elco-A	Oct. 3, 1944	Trans. to USSR in a knocked-down condition (kit form) Dec. 12, 1944, under Lend-lease. Returned July 14, 1955. Fate unknown.
PT 733	Elco-A	Oct. 10, 1944	See comments under PT 732.
PT 734	Elco-A	Oct. 10, 1944	Trans. to USSR in a knocked-down condition (kit form) Dec. 12, 1944, under Lend-lease. Returned July 20, 1955. Fate unknown.
PT 735	Elco-A	Oct. 24, 1944	See comments under PT 734.
PT 736	Elco-A	Oct. 24, 1944	See comments under PT 734.
PT 737	Elco-A	Nov. 14, 1944	See comments under PT 734.
PT 738	Elco-A	Nov. 14, 1944	Trans. to USSR in a knocked-down condition (kit form) Dec. 12, 1944, under Lend-lease. See comments under PT 414 for disposition.
PT 739	Elco-A	Nov. 21, 1944	Trans. to USSR in a knocked-down condition (kit form) Dec. 12, 1944, under Lend-lease. Returned July 2, 1955. Fate unknown.
PT 740	Elco-A	Nov. 21, 1944	See comments under PT 739.
PT 741	Elco-A	Nov. 25, 1944	Trans. to USSR in a knocked-down condition (kit form) Dec. 12, 1944, under Lend-lease. See comments under PT 414 for disposition.
PT 742	Elco-A	Nov. 25, 1944	Trans. to USSR in a knocked-down condition (kit form) Dec. 12, 1944, under Lend-lease. Returned July 25, 1955. Fate unknown.
PT 743	Elco-A	Nov. 30, 1944	See comments under PT 732.
PT 744	Elco-A	Nov. 30, 1944	Trans. to USSR in a knocked-down condition (kit form) Dec. 12, 1944, under Lend-lease. Returned July 9, 1955. Fate unknown.
PT 745	Elco-A	Dec. 9, 1944	Trans. to USSR in a knocked-down condition (kit form) Jan. 15, 1945, under Lend-lease. Returned July 25, 1955. Fate unknown.
PT 746	Elco-A	Dec. 9, 1944	See comments under PT 745.
PT 747	Elco-A	Dec. 14, 1944	Trans. to USSR in a knocked-down condition (kit form) Jan. 15, 1945, under Lend-lease. See comments under PT 414 For disposition.
PT 748	Elco-A	Dec. 14, 1944	Trans. to USSR in a knocked-down condition (kit form) Jan. 15, 1945, under Lend-lease. Returned July 20, 1955. Fate unknown.
PT 749	Elco-A	Dec. 23, 1944	Trans. to USSR in a knocked-down condition (kit form) Jan. 15, 1945, under Lend-lease. See comments under PT 414 For disposition.
PT 750	Elco-A	Dec. 23, 1944	Trans. to USSR in a knocked-down condition (kit form) Jan. 15, 1945, under Lend-lease. Returned July 9, 1955. Fate unknown.
PT 751	Elco-A	Dec. 30, 1944	See comments under PT 750.
PT 752	Elco-A	Dec. 30, 1944	See comments under PT 750.
PT 753	Elco-A	Jan. 4, 1945	See comments under PT 749.
PT 754	Elco-A	Jan. 4, 1945	See comments under PT 749.
PT 755	Elco-A	Jan. 10, 1945	Trans. to USSR in a knocked-down condition (kit form) Feb. 21, 1945, under Lend-lease. See comments under PT 414 for disposition.
PT 756	Elco- A	Jan. 10, 1945	Trans. to USSR in a knocked-down condition (kit form) Feb. 21, 1945, under Lend-lease. Returned July 14, 1955. Fate unknown.

Hull Number	Design/ Builder	Completed	Comments
PT 757	Elco-A	Jan. 20, 1945	Trans. to USSR in a knocked-down condition (kit form) Feb. 21, 1945, under Lend-lease. Returned July 14, 1955. Fate unknown.
PT 758	Elco-A	Jan. 20, 1945	See comments under PT 757.
PT 759	Elco-A	Jan. 26, 1945	See comments under PT 757.
PT 760	Elco-A	Jan. 26, 1945	See comments under PT 757.
PT 761	Elco-A	-----	Keel laid Mar. 19, 1945. Construction canceled Aug. 14, 1945. Completed under separate contract for commercial service. Still in existence in the Jacksonville, FL, area as a river cruiser under the ownership of Mr. Bob Whyte. In poor condition.
PT 762	Elco-A	-----	Keel laid May 10, 1945. Construction canceled Aug. 14, 1945. Hull broken up on stocks.
PT 763	Elco-A	-----	Keel laid May 15, 1945. Construction canceled Aug. 14, 1945. Completed under separate contract for commercial service. Cut down to 55 ft. during construction. Caught fire and burned in 1974.
PT 764	Elco-A	-----	Keel laid May 19, 1945. See comments under PT 762.
PT 765	Elco-A	-----	Keel laid May 24, 1945. See comments under PT 762.
PT 766	Elco-A	-----	Keel laid May 30, 1945. See comments under PT 762.
PT 767	Elco-A	-----	Keel laid June 5, 1945. See comments under PT 762.
PT 768	Elco-A	-----	Keel laid June 11, 1945. Construction canceled Aug. 14, 1945. Completed under separate contract for commercial service. Sunk in collision in 1969.
PT 769	Elco-A	-----	Keel laid June 16, 1945. See comments under PT 762 .
PT 770	Elco-A	-----	Keel laid June 22, 1945. Construction canceled Aug. 14, 1945. Completed under separate contract for commercial service as a 50-ft. passenger vessel. In 1956 she ran aground and was stranded.
PT 771	Elco-A	-----	Keel laid June 28, 1945. See comments under PT 762.
PT 772	Elco-A	-----	Keel laid July 4, 1945. See comments under PT 762.
PT 773	Elco-A	-----	Keel laid July 10, 1945. Construction canceled Aug. 14, 1945. Completed under separate contract for commercial service as a 65-ft. passenger vessel. Fate unknown.
PT 774	Elco-A	-----	Keel laid July 17, 1945. Construction canceled Aug. 14, 1945. Completed under separate contract for commercial service as a 58-ft. passenger vessel. Last reported as still in existence in 1975.
PT 775	Elco-A	-----	Keel laid July 23, 1945. See comments under PT 762 .
PT 776	Elco-A	-----	Keel laid July 30, 1945. See comments under PT 762.
PT 777	Elco-A	-----	Keel laid Aug. 3, 1945. See comments under PT 762.
PT 778	Elco-A	-----	Keel laid Aug. 9, 1945. See comments under PT 762.
PT 779– 790	Elco-A	-----	Construction canceled Aug. 14. 1945.
PT 791	Higgins	Sept. 19, 1945	Was to have been Lend-leased to USSR. Canceled. Trans. to the War Shipping Administration for disposal Oct. 11, 1946. Sold.
PT 792	Higgins	Sept. 20, 1945	Was to have been Lend-leased to USSR. Canceled. Trans. to the War Shipping Administration for disposal Oct. 31, 1946. Sold. Converted for commerical service. Last reported as still in existence in 1951.

Hull Number	Design/ Builder	Completed	Comments
PT 793	Higgins	Oct. 23, 1945	Was to have been Lend-leased to USSR. Canceled. Trans. to the War Shipping Administration for disposal Oct. 11, 1946. Sold. Converted for commercial service. Last reported as still in existence in 1976.
PT 794	Higgins	Oct. 24, 1945	Was to have been Lend-leased to USSR. Canceled. Trans. to the War Shipping Administration for disposal Oct. 31, 1946. Sold.
PT 795	Higgins	Oct. 25, 1945	Was to have been Lend-leased to USSR. Canceled. Reclass. as small boat "C 104350" Nov. 16, 1945. Sold Apr. 10, 1950.
PT 796	Higgins	Oct. 26, 1945	Was to have been Lend-leased to USSR. Canceled. Reclass. as small boat "C 104351" Nov. 16, 1945. Reclass. as "floating equipment" July 17, 1947. Acquired by PT Boats Inc., Memphis, TN, in 1970 and restored. Now on display at Battleship Cove, Fall River, MA.
PT 797	Higgins	----	Keel laid May 11, 1945. Launched July 5, 1945. Was to have been Lend-leased to USSR. Construction for the U.S. Navy canceled Sept. 7, 1945. Completed for the Argentine Navy as LT-1.
PT 798	Higgins	----	Keel laid May 19, 1945. Launched July 13, 1945. Was to have been Lend-leased to USSR. Construction for the U.S. Navy canceled Sept. 7, 1945. Completed for the Argentine Navy as LT-2.
PT 799	Higgins	----	Keel laid May 28, 1945. Launched July 23, 1945. Was to have been Lend-leased to USSR. Construction for the U.S. Navy canceled Sept. 7, 1945. Completed for the Argentine Navy as LT-3.
PT 800	Higgins	----	Keel laid June 14, 1945. Launched Aug. 4, 1945. Was to have been Lend-leased to USSR. Construction for the U.S. Navy canceled Sept. 7, 1945. Completed for the Argentine Navy as LT-4.
PT 801	Higgins	----	Keel laid June 22, 1945. Launched Aug. 14, 1945. Was to have been Lend-leased to USSR. Construction for the U.S. Navy canceled Sept. 7, 1945. Completed for the Argentine Navy as LT-5. Pulled ashore for use as an office at the Ushuaia Sailing Club, Tierra del Fuego, Argentina. Still in existence.
PT 802	Higgins	----	Keel laid June 30, 1945. Was to have been Lend-leased to USSR. Construction for the U.S. Navy canceled Aug. 27, 1945. Completed for the Argentine Navy as LT-6.
PT 803	Higgins	----	Keel laid July 12, 1945. Was to have been Lend-leased to USSR. Construction for the U.S. Navy canceled Aug. 27, 1945. Completed for the Argentine Navy as LT-7.
PT 804	Higgins	----	Keel laid July 23, 1945. Was to have been Lend-leased to USSR. Construction for the U.S. Navy canceled Aug. 27, 1945. Completed for the Argentine Navy as LT-8.
PT 805	Higgins	----	Keel laid Aug. 3, 1945. Was to have been Lend-leased to USSR. Construction for the U.S. Navy canceled Aug. 27, 1945. Completed for the Argentine Navy as LT-9.
PT 806–808	Higgins	----	Were to have been Lend-leased to USSR. Construction for the U.S. Navy canceled Aug. 27, 1945.

Hull Number	Design/ Builder	Completed	Comments
PT 809	Groton	Feb. 9, 1951	Taken out of service in Aug. 1986. Fate unknown.
PT 810	Bath	Dec. 5, 1950	Stricken on Nov. 1, 1959. Reinstated on Navy List and reclass. PTF 1 on Dec. 21, 1962. See comments under PTF 1 in table below.
PT 811	Trumpy-A	Mar. 6, 1951	Stricken on Nov. 1, 1959. Reinstated on Navy List and reclass. PTF 2 on Dec. 21, 1962. See comments under PTF 2 in table below.
PT 812	Phil.	May 3, 1951	Reclass. as small boat Nov. 1, 1959. Trans. to U.S. Army in 1959. Trans. S. Korea in Apr. 1967 as *Olpemi* (PB-1). Disposed of in 1968.
PT 813	Denmark	Nov. 1, 1954	Built under the U.S. Military Defense Assistance Program for Denmark. Commissioned as *Flyvefisken* (P-500). Sold for scrap May 1976.
PT 814	Denmark	May 20, 1955	Built under the U.S. Military Defense Assistance Program for Denmark. Commissioned as *Havkatten* (P-502). Sold for scrap in May 1976.
PT 815	Denmark	Sept. 10, 1955	Built under the U.S. Military Defense Assistance Program for Denmark. Commissioned as *Svaerdfisken* (P-505). Sold for scrap in May 1976.
PT 816	Copenhagen	Jan. 24, 1955	Built under the U.S. Military Defense Assistance Program for Denmark. Commissioned as *Hajen* (P-501). Sold for scrap in May 1976.
PT 817	Copenhagen	Apr. 25, 1955	Built under the U.S. Military Defense Assistance Program for Denmark. Commissioned as *Laxen* (P-503). Sold for scrap in May 1976.
PT 818	Copenhagen	June 24, 1955	Built under the U.S. Military Defense Assistance Program for Denmark. Commissioned as *Makrelen* (P-504). Sold for scrap in May 1976.
PT 819	Denmark	Oct. 4, 1962	Built under the U.S. Military Defense Assistance Program for Denmark. Commissioned as *Falken* (P-506). To reserve in 1977. Sold for scrap July 10, 1979.
PT 820	Denmark	Dec. 15, 1962	Built under the U.S. Military Defense Assistance Program for Denmark. Commissioned as *Glenten* (P-507). To reserve in 1977. Sold July 10, 1979, for scrapping.
PT 821	Denmark	Apr. 26, 1963	Built under the U.S. Military Defense Assistance Program for Denmark. Commissioned as *Gribben* (P-508). To reserve in 1977. Scrapped in 1979.
PT 822	Denmark	June 6, 1963	Built under the U.S. Military Defense Assistance Program for Denmark. Commissioned as *Hogen* (P-509). To reserve in 1977. Scrapped in 1979.

Motor Boats, Submarine Chaser

Hull Number	Design/ Builder	Completed	Comments
PTC 1	Elco-A	Feb. 13, 1941	Lend-lease to UK July 15, 1941, as MGB 82. Returned Mar. 9, 1945. Disposed of in Mar. 1946.
PTC 2	Elco-A	Feb. 17, 1941	Lend-lease to UK July 15, 1941, as MGB 83. Returned May 16, 1945. Disposed of in Mar. 1946.
PTC 3	Elco-A	Feb. 20, 1941	Lend-lease to UK July 15, 1941, as MGB 84. Returned July 21, 1945. Disposed of in Mar. 1946.
PTC 4	Elco-A	Mar 7, 1941	Lend-lease to UK July 15, 1941, as MGB 85. Returned July 21, 1945. Disposed of in Dec. 1947.
PTC 5	Elco-A	Feb. 17, 1941	Lend-lease to UK Apr. 4, 1941, as MGB 86. Returned July 21, 1945. Disposed of in Dec. 1947. Last reported as still in existence in 1991 and being restored.

Hull Number	Design/ Builder	Completed	Comments
PTC 6	Elco-A	Feb. 20, 1941	Lend-lease to UK Apr. 4, 1941, as MGB 87. Returned July 21, 1945. Disposed of in Dec. 1947.
PTC 7	Elco-A	Mar 7, 1941	Lend-lease to UK Apr. 4, 1941, as MGB 88. Returned June 19, 1945. Disposed of in Jan. 1948.
PTC 8	Elco-A	Mar 8, 1941	Lend-lease to UK Apr. 4, 1941, as MGB 89. Returned Apr. 3, 1945. Disposed of in Mar. 1946.
PTC 9	Elco-A	Mar 4, 1941	Lend-lease to UK Apr. 4, 1941, as MGB 90. Destroyed by accidental fire July 16, 1941.
PTC 10	Elco-A	Mar 20, 1941	Lend-lease to UK Apr. 4, 1941, as MGB 91. Returned July 6, 1945. Disposed of in Dec. 1947.
PTC 11	Elco-A	Mar 27, 1941	Lend-lease to UK Apr. 4, 1941, as MGB 92. Destroyed by accidental fire July 16, 1941.
PTC 12	Elco-A	Mar 28, 1941	Lend-lease to UK Apr. 4, 1941, as MGB 93. Returned to U.S. Sept. 13, 1945. Disposed of in Nov. 1946.
PTC 13–24	——	——	Reclass. PT 33–44 Mar. 24, 1941.
PTC 25, 26	——	——	Reclass. PT 57, 58 June 19, 1941.
PTC 27–36	——	——	Reclass. BPT 11–20 June 19, 1941. Reclass. PT 59–68 Dec. 12, 1941.
PTC 37	Trumpy-B	Oct. 16, 1943	Ex RPC 51. Reclass. PTC 37 Mar. 29, 1943. Reclass. as small boat Aug. 1, 1943. Lend-lease to USSR Oct. 21, 1943. Sunk during the war.
PTC 38	Trumpy-B	Oct. 22, 1943	Ex RPC 52. Reclass. PTC 38 Mar. 29, 1943. Reclass. as small boat Aug. 1, 1943. Lend-lease to USSR Dec. 8, 1943. Sunk during the war.
PTC 39	Trumpy-B	Oct. 30, 1943	Ex RPC 53. Reclass. PTC 39 Mar. 29, 1943. Reclass. as small boat on Aug. 1, 1943. Lend-lease to USSR Dec. 8, 1943. Sunk during the war.
PTC 40	Trumpy-B	Nov. 17, 1943	Ex RPC 54. Reclass. PTC 40 Mar. 29, 1943. Reclass. as small boat Aug. 1, 1943. Lend-lease to USSR Dec. 8, 1943. Sunk during the war.
PTC 41	Trumpy-B	Nov. 20, 1943	Ex RPC 55. Reclass. PTC 41 Mar. 31, 1943. Reclass. as small boat Aug. 1, 1943. Lend-lease to USSR Dec. 12, 1943. Returned June 16, 1954. Fate unknown.
PTC 42	Trumpy-B	Nov. 29, 1943	Ex RPC 56. Reclass. PTC 42 Mar. 31, 1943. Reclass. as small boat Aug. 1, 1943. Lend-lease to USSR Dec. 12, 1943. Returned May 17, 1954. Fate unknown.
PTC 43	Trumpy-B	Dec. 8, 1943	Ex RPC 57. Reclass. PTC 43 Mar. 31, 1943. Reclass. as small boat Aug. 1, 1943. Lend-lease to USSR Dec. 17, 1943. Sunk during the war.
PTC 44	Trumpy-B	Dec. 17, 1943	Ex RPC 58. Reclass. PTC 44 Mar. 31, 1943. Reclass. as small boat Aug. 1, 1943. Lend-lease to USSR Jan. 11, 1944. Fate unknown.
PTC 45	Trumpy-B	Dec. 28, 1943	Ex RPC 59. Reclass. PTC 45 Mar. 31, 1943. Reclass. as small boat Aug. 1, 1943. Lend-lease to USSR Jan. 17, 1944. Returned July 9, 1955. Fate unknown.
PTC 46	Trumpy-B	Jan. 7, 1944	Ex RPC 60. Reclass. PTC 46 Mar. 31, 1943. Reclass. as small boat Aug. 1, 1943. Lend-lease to USSR Jan. 17, 1944. Returned June 8, 1954. Fate unknown.

Hull Number	Design/ Builder	Completed	Comments
PTC 47	Trumpy-B	Jan. 10, 1944	Ex RPC 61. Reclass. PTC 47 Mar. 31, 1943. Reclass. as small boat Aug. 1, 1943. Lend-lease to USSR Jan. 21, 1944. Sunk during the war.
PTC 48	Trumpy-B	Jan. 19, 1944	Ex RPC 62. Reclass. PTC 48 Mar. 31, 1943. Reclass. as small boat Aug. 1, 1943. Lend-lease to USSR Feb. 24, 1944. Returned June 8, 1954. Fate unknown.
PTC 49	Trumpy-B	Jan. 27, 1944	Ex RPC 63. Reclass. PTC 49 Mar. 31, 1943. Reclass. as small boat Aug. 1, 1943. Lend-lease to USSR Feb. 24, 1944. Returned June 8, 1954. Fate unknown.
PTC 50	Trumpy-B	Feb. 5, 1944	Ex RPC 64. Reclass. PTC 50 Mar. 31, 1943. Reclass. as small boat Aug. 1, 1943. Fate unknown.
PTC 51	Trumpy-B	Feb. 19, 1944	Ex RPC 65. Reclass. PTC 51 Mar. 31, 1943. Reclass. as small boat Aug. 1, 1943. Fate unknown.
PTC 52	Trumpy-B	Feb. 23, 1944	Ex RPC 66. Reclass. PTC 52 Mar. 31, 1943. Reclass. as small boat Aug. 1, 1943. Fate unknown.
PTC 53	Trumpy-B	Feb. 26, 1944	Ex RPC-67. Reclass. PTC 53 Mar. 31, 1943. Reclass. as small boat Aug. 1, 1943. Fate unknown.
PTC 54	Trumpy-B	Mar. 13, 1944	Ex RPC 68. Reclass. PTC 54 Mar. 31, 1943. Reclass. as small boat Aug. 1, 1943. Lend-lease to USSR Aug. 11, 1944. Destroyed on purpose by USSR with demolition charges after the war.
PTC 55	Trumpy-B	Mar. 21, 1944	Ex RPC 69. Reclass. PTC 55 Mar. 31, 1943. Reclass. as small boat Aug. 1, 1943. Lend-lease to USSR Aug. 11, 1944. Destroyed on purpose by USSR with demolition charges after the war.
PTC 56	Trumpy-B	Mar. 31, 1944	Ex RPC 70. Reclass. PTC 56 Mar. 31, 1943. Reclass. as small boat Aug. 1, 1943. Lend-lease to USSR Aug. 11, 1944. Destroyed on purpose by USSR with demolition charges after the war.
PTC 57	Trumpy-B	Apr. 13, 1944	Ex RPC 71. Reclass. PTC 57 Mar. 31, 1943. Reclass. as small boat Aug. 1, 1943. Lend-lease to USSR Aug. 11, 1944. Destroyed on purpose by USSR with demolition charges after the war.
PTC 58	Trumpy-B	Apr. 21, 1944	Ex RPC 72. Reclass. PTC 58 Mar. 31, 1943. Reclass. as small boat Aug. 1, 1943. Lend-lease to USSR Aug. 11, 1944. Destroyed on purpose by USSR with demolition charges after the war.
PTC 59	Trumpy-B	May 2, 1944	Ex RPC 73. Reclass. PTC 59 Mar. 31, 1943. Reclass. as small boat Aug. 1, 1943. Lend-lease to USSR Aug. 11, 1944. Destroyed on purpose by USSR with demolition charges after the war.
PTC 60	Trumpy-B	May 9, 1944	Ex RPC 74. Reclass. PTC 60 Mar. 31, 1943. Reclass. as small boat Aug. 1, 1943. Lend-lease to USSR July 17, 1944. Destroyed on purpose by USSR with demolition charges after the war.
PTC 61	Trumpy-B	May 29, 1944	Ex RPC 75. Reclass. PTC 61 Mar. 31, 1943. Reclass. as small boat Aug. 1, 1943. Lend-lease to USSR July 9, 1944. Destroyed by the Soviet Navy June 29, 1956, in Pechenga Gulf, Barents Sea, USSR, under U.S. supervision.
PTC 62	Trumpy-B	June 6, 1944	Ex RPC 76. Reclass. PTC 62 Mar. 31, 1943. Reclass. as small boat Aug. 1, 1943. Lend-lease to USSR on July 9, 1944. Destroyed by the Soviet Navy June 29, 1956, in Pechenga Gulf, Barents Sea, USSR under U.S. supervision.

Hull Number	Design/ Builder	Completed	Comments
PTC 63	Trumpy-B	June 22, 1944	Ex RPC 77. Reclass. PTC 63 Mar. 31, 1943. Reclass. as small boat Aug. 1, 1943. Lend-lease to USSR July 9, 1944. Destroyed by the Soviet Navy June 29, 1956, in Pechenga Gulf, Barents Sea, USSR, under U.S. supervision.
PTC 64	Trumpy-B	Oct. 7, 1944	Ex RPC 78. Reclass. PTC 64 Mar. 31, 1943. Reclass. as small boat Aug. 1, 1943. Lend-lease to USSR Aug. 11, 1944. Returned July 9, 1955. Fate unknown.
PTC 65	Trumpy-B	July 21, 1944	Ex RPC 79. Reclass. PTC 65 Mar. 31, 1943. Reclass. as small boat Aug. 1, 1943. Lend-lease to USSR Aug. 11, 1944. Destroyed by the Soviet Navy June 29, 1956, in Pechenga Gulf, Barents Sea, USSR, under U.S. supervision.
PTC 66	Trumpy-B	Aug. 4, 1944	Ex RPC 80. Reclass. PTC 66 Mar. 31, 1943. Reclass. as small boat Aug. 1, 1943. Lend-lease to USSR Aug. 11, 1944. Destroyed by the Soviet Navy June 29, 1956, in Pechenga Gulf, Barents Sea, USSR, under U.S. supervision.

British Motor Torpedo Boats

Hull Number	Design/ Builder	Completed	Comments
BPT 1– 10	——	——	Reclass. from PT 49–58 July 3, 1941. See PT 49–58 for data.
BPT 11– 20	——	——	Ex PTC 27–36. Reclassified BPT 11–20 on June 19, 1941. Reclass. PT 59–68 Dec. 12, 1941.
BPT 21	Vosper-B	Mar. 2, 1943	Lend-lease to UK Mar. 2, 1943, as MTB-275. Manned by the Royal Indian Navy. Returned Mar. 15, 1946. Fate unknown.
BPT 22	Vosper-B	Nov. 10, 1942	Lend-lease to UK Nov. 10, 1942, as MTB-276. Manned by the Royal Indian Navy. Returned Mar. 17, 1946. Sold Mar. 17, 1946.
BPT 23	Vosper-B	Nov. 10, 1942	Lend-lease to UK Nov. 10, 1942, as MTB-277. Manned by the Royal Indian Navy. Returned Mar. 15, 1946, and sold the same date.
BPT 24	Vosper-B	Nov. 10, 1942	Lend-lease to UK Nov. 10, 1942, as MTB-278. Manned by the Royal Indian Navy. Returned Mar. 15, 1946, and sold the same date.
BPT 25	Vosper-B	Nov. 10, 1942	Lend-lease to UK Nov. 10, 1942, as MTB-279. Manned by the Royal Indian Navy. Returned Mar. 15, 1946, and sold the same date.
BPT 26	Vosper-B	Nov. 26, 1942	Lend-lease to UK Nov. 26, 1942, as MTB-280. Manned by the Royal Indian Navy. Returned Mar. 15, 1946, and sold the same date.
BPT 27	Vosper-B	Dec. 2, 1942	Lend-lease to UK Dec. 2, 1942, as MTB-281. Manned by the Royal Indian Navy. Returned Mar. 17, 1946, and sold the same date.
BPT 28	Vosper-B	Dec. 15, 1942	Lend-lease to UK Dec. 15, 1942, as MTB-282. Manned by the Royal Indian Navy. Returned Mar. 15, 1946, and sold the same date.
BPT 29	Vosper-C	Mar. 18, 1943	Lend-lease to UK Mar. 18, 1943, as MTB-287. Manned by the Royal Indian Navy. Wrecked Nov. 24, 1944. Blown up to prevent capture the same date.

Hull Number	Design/Builder	Completed	Comments
BPT 30	Vosper-C	Dec. 15, 1942	Lend-lease to UK Mar. 18, 1943, as MTB-288. Manned by the Royal Indian Navy. Sunk July 22, 1943, by German aircraft.
BPT 31	Vosper-C	Apr. 12, 1943	Lend-lease to UK Apr. 13, 1943, as MTB-289. Manned by the Royal Indian Navy. Returned Sept. 10, 1945. Destroyed Oct. 26, 1945.
BPT 32	Vosper-C	Apr. 12, 1943	Lend-lease to UK Apr. 13, 1943, as MTB-290. Manned by the Royal Indian Navy. Returned May 31, 1945. Destroyed Aug. 13, 1945.
BPT 33	Vosper-C	May 10, 1943	Lend-lease to UK May 10, 1943, as MTB-291. Manned by the Royal Indian Navy. Returned Mar. 15, 1946. Sold in Jan. 1948.
BPT 34	Vosper-C	May 10, 1943	Lend-lease to UK May 10, 1943, as MTB-292. Manned by the Royal Indian Navy. Returned Mar. 5, 1946. Sold Mar. 15, 1946.
BPT 35	Vosper-C	June 18, 1943	Lend-lease to UK June 29, 1943, as MTB-293. Manned by the Royal Indian Navy. Returned Mar. 15, 1946. Sold in Jan. 1948.
BPT 36	Vosper-C	May 10, 1943	Lend-lease to UK July 9, 1943, as MTB-294. Manned by the Royal Indian Navy. Returned Mar. 17, 1946, and sold the same date.
BPT 37	Vosper-A	Feb. 17, 1943	Lend-lease to UK Feb. 17, 1943, as MTB-295. Manned by the Royal Indian Navy. Returned Sept. 25, 1946. Sold in Feb. 1947 to the Italian Navy. Renamed GIS-0018. Cannibalized for spares and later scrapped.
BPT 38	Vosper-A	Mar. 3, 1943	Lend-lease to UK Mar. 3, 1943, as MTB-296. Manned by the Royal Indian Navy. Returned May 31, 1945. Destroyed Aug. 13, 1945.
BPT 39	Vosper-A	Feb. 6, 1943	Lend-lease to UK Feb. 6, 1943, as MTB-297. Manned by the Royal Indian Navy. Returned Sept. 10, 1945. Destroyed Oct. 26, 1945.
BPT 40	Vosper-A	Mar. 30, 1943	Lend-lease to UK Mar. 30, 1943, as MTB-298. Manned by the Royal Indian Navy. Returned Sept. 25, 1945. Sold Nov. 20, 1945.
BPT 41	Vosper-A	Mar. 17, 1943	Lend-lease to UK Mar. 17, 1943, as MTB-299. Manned by the Royal Indian Navy. Returned Mar. 5, 1946. Sold Mar. 15, 1946.
BPT 42	Vosper-A	Apr. 28, 1943	Lend-lease to UK Apr. 28, 1943, as MTB-300. Manned by the Royal Indian Navy. Returned Mar. 5, 1946. Sold Mar. 15, 1946.
BPT 43	Elco-B	Feb. 10, 1943	Lend-lease to UK Mar. 7, 1943, as MTB-301. Manned by the Royal Indian Navy. Returned Mar. 17, 1946 and sold the same date.
BPT 44	Elco-B	Feb. 10, 1943	Lend-lease to UK Mar. 7, 1943, as MTB-302. Manned by the Royal Indian Navy. Returned Mar. 17, 1946 and sold the same date.
BPT 45	Elco-B	Feb. 27, 1943	Lend-lease to UK Mar. 9, 1943, as MTB-303. Manned by the Royal Indian Navy. Returned Mar. 17, 1946 and sold the same date.
BPT 46	Elco-B	Feb. 27, 1943	Lend-lease to UK Mar. 9, 1943, as MTB-304. Manned by the Royal Indian Navy. Returned Mar. 16, 1946 and sold the same date.

Hull Number	Design/ Builder	Completed	Comments
BPT 47	Elco-B	Mar. 9, 1943	Lend-lease to UK Mar. 9, 1943, as MTB-305. Manned by the Royal Indian Navy. Returned Mar. 16, 1946, and sold the same date.
BPT 48	Elco-B	Mar. 31, 1943	Lend-lease to UK Mar. 31, 1943, as MTB-306. Manned by the Royal Indian Navy. Returned Mar. 16, 1946, and sold the same date.
BPT 49	Vosper-B	Apr. 3, 1943	Lend-lease to UK Apr. 3, 1943, as MTB-283. Manned by the Royal Indian Navy. Returned Mar. 17, 1946, and sold the same date.
BPT 50	Vosper-B	Apr. 3, 1943	Lend-lease to UK Apr. 3, 1943, as MTB-284. Lost Sept. 9, 1943, while being transported to India as deck cargo when her transport, the *SS Larchbank*, was torpedoed by a Japanese submarine.
BPT 51	Vosper-B	Apr. 3, 1943	See comments under BPT 50.
BPT 52	Vosper-B	Apr. 3, 1943	Lend-lease to UK Apr. 3, 1943, as MTB-286. Manned by the Royal Indian Navy. Returned Mar. 17, 1946, and sold the same date.
BPT 53	Vosper-B	Sept. 30, 1943	Lend-lease to UK Oct. 5, 1943, as MTB-363. Retrans. to USSR under Lend-lease Feb. 15, 1944, as TKA-221. Returned Feb. 16, 1954. Sold Aug. 11, 1954.
BPT 54	Vosper-B	Nov. 18, 1943	Lend-lease to UK Nov. 18, 1943, as MTB-364. Retrans. to USSR under Lend-lease Feb. 8, 1944, as TKA-222. Sunk in Oct. 1944 in the Barents Sea by the German Navy.
BPT 55	Vosper-B	Dec. 15, 1943	Lend-lease to UK Dec. 15, 1943, as MTB-365. Retrans. to USSR under Lend-lease Feb. 8, 1944, as TKA-223. Returned June 16, 1954. Sold Aug. 11, 1954.
BPT 56	Vosper-B	Nov. 29, 1943	Lend-lease to UK Nov. 29, 1943, as MTB-366. Retrans. to USSR under Lend-lease Feb. 15, 1944, as TKA-226. Returned July 9, 1955. Fate unknown.
BPT 57	Vosper-B	Nov. 19, 1943	Lend-lease to UK Nov. 19, 1943, as MTB-367. Retrans. to USSR under Lend-lease Feb. 15, 1944, as TKA-227. Returned June 16, 1954. Sold Aug. 11, 1954.
BPT 58	Vosper-B	Nov. 22, 1943	Lend-lease to UK Nov. 22, 1943, as MTB-368. Retrans. to USSR under Lend-lease Feb. 15, 1944, as TKA-228. Returned July 9, 1955. Fate unknown.
BPT 59	Vosper-B	Nov. 22, 1943	Lend-lease to UK Nov. 22, 1943, as MTB-369. Retrans. to USSR under Lend-lease Feb. 15, 1944, as TKA-229. Returned June 16, 1954. Sold Aug. 11, 1954.
BPT 60	Vosper-B	Nov. 29, 1943	Lend-lease to UK Nov. 29, 1943, as MTB-370. Retrans. to USSR under Lend-lease Feb. 16, 1944, as TKA-230. Returned July 2, 1955. Fate unknown.
BPT 61	Vosper-B	Oct. 10, 1943	Lend-lease to UK Oct. 20, 1943, as MTB-371. Wrecked Nov. 24, 1944. Blown up to prevent capture the same date.
BPT 62	Vosper-B	Sept. 30, 1943	Lend-lease to UK Oct. 5, 1943, as MTB-372. Sunk July 23, 1944, by gunfire from German Navy surface ships.
BPT 63	Vosper-B	Oct. 9, 1943	Lend-lease to UK Oct. 9, 1943, as MTB-373. Returned Oct. 16, 1945. Sold in Feb. 1947 to the Italian Navy. Renamed GIS-014. Cannibalized for spares and later scrapped.
BPT 64	Vosper-B	Oct. 20, 1943	Lend-lease to UK Nov. 19, 1943, as MTB-374. Returned Oct. 23, 1945. Sold in Feb. 1947 to the Italian Navy. Renamed GIS-015. Cannibalized for spares and later scrapped.

Hull Number	Design/Builder	Completed	Comments
BPT 65	Vosper-B	Nov. 19, 1943	Lend-lease to UK Nov. 19, 1943, as MTB-375. Returned Oct. 15, 1945. Sold in Feb. 1947 to the Italian Navy. Renamed GIS-009. Cannibalized for spares and later scrapped.
BPT 66	Vosper-B	Dec. 2, 1943	Lend-lease to UK Dec. 2, 1943, as MTB-376. Returned on Nov. 7, 1945. Sold in Feb. 1947 to the Italian Navy. Renamed GIS-010. Cannibalized for spares and later scrapped.
BPT 67	Vosper-B	Dec. 2, 1943	Lend-lease to UK Dec. 2, 1943, as MTB-377. Returned Oct. 18, 1945. Sold in Feb. 1947 to the Italian Navy. Renamed GIS-016. Cannibalized for spares and later scrapped.
BPT 68	Vosper-B	Dec. 15, 1943	Lend-lease to UK Dec. 15, 1943, as MTB-378. Returned Oct. 15, 1945. Sold in Feb. 1947 to the Italian Navy. Renamed GIS-017. Cannibalized for spares and later scrapped.

Russian Motor Torpedo Boats

Hull Number	Design/Builder	Completed	Comments
RPT 1–12	——	——	Reclass. PT 372–383 Nov. 21, 1942.
RPT 13–30	——	——	Reclass. PT 546–563 May 10, 1943.

Fast Patrol Boats

Hull Number	Design/Builder	Completed	Comments
PTF 1	Bath	(see PT 810)	Orig. built as PT 810. Reactivated in Oct. 1962–Jan. 1963. Instated on the Navy List and reclass. PTF 1 Dec. 21, 1962. Leased to S. Vietnam Jan. 26, 1965. Returned to the U.S. Navy. Stricken from the U.S. Navy List Aug. 1, 1965. Sunk as target Dec. 10, 1966, by a Mark 37 torpedo fired by USS *Blackfin* (SS-322).
PTF 2	Trumpy-A	*see PT 811)	Orig. built as PT 811. Instated on the Navy List and reclass. PTF 2 Dec. 21, 1962. Placed in service Jan. 9, 1963. Leased to S. Vietnam Jan. 26, 1965. Returned to the U.S. Stricken from the U.S. Navy List Aug. 1, 1965. Sunk Dec. 20, 1966, by gunfire from *USS Coucal* (ASR 8) "after machinery derangement (sic) caused craft to become hazard to navigation."
PTF 3	Norway-A	Jan. 1, 1963	Ex-Norwegian *Skrei*. Acquired in Dec. 1962. Instated on the Navy List Jan. 1, 1963. Placed in service Mar. 25, 1963. Leased to S. Vietnam Jan. 26, 1965. Returned to the U.S. in 1970. Sold Dec. 9, 1977, for scrapping.
PTF 4	Norway-A	Jan. 1, 1963	Ex-Norwegian *Hvass*. Acquired Dec. 1962. Instated on the Navy List Feb. 15, 1963. Placed in service May 3, 1963. Leased to S. Vietnam Jan. 26, 1965. Sunk Nov. 4, 1965. Stricken from the U.S. Navy List Dec. 1, 1965.
PTF 5	Norway-A	Mar. 1, 1964	Ex-Norwegian *Knurr*. Instated on the Navy List March 1, 1964. Leased to S. Vietnam Jan. 26, 1965. Returned in 1970. Sold June 29, 1977, for scrapping.

Hull Number	Design/ Builder	Completed	Comments
PTF 6	Norway-A	Mar. 1, 1964	Ex-Norwegian Lyr. Instated the Navy List Mar. 1, 1964. Leased to S. Vietnam Jan. 26, 1965. Returned to U.S. in 1970. Sold Dec. 9, 1977, for scrapping.
PTF 7	Norway-A	Mar. 1, 1964	Ex-Norwegian *Skrei*. Instated on the Navy List Mar. 1, 1964. Placed in Service June 16, 1964. Leased to S. Vietnam Jan. 26, 1965. Returned to U.S. 1970. Sold Dec. 9, 1977, for scrapping.
PTF 8	Norway-A	Mar. 1, 1964	Ex-Norwegian Delfin. Instated on the Navy List Mar. 1, 1964. Placed in service June 16, 1964. Leased to S. Vietnam Jan. 26, 1965. Sunk June 16, 1966. Stricken from the U.S. Navy List July 1, 1966.
PTF 9	Norway-A	Apr. 22, 1965	Leased to S. Vietnam Jan. 26, 1966. Sunk Mar. 7, 1966. Stricken from the U.S. Navy List Apr. 1, 1966.
PTF 10	Norway-B	Apr. 22, 1965	Sold in Feb. 1980 for scrapping.
PTF 11	Norway-B	July 7, 1965	Sold June 29, 1977, for scrapping.
PTF 12	Norway-B	July 7, 1965	Sold Dec. 9, 1977, for scrapping.
PTF 13	Norway-B	Aug. 31, 1965	Reclass. as small boat "80PB651323" Sept. 23, 1970. Sold Dec. 9, 1977, for scrapping.
PTF 14	Norway-B	Oct. 14, 1965	Leased to S. Vietnam Feb. 23, 1966. Sunk Apr. 22, 1966. Stricken from the U.S. Navy List May 1, 1966.
PTF 15	Norway-B	Nov. 29, 1965	Leased to S. Vietnam Apr. 18, 1966. Sunk Apr. 22, 1966. Stricken from the U.S. Navy List July 1, 1966.
PTF 16	Norway-B	Nov. 29, 1965	Leased to S. Vietnam Apr. 18, 1966. Sunk Aug. 19, 1966. Stricken from the U.S. Navy List Oct. 1, 1966.
PTF 17	Trumpy-A	July 1, 1968	Museum at Naval & Servicemen's Park, Buffalo, NY, since August 1, 1979.
PTF 18	Trumpy-A	July 1, 1968	Sold in Apr. 1980 for scrapping.
PTF 19	Trumpy-A	Oct. 5, 1968	Sold in Apr. 1980 for scrapping.
PTF 20	Trumpy-A	Oct. 5, 1968	Trans. to Point Mugu Missile Test Facility, in Feb. 1977 for use as a target.
PTF 21	Trumpy-A	May 14, 1969	See comments under PTF 20.
PTF 22	Trumpy-A	May 14, 1969	Severely damaged by grounding in March 1976. Beyond repair. Sold. Hull repaired and used as a commercial fishing boat.
PTF 23	Sewart	Mar. 13, 1968	Sold for service as a commercial oceanographic vessel.
PTF 24	Sewart	Mar. 13, 1968	Sold in 1985 for use in a movie.
PTF 25	Sewart	Apr. 8, 1968	Deactivated Jan. 23, 1978, for conversion to a test platform for gas turbine propulsion. Was to have been fitted with (2)5,000 shp gas turbines under the "Osprey 990" program. Canceled due to budget constraints. Sold in March 1980.
PTF 26	Sewart	Apr. 8, 1968	Trans. to Point Mugu Missile Test Facility in Feb. 1977 for use as a target. Sold 1984. Still in existence in 1998 owned by the Sea Scouts of West Sacramento, CA. Operated as a sea-going training boat under the name *Liberty*.

(All surviving PTFs were reclassified as "boats" Sept. 23, 1970. This removed them from the Naval Vessel Register and they are operated as "floating equipment.")

Appendix D

PT Boat Squadrons

Squadron	Campaigns	Type of Boat	Period of Service
MTBRon 1	Pearl Harbor, Midway, Aleutians	77' Elco	July 24, 1940 – Feb. 9, 1945
MTBRon 1 (ii)	None	Postwar Prototypes (PT 809–812)	1954 – 1959
MTBRon 2	South Pacific	70' Elco 77' Elco 80' Elco	Nov. 8, 1942–Nov. 11, 1943
MTPRon 2(ii)	English Channel	78' Higgins	Mar. 23, 1944–Sept. 21, 1945
MTBRon 3	Philippines	77' Elco	Aug. 12, 1941–Apr. 15, 1942
MTBRon 3(ii)	South Pacific	77'Elco	July 27, 1942–Aug. 7, 1944
MTBRon 4	Training Squadron	77' Elco 78' Huckins 70' Higgins 78' Higgins 80' Elco	Jan. 13, 1942–Apr. 15, 1946

A rare photo of the first MTB tender, the *Niagara*. Elco 77-foot PT boats are in the foreground. The converted yacht *Niagara* was the only MTB tender to be lost during the war, being sunk in a Japanese air attack. *Electric Boat Co.*

The *Niagara* under way, her sleek lines showing her origins as a yacht. As a gunboat and subsequent MTB tender, she mounted two 3-inch anti-aircraft guns; they proved inadequate when she came under attack by Japanese bombers.

Squadron	Campaigns	Type of Boat	Period of Service
MTBRon 5	Panama, S. Pacific, Southwest Pacific	77' Elco	June 16, 1942 – Feb. 16, 1945
MTBRon 6	South Pacific, Southwest Pacific	80' Elco	Aug. 4, 1942 – May 29, 1944
MTBRon 7	Southwest Pacific	77' Elco 80' Elco	Sept. 4, 1942 – Feb. 15, 1945
MTBRon 8	Southwest Pacific	77' Elco 80' Elco	Oct. 10, 1942 – Oct. 28, 1945
MTBRon 9	South Pacific, Southwest Pacific	80' Elco	Nov. 10, 1942 – Nov. 10, 1945
MTBRon 10	South Pacific	80' Elco	Dec. 9, 1942 – Nov. 11, 1945
MTBRon 11	South Pacific, Southwest Pacific	80' Elco	Jan. 20, 1943 – Nov. 11, 1945
MTBRon 12	Southwest Pacific	80' Elco	Feb. 18, 1943 – Oct. 26, 1945
MTBRon 13	Aleutians, Southwest Pacific	78' Higgins	Sept. 18, 1942 – Nov. 23, 1945
MTBRon 14	Panama Sea Frontier	78' Huckins	Feb. 17, 1943 – Sept. 16, 1944
MTBRon 15	Mediterranean	78' Higgins	Jan. 20, 1943 – Oct. 17, 1944
MTBRon 16	Aleutians, Southwest Pacific	78' Higgins	Feb. 26, 1943 – Nov. 26, 1945
MTBRon 16 (B)	In transit Aleutians	78' Higgins	Mar. 1943 – May 31, 1944
MTBRon 17	Hawaii Southwest Pacific	78' Higgins	Mar. 29, 1943 – Nov. 19, 1945
MTBRon 18	Southwest Pacific	80' Elco 70' Scott-Paine	Mar. 27, 1943 – Nov. 1, 1945
MTBRon 19	South Pacific	78' Higgins	Apr. 22, 1943 – May 15, 1944
MTBRon 20	South Pacific, Southwest Pacific	78' Higgins	June 3, 1943 – Nov. 24, 1945
MTBRon 21	Southwest Pacific	80' Elco	Apr. 8, 1943 – Nov. 10, 1945
MTBRon 22	Mediterranean	78' Higgins	Nov. 10, 1943 – Nov. 15, 1945

The tender *Hilo*, shown here, and the similar *Jamestown* were, like the *Niagara*, converted from large yachts. They were originally taken over by the Navy for use as patrol vessels. As MTB tenders they had a severely limited repair and supply capabilities. *U.S. Navy*

Right
The *Varuna* was one of ten LSTs converted to MTB tenders during the war. Note the large deckhouse amidships containing various ships and storage areas. There is a heavy-lift boom forward. Several 40-mm and 20-mm guns are fitted for self-defense. *James C. Fahey collection (USNI)*

The *Callisto* was converted to an MTB tender from a later-series LST. The mast and bridge differ from the earlier LSTs. The bow doors and ramp for unloading vehicles onto the beach have been sealed shut in the AGP role. *James C. Fahey collection (USNI)*

An MTB tender revealing her origins as a landing ship tank. The LST was one of the most important ships of World War II. However, MTB tenders and repair ships were also needed, with many LSTs being converted to those roles.

The *Willoughby* was one of four small seaplane tenders completed as MTB tenders. Designed to support seaplanes, they proved well suited to support PT boats. The large enclosed mount forward has a 5-inch gun; a second 5-inch open mount amidships is aft of the crane, lost in topside clutter. *U.S. Navy*

The *Acontius*, shown here, and the *Cyrene*, were C2-type merchant hulls converted during construction to support PT boats. There is a cradle forward for holding a PT boat, beneath the 50-ton-capacity cargo boom. The ships mounted a 5-inch gun after and several 40-mm and 20-mm anti-aircraft guns. *U.S. Navy*

Squadron	Campaigns	Type of Boat	Period of Service
MTBRon 23	South Pacific, Southwest Pacific	78′ Higgins	June 28, 1943 – Nov. 26, 1945
MTBRon 24	Southwest Pacific	80′ Elco	May 10, 1943 – Nov. 6, 1945
MTBRon 25	Southwest Pacific	80′ Elco	June 17, 1943 – Nov. 9, 1945
MTBRon 26	Hawaiian Sea Frontier	78′ Huckins	Mar. 3, 1943 – Dec. 3, 1945
MTBRon 27	South Pacific, Southwest Pacific	80′ Elco	July 23, 1943 – Oct. 19, 1945
MTBRon 28	South Pacific, Southwest Pacific	80′ Elco	Aug. 30, 1943 – Oct. 21, 1945
MTBRon 29	Mediterranean	80′ Elco	Oct. 22, 1943 – Nov. 23, 1943
MTBRon 30	English Channel	78′ Higgins	Feb. 15, 1944 – Nov. 15, 1945
MTBRon 31	Pacific Fleet	78′ Higgins	Apr. 5, 1944 – Dec. 17, 1945
MTBRon 32	Pacific Fleet	78′ Higgins	June 10, 1944 – Dec. 18, 1945
MTBRon 33	Southwest Pacific	80′ Elco	Dec. 2, 1943 – Oct. 24, 1945
MTBRon 34	English Channel	80′ Elco	Dec. 31, 1943 – Mar. 9, 1945
MTBRon 35	English Channel	80′ Elco	Feb. 15, 1944 – Apr. 10, 1945
MTBRon 36	Southwest Pacific	80′ Elco	Apr. 3, 1944 – Oct. 29, 1945

Squadron	Campaigns	Type of Boat	Period of Service
MTBRon 37	Pacific Fleet	80' Elco	June 5, 1944 – Dec. 7, 1945
MTBRon 38	Southwest Pacific	80' Elco	Dec. 20, 1944 – Oct. 24, 1945
MTBRon 39	Pacific Fleet	80' Elco	Mar. 6, 1945 – Dec. 24, 1945
MTBRon 40	Pacific Fleet	80' Elco	Apr. 26, 1945 – Dec. 21, 1945
MTBRon 41*	None	80' Elco	June 21, 1945 – Feb. 6, 1946
MTBRon 42*	None	80' Elco	Sept. 17, 1945 – Feb. 8, 1946
MTBRon 43*	None	78' Higgins	Dec. 12, 1944 – Mar. 16, 1945
MTBRon 44*	None	78' Higgins	Never Commissioned
MTBRon 45*	None	78' Higgins	Never Commissioned
PTC Ron 1**	None	70' Elco	Feb. 20, 1941 – July 17, 1941

Notes:

* All five squadrons were assigned to the Pacific Fleet. MTBRons 41 and 42 were still running trials when Japan surrendered and never were shipped to the Pacific. Boats assigned to MTBRons 43 through 45 were all transferred to Russia under Lend-lease.

** Included PTC 1–12. The PTC concept was abandoned due to failure to develop adequate sound gear for these boats. The entire squadron was transferred to Great Britain, where they were converted to gunboats. The small size and limited provisions, accommodations, and torpedoes of motor torpedo boats necessitated the availability of MTB tenders to support boats operating in forward areas. During World War II the Navy modified 19 ships to serve as MTB tenders. They were given the designation AGP––AG indicating miscellaneous auxiliary and *P* indicating PT boats. The first AGPs were the *Niagara*, *Jamestown*, and *Hilo*, all built as large civilian yachts. They were taken over by the Navy and converted to gunboats (PG) but primarily employed as MTB tenders:

MTB tenders also provided divers to inspect and work on the underwater hulls of PT boats while they were in the water. Here a "hard-hat" diver is helped over the side to inspect the screws and rudders of a boat.

A January 3, 1945 closeup photo of the Elco 80-ft. PT 192 being hoisted out of the water, on to the forecasltle of the MTB tender *Cyrene*, for major hull repairs. Running in shallow water, the PTs often damaged their underwater hulls and propellers. Note the gun armament and lightweight torpedo launch racks (seen on the main deck forward below the starboard .50 cal. machine gun and aft opposite the radar dome on the folded down mast). *U.S. Navy*

Another view of the AGP *Harnett County*, tending her brood in South Vietnamese waters. On occasion these ships would provide support to PTFs. The *Harnett County* was moored just south of the Ben Loc bridge on the Vam Co Dong River in this photo. *U.S. Navy*

Left

The AGP *Harnett County* was one of four LSTs modified—but not fully converted—to support riverine and coastal craft during the Vietnam War. Here, the ship was supporting small craft and Navy UH-1 Huey helicopters on the Bassac River in South Vietnam. *U.S. Navy*

Appendix E

Boat Tenders

The small size and limited provisions, accomodations, and torpedoes of motor torpedo boats necessitated the availability of MTB tenders to support boats operating in forward areas. During World War II the Navy modified 19 ships to serve as MTB tenders. They were given the designation AGP—Motor Torpedo Boat Tenders.

The first AGPs were the *Niagara*, *Jamestown*, and *Hilo*, all built as large civilian yachts. They were taken over by the Navy and converted to gunboats (PG), but were primarily employed as MTB tenders.

- AGP 1 *Niagara* (ex–PG 52) built in 1929; acquired in 1940
- AGP 2 *Jamestown* (ex–PG 55) built in 1928; acquired in 1940
- AGP 3 *Hilo* (ex–PG 58) built in 1931; acquired in 1941

Each ship was fitted with one or two 3-inch guns in the PG/AGP role, plus machine guns.

In the spring of 1941 the *Niagara* was sent with several PT boats to Newport, Rhode Island, to serve as the headquarters for an MTB school. However, she was needed in the Pacific and, on August 30, 1941, departed from New York for the Pacific. Initially she was employed as a convoy escort.

Subsequently, the *Niagara* did serve as a tender for PT boats. On May 23, 1943, while she was steaming with six PT boats from Tulagi in the Solomons to New Guinea, she was attacked by Japanese aircraft. Seriously damaged, the ship was scuttled, and her crew was rescued by the MTBs. She suffered no casualties in the attack (see Chapter 5). The *Niagara* was the only MTB tender sunk during the war.

The two other ex–gunboats served as MTB tenders. The *Jamestown* briefly served as a training ship for Naval Academy midshipmen in the summer of 1941, and then assisted in establishing the MTB training center at Melville, Rhode Island. She then sailed for the South Pacific to support PT boats. The *Hilo*, commissioned in 1942, immediately began service as a tender.

In the role of tenders these ships had very limited repair, virtually no fuel and weapons-storage capabilities, and few messing, berthing, or medical facilities for PT boat crews. Subsequently, the Navy took in hand ten of the ubiquitous tank landing ships (LST) for conversion to MTB tenders; the conversion of an 11th ship was canceled:

AGP 4 *Portunus* (ex–LST 330) completed in 1943
AGP 5 *Varuna* (ex–LST 14) completed in 1943
AGP 10 *Orestes* (ex–LST 135) completed in 1944
AGP 11 *Silenus* (ex–LST 604) completed in 1944
AGP 14 *Alecto* (ex–LST 558) completed in 1945
AGP 15 *Callisto* (ex–LST 966) completed in 1944
AGP 16 *Antigone* (ex–LST 773) completed in 1944
AGP 17 *Brontes* (ex–LST 1125) completed in 1945
AGP 18 *Chiron* (ex–LST 1133) completed in 1945
AGP 19 canceled
AGP 20 *Pontus* (ex–LST 201) completed in 1943

These were large ships, 328 feet in length with a standard displacement of just over 1,600 tons; fully loaded, they were rated at 4,080 tons. Their large open upper deck and cavernous tank deck provided considerable space for MTB support facilities. Further, the LSTs already had accommodations for 147 troops in addition to their crew spaces, providing space for maintenance personnel.

In their conversion to AGPs the bow door was sealed and bow ramp removed; ramp or elevator to the tank deck (depending on the LST class) was removed, and each ship was fitted with a variety of shops and storage spaces. Forward, a 50-ton-capacity A-frame was installed for lifting PT boats. Additional high-octane fuel tanks and weapons stowage were provided. Two 40-mm quad anti-aircraft gun mounts were provided. (Another 53 LSTs were similarly converted to repair ships.)

Four Barnegat-class small seaplane tenders (AVP) were completed as AGPs:

AGP 6 *Oyster Bay* (ex–AVP 28) completed in 1943
AGP 7 *Mobjack* (ex–AVP 27) completed in 1943
AGP 8 *Wachapreague* (ex–AVP 56) completed in 1944
AGP 9 *Willoughby* (ex–AVP 57) completed in 1944

These ships, 310 3/4 feet long displacing 1,695 tons, were intended to support flying boats, thus they already had excellent features for supporting PT boats. The Barnegats carried a heavy gun armament with the AGPs each armed with two 5-inch dual-purpose guns plus four twin 40-mm mounts. (An additional 31 ships of this class were completed as small seaplane tenders.)

The ships already had extra accommodations (for seaplane crews), storage for high-octane gasoline and torpedoes, and other facilities that could easily be modified to support MTBs.

The final two AGPs of the war period were merchant ships completed to an AGP configuration:

AGP 12 *Acontius* completed in 1944
AGP 13 *Cyrene* completed in 1944

Built to a basic merchant ship design, the AGP 12 and AGP 13 were the largest ships employed as MTB tenders being 412 feet long and displacing just over 5,800 tons. They were provided with extensive support facilities. An armament of one 5-inch dual-purpose gun and four twin 40-mm mounts was provided.

None of these ships was retained in the AGP role after the war. Only the four Barnegat–class ships saw postwar service: The *Mobjack* was transferred to the U.S. Coast and Geodetic Survey in 1946 for use as a surveying ship, serving in that role for two decades. The *Wachapreague* and *Willoughby* were transferred to the U.S. Coast Guard in 1948 and saw extensive service as patrol ships into the 1970s; the *Wachapreague* was transferred to the South Vietnamese Navy in 1972, and then to the Philippines Navy in 1976, where she served for almost ten years. The *Oyster Bay*, laid up in reserve after the war, was transferred to the Italian Navy in 1957 and remained in service as a tender until 1994.

During the Vietnam War four long-serving LSTs were employed in the AGP role, that designation being reactivated as patrol craft tender (vice PT boat tender). These ships primarily supported riverine and coastal patrol craft, which were procured in prodigious numbers during that conflict, but on occasion they provided services to the fast patrol craft (PTF), descendants of the PT boat. On September 29, 1970, after four of the ships had served in the AGP role for five years, three were redesignated as AGP but retained their LST hull numbers:

AGP 786 *Garrett County* (ex–LST 786)
AGP 821 *Harnett County* (ex–LST 821)
AGP 838 *Hunterdon County* (ex–LST 838)

The fourth ship, the *Jennings County* (LST 846), for unknown reasons, retained her LST classification. Their modification to the AGP role was far less elaborate than that of the World War II LST/AGP tenders.

Another post-World War II AGP was the *Graham County* (LST 1176), modified in the 1970s to support patrol gunboats (PGM) in the Mediterranean and reclassified AGP 1176.

One additional ship was intended to serve in an AGP role. In the early 1970s the U.S. Navy built six hydrofoil missile craft (PHM). The *Wood County* (LST 1178), like the *Graham County*, an improved, postwar landing ship, was designated to serve as a tender to these craft and planned for reclassification to a patrol combatant support ship––AGHS 1178, the H indicating hydrofoil and the S for support. However, her conversion was canceled with the decision not to deploy the PHMs to the Mediterranean Sea.

Glossary

AGP .... motor torpedo boat tender

AVP .... small seaplane tender

BPT .... British PT boat

Elco .... Electric Boat Company

LCG .... landing craft gunboat (British)

LCI .... landing craft infantry (153 feet)

LCM .... landing craft mechanized (36 feet)

LST .... landing ship tank (328 feet)

MGB .... motor gunboat

mm .... millimeter

MTB .... motor torpedo boat

OSS .... Office of Strategic Services

TF .... Task Force

TG .... Task Group

PG .... gunboat

PT .... motor torpedo boat (not patrol torpedo boat)

PTC .... motor boat submarine chaser

PTF .... fast patrol boat

RPT .... Russian motor torpedo boat

[All miles for water distances are nautical miles
(i.e., 1.15 statute miles).]

About the Authors

Norman Polmar has written or coauthored more than 30 books on naval, aviation, and intelligence subjects. Also serving as a consultant to several officials in the Department of Defense and to members of Congress, he is best known in naval circles as author of the Naval Institute's reference books *Ships and Aircraft of the U.S. Fleet* and *Guide to the Soviet Navy*. He also writes regular columns for the Naval Institute *Proceedings* and *Naval History* magazines. He previously was a member of the Secretary of the Navy's Research Advisory Committee (NRAC).

Samuel Loring Morison, a freelance writer, historian, and researcher, has been described as "an accomplished writer of naval history and a nonpareil researcher: if a document exists, I believe he can find it. His mental catalogue of World War II naval facts is encyclopedic," according to John A. Lorelli, author of *To Foreign Shores: U.S. Amphibious Operations in World War II*. Mr. Morison has written or coauthored five books, and writes regularly for *Navy News* and *Undersea Technology*, Naval Institute *Proceedings*, and *Navy Times*. He served as an officer on an escort ship during the Vietnam War and, subsequently, was assigned to the Naval History Division.

Index